My Costume, Myself

Celebrating Stories of Cosplay and Beyond

THOMAS G. ENDRES, PHD

My Costume, Myself: Celebrating Stories of Cosplay and Beyond
Copyright © 2023 by Thomas G. Endres, PhD

All rights reserved. No part of this book may be used or reproduced in any manner whatsoever without the author's written permission except in the case of brief quotations embodied in critical articles and reviews.

The information in this book is distributed on an "as is" basis, without warranty. Although every precaution has been taken in the preparation of this work, neither the author nor the publisher shall have any liability to any person or entity with respect to any loss or damage caused or alleged to be caused directly or indirectly by the information contained in this book.

Paperback ISBN: 978-1-959681-09-0
eBook ISBN: 978-1-959681-10-6
Hardcover ISBN: 978-1-959681-11-3

Library of Congress Number: 2023906818

Written and photographed by Thomas G. Endres, PhD
Foreword by "Founding Father of Cosplay" Nobuyuki Takahashi
Cover and Interior Design by Ann Aubitz
Published by Kirk House Publishers

Kirk House Publishers
1250 E 115th Street
Burnsville, MN 55337
612-781-2815
kirkhousepublishers.com

*To the amazing women who, by example, taught me
everything I know about family, faith, strength, serenity,
compassion, creativity, life, and love*

*Mom, my memory
Maki, my miracle
Daughters, my delight
Granddaughters, my gift*

Thank You

TABLE OF CONTENTS

Foreword by Nobuyuki Takahashi |7
Preface |11

PART I: COSPLAY |15
Chapter 1   History and Definitions |17
         Costume Conversation
             #1: Eric Adams |37
         Costume Conversation
             #2: Kat Sawyer and Lee Montgomery |41
         Costume Conversation
             #3: Casey Barrett |48
Chapter 2   Con(ventions) |55
         Costume Conversation
             #4: Ken Barrett and Brianna Cecil-Barrett |78
         Costume Conversation
             #5: Voniè and Chase Stillson |85
         Costume Conversation
             #6: Elaine and Ember Waterman |92
Chapter 3   Identity and Representation |99
         Costume Conversation
             #7: Gracie Villa |127
         Costume Conversation
             #8: Jonathan Alexandratos |134
         Costume Conversation
             #9: Samantha Nord |141

PART II: AND BEYOND		|149
Chapter 4	Professional and Work Costumes	|151
	Costume Conversation #10: David Blevins	|175
	Costume Conversation #11: John C. Luzader	|182
	Costume Conversation #12: Andy Mosher	|190
Chapter 5	Fashion and Lifestyle Costumes	|197
	Costume Conversation #13: Michael Schluter	|222
	Costume Conversation #14: Angel Cardon	|229
	Costume Conversation #15: Erin B. and Jesus G.	|236
Chapter 6	Research, Rules, and Wrapping Up	|243
	Costume Conversation #16: Bond Family	|269
	Costume Conversation #17: Rachel Taulbee	|276
	Costume Conversation #18: George Gray	|283
References		|291
Appendix: Studies from Around the World		|303
Color Photos		|313

FOREWORD
The Breakthrough of Cosplay Culture
by Nobuyuki Takahashi

This year marks 40 years since our team created the name of an otaku culture activity called "*kosupure*: COSPLAY."

This word, with unfamiliar spelling, was used as the title of an article in a series that began in the June 1983 issue of the Japanese animation magazine *My Anime*. Since the preceding year, we had been thinking about what to call the activities of the youth subculture.

In the United States, fans dressing up as characters from movies, dramas, anime, and manga existed since the 1970s at science fiction conventions (e.g., Worldcon) and Trekkies fan conventions. The existence of costumes of Disney Studio characters can even be confirmed from the 1940s.

However, there was no name for that action.

At the SF convention, it was called costuming and dressing up. The attraction for the visitors was a show called "Masquerade" where they competed in costumes and stage performances. This tradition continues today at many anime and manga conventions around the world.

We looked up theater terms in the English dictionary and found the phrase "Costume Play." I learned that it was a historical drama performed in classic theater, such as Shakespeare, in the costumes of the era, and that was sometimes ridiculed as "an unsophisticated play where the costumes are emphasized much more than the actors' performances."

We dared to create the word "COSPLAY" by combining short words based on this "Costume Play."

Cosplay is not a theatrical performance in which individual actors emote, but an activity in which those who love the character "capture the character's appearance" and "claim their deep affection for the work."

"Costume Play," which is often ridiculed in the world of theater, was deliberately used as the base of the name "COSPLAY," because it conveyed the message that what matters most in portraying the character is "capturing the appearance in costume."

The source of inspiration is American fan culture, but I believe the act of naming it "COSPLAY" is what caused the culture to spread to younger fans and the general public.

Similarly, Japanese production companies, learning from the "Animation" works of Disney and Fleischer's studios, created "ANIME" in their own style. Learning from "American Comics," "MANGA" was born. Television receivers, video recorders, video games, and portable music players are all entertainment products, born in the United States, that have spread around the world after Japanese enhancements. I believe that Japan, learning and adapting to the cultures and industries of the world, not just those of Europe and the United States, gained the ability to make improvements and advances.

There are now more than 1,000 COSPLAY events a year in Japan. Large events include the *World Cosplay Summit*, which attracts 1,000 cosplayers and tens of thousands of visitors, anime and game events where hundreds of people show off their outstanding costumes, and small parties and photo shoot events that attract dozens of people.

Also, more than 300 fan conventions – events for fans of Japanese anime, manga, and games - are held annually in over 100 countries around the world. And cosplay is present at almost all events.

Cosplay is more than just a fan festival, it is an animistic ritual that connects performers with favorite characters, sometimes drawing life force from the characters, and is also a unifying symbol for a tribe that connects like-minded people.

People who like anime, manga, and games are generally shy people regardless of age or gender. As a tool to support communication, cosplay is a way for strangers to meet people who share "characters they like," and to become friends through mutual enthusiasm. I believe that fans around the world will continue to be connected through "cosplay".

I have big expectations of what's to come, now that "cosplay" and "fan culture" are finally accepted as academic research at universities. I would like to commend the activities of subculture researcher Thomas Endres, who wrote this book, and his partner, Maki Notohara Endres.

Let's continue to work together to realize "one world united by cosplay."

March 10, 2023 *(Translated from the original Japanese. Thank you to Maki Notohara Endres for her help in transcribing.)*

PREFACE

Borrowing a term from Henry Jenkins, Nichols (2019) would call me an *aca-fan*: an academic and a fan. I am a scholar who does cosplay. I am a cosplayer who conducts research. I want to thank the University of Northern Colorado, Greeley, CO, for their assistance, both intellectually and financially. In addition to ongoing encouragement from faculty colleagues in my home discipline of Communication Studies, and multiple other programs and departments, institutional support included a Spring 2022 sabbatical, a Provost Award for Travel (PAT) grant, and a grant from the University's Fund for Faculty Publications.

Though I will cite a few throughout, this is not a study of *professional* cosplayers. They already have a platform and a voice. I was seeking out those who rarely have a chance to share their story. This is also not a study of cosporn which, as Winge (2019) points out, are porn actors in costumes and not real cosplayers. Again, they get enough hits. Granted, some cosplayers engage in erotic performance. We'll investigate that a little. Honestly, who and what gets talked about in the forthcoming pages is all a matter of what was uncovered during an almost two-year search. A broad net was cast, and you'll get to read about everything found in the catch.

During that long research process, my wife Maki and I traveled to most areas in the United States. We flew to Florida, New York, California, and Louisiana, where we rented cars, hired Ubers, hailed taxis, rode subways, and walked, walked, and walked. A train brought us home from Chicago. We drove through the Badlands and Black Hills of the Dakotas, and back and forth and back and forth through the Central

West. This project also took us to Japan, where we met the engaging Nobuyuki Takahashi, who graciously wrote the foreward.

The word that hummed within me during these travels was *sonder*; the realization that every person who passes by has a life as complicated and intricate as your own. All those people in New York City. All those homes and apartments viewed through the window of an Amtrack or *Shikansen* (bullet train) car. The drivers and passengers all along the Pacific Coast Highway heading to and from Los Angeles. The partiers on Bourbon Street and the *otaku* (geek) youth in Tokyo's Akihabara district. Each one with a full and complex life. Most of whom I will never, ever have the chance to meet. The thought makes you feel both small and connected at the same time. I met a number of them, however, and now you get to meet them, too.

The title of this book is in honor of a groundbreaking feminist publication I greatly respected in my college days. Frustrated with the lack of medical information available on female health topics like birth control, rape, venereal disease, childbearing, and menopause, a group of women known as the Boston Women's Health Book Collective published a compilation in 1971 titled *Our Bodies, Ourselves: A Book By and For Women* (New York, NY: Simon and Schuster). Updated versions were published over several years. Their stated goal was to reclaim the strength of femininity without becoming or discarding the male. "We want, in short, to create a cultural environment where all qualities can come out in all people" (p. 6). I always respected that goal and want to embody that same "all qualities" and "all people" principle in this unpacking of cosplay and costume environments. The preface to *Our Bodies, Ourselves* is titled "A Good Story." That is powerful, for, as I continually tell my students, the person who tells the best story rules the world.

In addition to my university, there are others I need to thank. To the organizers of gatherings like FanExpo Denver, Big Apple Comic Con, Colorado Anime Fest, Comic Con Revolution Ontario (CA), and other venues hosting costume events, I thank you for the day passes, press I.D.s, and other forms of assistance and access.

Thank you to the dozens of individuals who participated in the interview process. They gave of their time and they shared their hearts. And, given that I am but an amateur photographer at best, they tolerated my fumbling with two cameras, lens adjustments, pop up flashes getting snagged in my cap, and the occasional delay while I deleted old shots to make room on the SD Card for more pics. I hope I have done justice to your story.

To Ann Aubitz and all those at Kirk House who assisted in the production of this book. Words can hardly express my gratitude. This is the second book I've published with Kirk House, and I'm beyond delighted that the titles of both books contain the words "celebrating" and "stories." They have taken my dreams and made them happen.

To my family, who stands beside me in all my projects and endeavors. You lift me up and keep me going. As the old saying goes, "Families are like branches on a tree. We grow in different directions, yet our roots remain as one." Our roots run deep.

And to Maki. My wife. My partner. You've heard me say it many times, but all these readers need to know, that this book would not exist without you. Amid my health concerns, you did all the things I could not do. You drove. You handled the paperwork. You carried the bag. You helped the interviewees into their costumes, fixed their hair, and hugged the ones who needed to cry. You took your own photos to chronicle our journey. And you were patient with me when writing consumed my days, nights, weeks, and months. Every cup of tea you delivered to my desk was a tenfold blessing I can never repay. I thank God for you.

Part I
Cosplay

They have lived among us for decades. For a long time, they stayed hidden. They shied away from passersby and gathered behind closed doors. Traditionally confined to parallel universes, they now come out into the open. Formerly marginalized, today their numbers are growing, numbering thousands, even millions. Perhaps you've seen them near you? They change their appearance, their clothes, their very skin. Welcome to Cosplay Culture.
~Opening monologue, *Cosplay Culture* **documentary, 2017**

CHAPTER 1
History and Definitions

You probably know a few things about me. If you perused the author blurb on the back cover or read my Preface, you picked up a few details, such as the fact that I'm a professor of Communication Studies. You could find out more by checking my name on places like LinkedIn or Facebook. But there are a few things about me that such a superficial search won't uncover. For example...

I. Am. Batman.

I am also Santa Claus.

And, depending on my mood or the occasion, I also tend to be a pirate, a Harley-riding biker, a Clint Eastwood-inspired cowboy, the Phantom of the Opera or, most recently, Ego the Living Planet from *Guardians of the Galaxy 2*. How do you know which of these many personas I happen to be at a given moment? You look, of course, at my costume (see Images 1.1 and 1.2).

The big question is, does seeing me in that costume tell you *more* about me, or does it confuse and confound your sense of who I am? Here's a hint. In the Communication Studies discipline, we frequently present our students with this credo regarding our field: *You cannot not communicate.* That is, we are in a constant, 24-hour-a day state of communication. You cannot turn off the message machine. You are always sending, which opens the door to constant and ongoing interpretation from others. At this point students try to stump me:

"What if I'm just sitting here in class, not saying anything?"

"You are communicating your willingness, or lack thereof, to listen to the lesson."

Images 1.1 and 1.2 *Your author, dressed as Knightmare Batman from* Batman v. Superman: Dawn of Justice *(left) and Kurt Russell-inspired Santa Claus from* The Christmas Chronicles.
PHOTO CREDITS: Kellsie Moore (1.1) and Maki Endres (1.2)

"What if I'm sleeping?"

"You are communicating that you are tired."

"What if I go off into the woods, and nobody knows I'm there, and I don't say anything to anyone?"

"Hmm. The very fact that you *chose* to go off into the woods by yourself, without telling *anybody*, says *a lot* about you!"

Yes, we are always sending information whether we intend to or not. Even in costume. *Especially* in costume. Why did you choose this persona? Why did you spend so much time and money, or so little, on its creation? How do you feel when you are wearing it? What are you telling me about who you are, what you fear, and how you see yourself?

The communicative process never ends. Kirkpatrick (2015) says that putting on a costume "visualizes a subject's desire to change their locus, to cross a border, and it is always a meaningful move. It affects all. In fictional worlds, we have no special name for this practice – characters simply just suit up – but in the real world we call it cosplay" [2.8].

That's what this book is about. Cosplay. Actually, that is what it started to be about, but it exploded from there to look at costumes in a variety of settings: drag, celebrity impersonations, historical reenactments, and more. Hence the book's subtitle regarding *cosplay and beyond*. Collectively, it is that dynamic and meaningful process of sending and receiving information using a *costume* as both the message and the medium. One of the best ways to get at that communication is by conducting in-depth interviews with participants of the activity. In these pages, you'll learn about a variety of factors that go into costume wearing, and get to meet a number of individuals in what we call "Costume Conversations."

As we begin this journey together, let's set a foundation and first take a quick look at some history of costume usage.

History

To dress in costume, states Liptak (2022), is "a form of play or communication that allows the wearer to enhance or immerse themselves and their audience in a fictional construct, whether that's reenacting a story or trying to communicate with a deity." He adds that our earliest ancestors "might have grabbed some sort of prop to aid in telling a story over the flickering light of a fire, or adorned themselves with something to better convey the particular traits of a character or creature" (p. 173).

In fact, drawings of shamans wearing animal costumes – dating back 15 to 20 thousand years - were found in prehistoric caves of Lascaux and Trois-Freres in Southwestern France. In the drawings, the shamans are shown dancing and performing, leading Barbieri (2017) to conclude this wearing of animal skins by a shaman "may be a negotiation between his humanity and animality, through a process of metamorphosis to which costume is critical" (p. 3). Similarly, 24 red deer headdresses were found at a site named Star Carr in North Yorkshire, UK. Little et al. (2016) report the headdresses date to c.11 kyr (a scientific measurement of approximately 11,000 years, i.e., 9,000 BCE), pointing out that similar headdress, linked to shamanic practices, were common in iconography from Siberian reindeer cultures in the Pleistocene era (11,700 years and older). Pushkareva and Agaltsova (2021) claim that primeval rituals marking the end of hunting season by dancing with animal skins were in turn a prelude to early theater and the medieval carnival.

That makes sense. Very few people are showing up at comic conventions dressed as a Pleistocene Siberian reindeer shaman. Though it took generations to evolve, our current practices are more likely an extension of Victorian Masquerade balls (Cline, 2017). The first example of character cosplay may be in 1877, when Jules Verne hosted a masked ball where guests dressed as characters from his novels (Winge, 2019; citing Unwin, 2005).

Such events really came into public consciousness in the early 1900s. Most cosplay historians cite the same basic stories, though the facts and specifics get jumbled from source to source. Most sources tell the story of Myrtle R. Douglas. Presumably, a 1910 newspaper article published in the *Tacoma Times* of Washington describes her as going to a party dressed as Mr. Skygack from Mars, a popular newspaper comic character of the time (Cline, 2017; Crawford & Hancock, 2019; Han, 2020; Winge, 2019). Liptak (2022) says the seminal article is instead about a man named Otto James, who was arrested for wearing a Skygack costume to promote the opening of a roller rink, thus violating a city ordinance about wearing costumes. Perhaps Otto borrowed the costume from Myrtle?

Turning back to Myrtle, other newspaper accounts report her association with Forrest J. Ackerman. Together the two published a science fiction magazine and attended the first World Science Fiction Convention in 1939 dressed as characters from H.G. Wells 1936 *Things to Come* (see, for example, Brochu, 2017; Cline, 2017; Crawford & Hancock, 2019; Pushkareva and Agaltsova, 2021). Where the stories seem to disagree is whether Myrtle and Forrest are husband and wife, boyfriend and girlfriend, or father and daughter. For those interested in history, Liptak (2022) seems to have the best research, and shows the most photos from early days.

Despite the variations of the Myrtle and Forrest story, there is one thing on which all costume historians agree. They agree that the term "cosplay" is a portmanteau, or contraction, of the words "costume" and "play." They also agree that the first person to publish that word was Japanese writer Nobuyuki Takahashi (who graciously penned the Foreword to this book). Sources all tell a similar tale. They say he coined the term after attending the 1984 Worldcon science fiction convention in Los Angeles, and seeing attendees dressed in costumes from fandoms like *Star Trek* and *Star Wars* (Liptak, 2022). On his return, Takahashi – who wrote for a manga magazine – needed a term to explain the phenomenon to his Japanese readers. He wanted to encourage Japanese *otaku* (essentially, pop culture geeks or nerds) to participate in similar events. The closest word he had was a Japanese version of "masquerade," which was too formal. Using the practice of *gairaigo*, appropriating "loan words" from foreign languages for Japanese usage, Takahashi joined *kosu* (costume) and *pure* (play) to create *kosupure* (cosplay) (Brochu, 2017; Cline, 2017; Crawford & Hancock, 2019; Mountfort, Peirson-Smith, and Geczy, 2019; Winge, 2019; Han, 2020; Liptak, 2022).

A Trip to Japan

The most exciting thing about this historical retelling from the sources above is that it is *almost* completely accurate! Maki and I had the pleasure of traveling to Japan in October of 2022 to present early pieces of this work at the International Academic Forum's (IAFOR) *MediAsia* conference, and to take photos and get quotes for the book. While there, I had the chance to interview Takahashi-san personally in his Tokyo office. We discussed the word's creation, and our conversation mirrored much of what he shared in the Foreword. In reality, he and his colleagues had played with the term a year *prior* to the convention in Los

Angeles. In a 1983 article on college manga clubs, in *My Anime* magazine, he offered the phrase to explain what was happening on local campuses, as students were attending meetings dressed as their favorite *manga* (printed comics) and *anime* (animation) characters. After the convention, finding he needed to use the term on a much larger scale, he edited and reprinted the piece titled *Operation Cosplay* (see Image 1.3). At that point, it caught on, and a new world was born.

Image 1.3 *Nobuyuki Takahashi (left) shares with author Thomas Endres the 1983* My Anime *magazine in which he first used the word "cosplay"*
PHOTO CREDIT: Maki Endres

On this topic, Winge (2019) suggests that many overemphasize Japan's role and involvement in cosplay. She acknowledges that Japan is where the term cosplay was coined, but argues it is limited in scope to anime and manga, and that it is repressed as a subcultural activity due to parental displeasure (p. 8). As Takahashi confirms, the inspiration did come from American fandom, but it was he and his team who gave it a name. And having a name – a label, a symbol – is what contributed to the worldwide explosion of the cosplay phenomenon.

As for the repressed activity, Takahashi confirms that otaku youth are often reluctant to showcase their fandom in public. He explains that 60-70% of Japanese cosplayers are female and that all cosplayers, regardless of gender, wait until they get to the convention center to change and put on makeup. Then, at the end of the day, they change back into street clothes before heading home. Unless there is a special cosplay parade, the costumes never see the light of day. Yes, this is very different from an American convention, where you see cosplayers wandering all over the city streets, and eating and drinking in local bars and restaurants, on their way to and from the event. In Japan, Takahashi explains, it is almost invisible to the outsider. But the convention hall itself is a "secret place," and once the cosplayer enters, they are in "paradise."

While traveling around Tokyo, Kyoto, Osaka, and other locales, it was clear to see that Takahashi was correct. Seeing anyone dressed outside of the norm was a rare occurrence. There were a handful of frilly schoolgirl variations, kind of Lolita-light (to be explained later), but not much more. The only exception, in select districts known to attract otaku youth, was the preponderance of Maid Cafes; restaurants where the waitstaff was primarily young females dressed in lacy French maid outfits. While certain neighborhoods had a dozen or more young Maids standing outside the establishments, trying to drum up business, it was clear that photographs were not to be taken. Part of the problem lies in the fine line between innocent frills and fun, and more adult-oriented entertainment. Unauthorized photos are often exploited in erotica and porn. Takahashi laments that many in Japanese culture equate the concept of cosplay with suggestive outfits worn by women in gentlemen's clubs. Worse yet, when he is associated with the term, some think of him as more of a Hugh Hefner type than someone whose focus is on anime, manga, and youth.

While we're on the topic of Japan, I'll also point out that the most popular costume of all – the geisha – is equally challenging to find in the wild. Tourists renting and wearing traditional Japanese clothing abounds, but seeing a true geisha – a woman trained in ancient arts of hospitality and entertainment – occurs only in private settings like tea ceremonies. Again, photography in public is forbidden; the result of bad behaviors from locals and tourists. Additionally, ceremonial opportunities decreased significantly due to COVID, and the country was very slow in re-introducing such traditions.

Back to U.S. History
The science fiction conventions about which Takahashi wrote began to grow in popularity. In particular, fan bases grew around the 1960s *Star Trek* television series, and 1970s and 80s *Star Wars* trilogy (Liptak, 2022). The public at large was exposed to the cosplay phenomenon on January 26, 1979, in an episode from the extremely popular TV show *Wonder Woman* starring Lynda Carter. The episode, titled "Space Out," filmed at the actual 1978 GalatiCON gathering in Los Angeles, found Wonder Woman searching for the bad guy amid a sea of costumed fans (Winge, 2019).

It is not the intent here to go into detail on the interplay between television and movies and the activity of cosplay. Obviously, TV and film provide a great deal of source material for costume ideas. There were key moments that raised the "costume consciousness" of the general viewing audience. Movies like *Blade* (1998) and *Spider-Man* (2002) set the stage for the DC and Marvel universe explosion, which now dominate our cinema screens. Movie franchises such as *Harry Potter* and *Lord of the Rings* also contributed greatly to both costume ideas and overall public acceptance. On our TV screen, shows like the *Big Bang Theory* regularly showed Sheldon, Leonard, and crew attending comic conventions. This opened the door for actual television series about cosplay such as *Heroes of Cosplay* and *Cosplay Melee*. As those entities already have their own websites and social media platforms, we will return our focus here to the everyday fans who love to dress up.

Defining Costume

Talk to any cosplayer and you'll likely find that they enjoyed dressing up for Halloween as a kid. (Liptak, 2022, p. 168).

In an interview for the 2007 documentary *Confessions of a Superhero*, Marvel comic book legend Stan Lee said, "I always felt if I had a superpower, I wouldn't wear a costume. I'm a showoff. I wouldn't wear a mask and conceal my identity, and I wouldn't want to look like an idiot in some costume." That's ironic language coming from a man credited with creating (or co-creating) over 350 costumed heroes including Captain America, Spider-Man, the Fantastic Four, X-Men, the Black Panther, Dr. Strange, and the Incredible Hulk.

Well, even if Stan would opt not to wear a costume, many of us – with or without superpowers – are willing to put one on. With that, I needed to come up with a definition of what constitutes a *costume*. Foolishly thinking this would be an easy task, I found it to be a complicated continuum, with no clear starting or ending point. To help, let's first examine what others have to say.

Fudimova (2021) defined costumes by their function more so than their appearance, saying they serve as "a protective shell" and a "carrier of cultural tradition" (p. 1). I like that. Lamerichs (2011) defined costume more by the locale of their usage, including comic cons, Renaissance fairs, historical reenactments, and LARPs (live action role plays). While we meet people from all those venues in these pages, this definition is still more *where* than *what*. Scott (2015) explained costumes by examining their fabrication techniques, observing there is sometimes a gender distinction between men, who often work on resin casting, plaster or latex molding, and wiring LED components, and women, who do sewing, makeup application, and wig styling. Practical, but still not a definition.

Broader insight is provided by Peirson-Smith (2013), who argued that we all have a public self (which all see), a private self (which those closest to us see), and a secret self (an imagined fantasy). Cosplay can produce a "publicly exhibited secret self, and the players are not only visually transformed by the costume, but often become the imagined persona, both cognitively and affectively, carrying this into their daily lives and other social worlds" (p. 90).

Ultimately, I was most persuaded by French and Reddy-Best, who defined costume as "intentional as it indicates clothing worn with an intended meaning in a particular context that is typically outside of everyday roles or activities that often takes the wearer through a transformational experience via 'mythical places' or 'emotional depths'" (2021, p. 2). Close on its heels is the following observation by Shukla:

> Costume is usually set apart from dress in its rarity, cost, and elaborate materials, trims, and embellishments, and in its pronounced silhouette or exaggerated proportions. It is not meant to be ordinary, but, rather, evocative, urging the daily further along an artistic trajectory that leads to heightened communication and often culminates in a spectacle for public consumption. (2015, p. 4)

In pulling forward the best elements of those works, and combining them with elements of my home discipline, I offer the following definition for this book: *A costume is a conscious decision about clothing, recognizable as outside the everyday norm, that an individual wears in specific or public locales, in order to make a statement or send a message.* Essentially, a costume exists when the wearer *intentionally* selects the outfit; they know that their attire is *different* from everyday clothing; and they understand that the outfit *communicates* something to others.

It is different than a uniform. Thus, the person who helps you at Best Buy is not in costume, even though their blue shirt with the yellow logo is outside of the daily norm. However, if that salesperson has augmented that blue shirt with matching blue hair/lipstick/eye shadow/nails, or is wearing a Pennywise the clown mask, or paisley bellbottoms with platform shoes, or a kilt and sporran, we can safely say they have entered costume territory. It might not be a full-blown and complete costume, but – because it is intentional, outside of the norm, and makes a statement – we can place it within our costume continuum (we will discuss these distinctions more in Chapter 4).

Copyright

Before digging deeper, let's get one question out of the way. Is there a point at which we accuse these costume-wearers of copyright infringement? Is that person dressed as the Scarlett Witch going to be sued by Marvel for her choice? Madonia (2016) clearly explains that costumes and cosplay generally fall under the Fair use clause of the Copyright Act of 1976. First and foremost, most cosplayers do this as a hobby. Most of them pay to go to a convention, rather than get paid. We are part of a collage. Our pastiche of costumed characters is not a direct threat to the copyright holder. What about professional cosplayers, or those who accept money for their costumed performance? Generally, there is no copyright infringement because it is often not a verbatim replica; even the most professional of reproductions has a personal spin (also discussed in Chapter 4). But the biggest reason she won't get sued is because her costume does not impact the Market Value of the copyright holder. Seeing a costumed character out in public won't stop you from buying the comic or seeing the movie. No one will say, "Hmm, I just saw someone dressed as the Black Panther. Now I can skip going to see *Wakanda Forever*." Not going to happen. Having fans dress up as superhero or anime characters will not have a negative impact on the original. In fact, it may very well have a positive one; seeing that person dressed as Black Panther may instead prompt you to go see *Wakanda Forever*. Everybody benefits.

With a working definition in hand, and a degree of comfort that we won't be party to any lawsuits, we can start to dig into the *why* of costumes. Ed Hoff, who managed communications for the 2016 World Cosplay Summit (an international competition held in Nagoya, Japan, since 2003), observes: "When human beings have a little bit of free time, and a little bit of money, we dress up. We put on costumes. We get up on stage and we watch people get up on stage and enjoy flipping over the world." He adds, "This is what differentiates humans from animals, in a way. Costuming is a part of us" (2017, *Cosplay Culture*).

I wholeheartedly agree with this notion that costuming is a part of us; of who we are and how we present ourselves to the world. And that, for me, is where it starts to get interesting.

Costume and Identity

Are we the mask we present to others, or whatever is behind the mask?
                        Casanova, Levoy, and Weirich (2020, p. 800)

During the months I was traveling the country conducting interviews for this book, people frequently asked me to explain what the project was about. My short answer was "costume and identity," though often that only resulted in quizzical expressions and confused looks. I'd follow up by saying something like, "It's a look at how people use costumes, not to cover up who they are, but to reveal aspects of themselves that often don't see the light of day." Most often, that explanation led to head nods and knowing expressions. Not only did people get it; they agreed.

"What if I told you," asks PhD and psychologist Andrea Letamendi, "that persons who cosplay actually feel more like themselves when they are in costume? What if looking like someone else makes them feel like who they really are? And what if that process is a completely normal one?" (2015, p. 273). Letamendi then shares a story of a woman who was interested in cosplay but was reluctant to participate. The woman was worried that the costume would "expose her face," and she was unsure how she'd be treated, as people would then see her true self (p. 277).

This "expression of the interior" is a theme repeated consistently in the literature. "Despite an emphasis on the exterior, cosplay is an internal transformation," argues Letamendi (2015), "It's neither shielding nor displaying our identity; it's somewhere in between. Cosplay is an integration of our identity and the character we are embodying" (p. 273).

Similarly, Nichols (2021) claims that cosplay moves deeper than simple masquerade, "to include the affective resonance between the identity of cosplayer and that of the character that they are seeking to portray" (p. 60). Rahman, Sun, and Cheung (2012) make analogous observations. They describe cosplay as a fun and playful activity that "enables enthusiasts to imitate the personas of their adored characters and to re-create an imaginative self in reality" (p. 321). For them, it is a form of "escapism" in the "boundaries between reality and fantasy" through which cosplayers can "enter into an imaginative world or into dreamlike states of hyperreality" (p. 333). They conclude:

> Through cosplay, the identity of a person can be transformed from a high-school student to a hero, from a woman to a beautiful boy, from an ordinary person to a celebrity – this changing identity of performativity is a magic wand or time machine which can offer excitement, contentment, escapism, and empowerment. (p. 334)

On the one hand, those are powerful statements. They agree that cosplay is clearly transformative, but are careful not to delve too far into the psyche of the players. There may be aspects of one's true identity driving the car, but the destination is still within the realm of make-believe. Other scholars take a stronger stance. Crawford and Hancock (2019) speak to this specifically:

> Many writers are keen to emphasise [sic] that though cosplay may appear to be primarily about escapism – such as in terms of escaping oneself and becoming someone else – on closer inspection it would appear to be much more complex than this…. This is certainly how many of those we spoke to saw cosplay – not necessarily as a mechanism for playing out another character, or imitation, but rather, as a way of exploring aspects of what they saw as their existing identity. (p. 135)

That is the stance of this book. Sure, there are a lot of people who are just dressing up for the fun of it, with no real thought put into it. But for many – like the people showcased in each chapter's "Costume Conversations" – putting on a costume is done to reveal, not conceal. I love Yamato's (2020) suggestion that "cosplay activity prompts a self-identification process that enables people to experience the acts of searching, revealing, and/or reflection as well as a prolonged process of self-identification of 'what I am becoming.'" [5.7]. It runs deeper than just being excited to dress as a loved character, observed Aljanahi and Alsheikh (2021), as "they felt it was important to express themselves and their identities through these characters" (p. 213). The authors continue, noting that cosplayers "assume, negotiate, and share different facets of their identities" and, using their own "symbols, lingua franca, and facts, they found ways to remix texts and insert their own semiotics" (2021, p. 216). Put simply, in their personal journey of self-discovery, cosplayers meld aspects of their inner selves with empowering attributes of their characters, and display something new, personal, and unique to the world.

The biggest reason seems to be empowerment. "Empowerment," notes Mountfort et al. (2019), is "at the core of the rhetoric of power in cosplay" (p. 122). Winge (2019) agrees, pointing out that cosplayers, by imbuing the power of their character, provides them "the opportunity for empowerment, agency, and self-determination" (p. 86). This is important for many because, as we'll see throughout this book, cosplayers are often somewhat shy and reserved in real life. This probably comes as no surprise, but it is important to note that this assumption about cosplayers is indeed validated in study after study. For example, following numerous in-person interviews with cosplayers, Rosenberg and Letamendi (2018) conclude that many cosplayers are shy when out of costume, and that "engaging in cosplay allows them to be more outgoing than their usual selves" [1.4]. Many of their subjects opted for characters whose personalities were venturesome, sensation-seeking, and sociable. In that way, they could integrate those qualities into their costumed self. Among the many byproducts of such integration, notes Letamendi, are a full range of human emotions and "something we often struggle to find: a feeling of acceptance" (2015, p. 273). Cline (2017) equates the benefits of cosplay to those of role play therapy, helping participants with social anxiety and even PTSD to overcome phobias and social awkwardness.

Does that make cosplay a deceitful practice? Is putting a costume over our passive and anxious shell a fraudulent act? Not at all. In fact,

Casanova, Levoy, and Weirich (2020) found that their interviewees believed they had *one true self*, and they could choose what aspects to reveal based upon their embodied portrayal. Again, they were taking what was already inside them, and using the cosplay persona to bring it more fully to the surface. "It seems surprising," concluded Casanova et al. "that these cosplayers claim to feel more comfortable with their presentation of self in costume than out of costume" (p.811). So, if anything, the presentation of self while in costume may be the most honest portrayal possible. As Mongan concludes, "Upon reflection, the act of cosplaying is a practice in finding truths, not manufacturing lies" (2015, para. 0.1).

On this topic, Crawford and Hancock once again provide some powerful commentary about self and identity:

On the one hand, most of us like to hold onto the idea that there is a real and true us, which is fairly constant and consistent. When we do something that we feel is out of character, we often apologise *[sic]* and say that it was not like us, or not who we really are. Similarly, often we can accuse others of not being themselves, or putting on a front or an act, which deceives and hides who they really are. On the other hand, contemporary society has multiple large and profitable industries based around helping us improve or change who we are. So, the assumption is that there is a real us, but this real us can be improved; there can be a better version of us we can work towards. (2019, pp. 124-25)

For all those who asked me what this book was about, a rare few got to hear this much detail in my reply. But it is ultimately the reason I started the project. I believe that costumes allow an individual to make conscious choices about public representation that allow dormant aspects of their personality, mostly those associated with confidence and sociability, to come to the fore. It is not an act of deception; it is an act of transformation on the journey to the best version of us that we can be. There is some truth to that old "fake it until you make it" credo. And if the act of costuming allows individuals to practice and eventually embody a new and stronger self, then we should of course support the activity. Dress up!

Pulling it all together, Mountfort et al. (2019) provide the following description, which I believe nicely sums up the activity. "Cosplayers are constantly traversing boundaries: physically when they put on the costume and transform their appearance, cognitively as they think like the character and feel consequently empowered, affectively as they experience a changed emotional state, behaviourally when they pose and act 'in character' and virtually when they share their captured cosplay images across multiple digital platforms" (p. 152). Traversing boundaries. Transforming appearance. Cognition and empowerment. Emotional affect. Behavior and action. Sharing across platforms. All these things are worthy of further investigation and discussion.

Before leaving this chapter, I want to make quick mention of a select group of individuals who, in the expression of inner qualities, move beyond *self*-improvement and devote their energies to the improvement of *others*. Letamendi says that cosplay "lifts up and makes accessible our own capacity to experience and express wonderful human emotions" (2015, p. 273). Among those qualities she lists, perhaps the most important of them all is altruism.

Cosplay and Charity
One of the more exciting things I've encountered in the cosplay community is the extent to which so many are willing to use their costumed personas to the betterment of humanity. Whether it be the Battlin' Betties visiting V.A. hospitals, or the Star Wars 501st Legion hosting an anti-bullying campaign, the use of cosplay for charitable purposes is growing fast. A quick Google search finds numerous organizations, including Costumers for a Cause (FL), Guardians of Justice (FL), Kids Can Cosplay (CA), the Justice League of WNY (NY), the League of Enchantment (IL), Phoenix Fan Fusion (AZ), Cosplay Supporting Charity (GA), Heroes, Inc. (UT), or Cosplay for a Cause (KY), to name just a few. I've had the good fortune to participate in a handful of events,

including fundraising for the Geeks of Grandeur project to bring anti-microbial video gaming equipment to hospitalized children. You'll hear many tales of altruism throughout this book, including the touching story of Hospital Batman at the end of this chapter.

Though it is impossible to capture the full scope of this emerging phenomenon, we can narrow the field of focus and briefly meet Matt Gnojek, better known as the Colorado Captain. Dressed as Captain America, and riding around on a Harley-Davidson painted in a WWII motif, Matt volunteers time at numerous charity events and spearheads cross-country rides to raise money for pediatric cancer. I caught up with Matt at a youth event and, when the tsunami of children around him finally subsided, got to talk about his work. Even with no children around, Matt is careful to watch his language and speak in the fresh and clean Chris Evans-style we've grown accustomed to in the Marvel movies.

"I started doing it because I was an out-of-work actor, and I started working for a birthday party company," he explained. "I ended up borrowing one of their Captain America suits to go to the kid's birthday party, and along the way I noticed that folks on the highway thought it was really fun when they saw Captain America riding a motorcycle. It occurred to me that maybe this was an opportunity to keep on making people smile. Maybe if I could make them smile, I could take them out of their day, and give them an opportunity to feel that hope, and that joy, again. After that, it turned into volunteering for charity, and I've been doing it ever since."

The number of events he does each year depends in part on the weather, which impacts his ability to ride. "My active months are typically between March and December. During that time period I always do a motorcycle trip across the country. That usually takes me anywhere between 15-17 states, and there's always one event like a comic con and one hospital stop. I also make a point to stop at LGBT centers, refugee centers, veterans memorials, things that I think really bring the country together and unite us under a flag of positive American unification."

Image 1.4 *Colorado Captain Matt Gnojek*

Here we have a young man, initially unemployed, who found the better part of himself after donning a Captain America costume. And what did this transformation evoke? How does it make him feel? "I get to be a part of peoples' day," he says, beaming. "There's no better feeling than knowing that the smile you're getting from someone else, you got to give to them in return. It feels like a million bucks." (Unfortunately, about a month after our interview, Matt was involved in a motorcycle accident. His bike and costume were largely destroyed. More frightening, he experienced head injuries which will leave him with nerve damage on his face. At the time of this writing, he is on the mend, optimistic about his recovery, and plans to return to fundraising in the very near future.)

Summary

We are in a constant state of communication; everything we do sends some type of message about us. Nowhere is this more true than when we are in costume. The activity of costuming has been around a long time, perhaps tens of thousands of years. In more contemporary times, we picture masquerade balls and, most recently, comic conventions. The word *cosplay* has been around to describe that latter activity since the early 1980s. Since then, the popularity of the activity, and the public's general awareness thereof, has increased significantly. To better examine the phenomenon, a definition of costume – which includes intention, being outside the norm, and message conveyance – is offered. When costumes are worn in activities such as cosplay, there is often a message about self-identification. As Lamerichs argues:

> Thus, when we speak of identity and identification in cosplay, we speak of two things. On the one hand, players actualize a narrative and its meaning; on the other hand, they actualize their own identities. To put it bluntly, by stating that a narrative or character is related to me – that I can identify with this particular story or person – I make a statement about myself. There is a transformative potential in this ability to express who we are through fiction. (2014, [5.4])

Via this transformative potential, cosplayers can capitalize on their character's strongest attributes and align them with their own corresponding traits. Primarily a form of empowerment used to strengthen social skills, other positive traits can be elicited. Most rewarding are those which focus on the benefit of others, and manifest themselves in a variety of charitable activities. We will see how these decisions about costume align with identity in the three Costume Conversations that follow, focusing on family connections, fandom, and giving.

COSTUME CONVERSATION # 1
Eric Adams
a.k.a. Gene Simmons from KISS

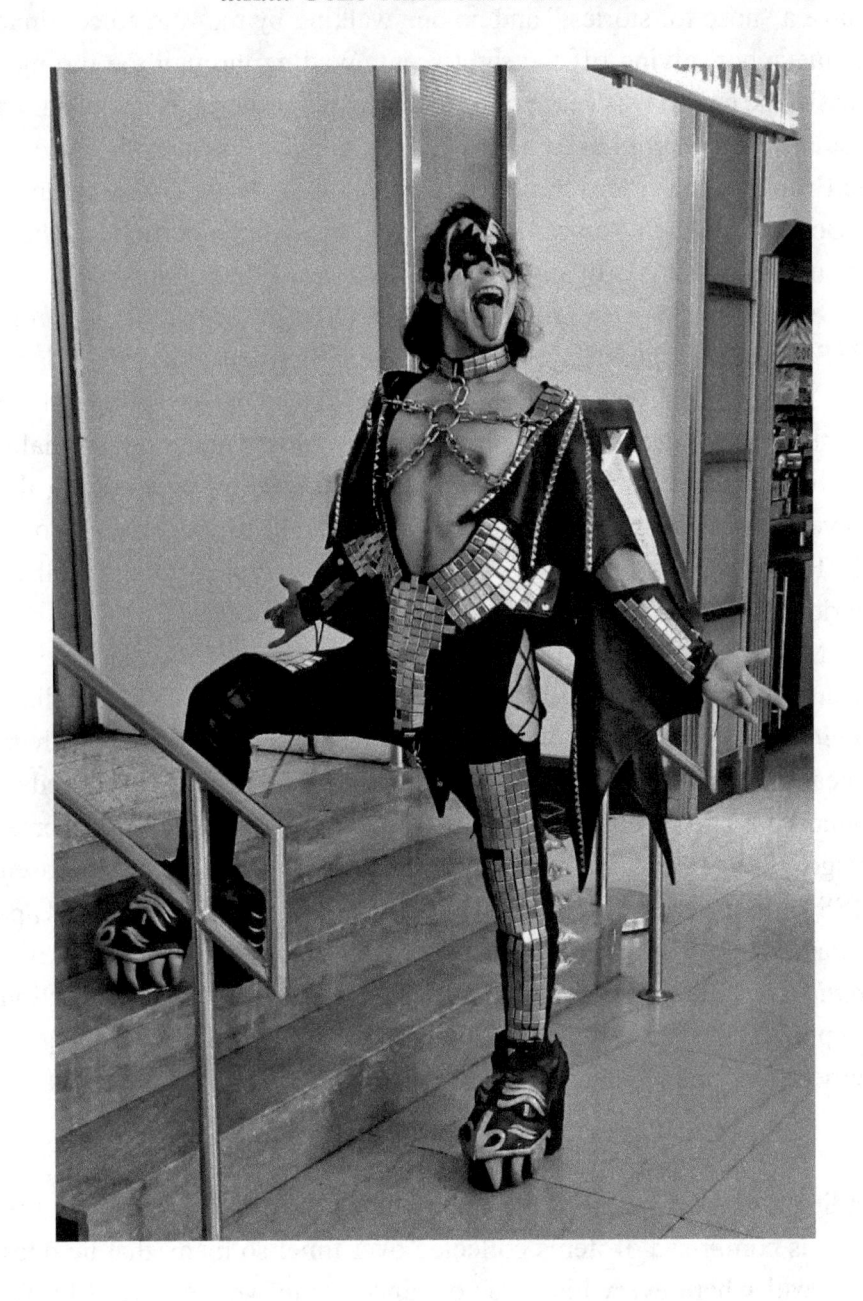

Walking around the Big Apple Comic Con in New York City, held in the iconic 1929 art deco New Yorker Hotel, it took a while to find the right person to interview. I've been told I have a "nose for stories," and no one walking by me was, to continue the metaphor, giving off the right scent. Wading through the throngs, most of the crowd was very young, and dressed in a prefabricated anime costume picked up in one of New York's popular costume shops (e.g., the Brooklyn Superhero Supply Co. in Midtown, New York Costumes in Boerum Hill, or Abracadabra in the Flatiron neighborhood). There was nothing wrong with any of this; I just wasn't finding my story.

Suddenly, Gene Simmons, the 1980s-through-today rock god from KISS walked by me. Okay, not really Gene Simmons, but Eric Adams – a 30-ish Brooklyn cook and tattoo artist from the Long Island Bayshore area – decked out in very realistic garb and make-up. I initially lost him in the crowd but, standing atop the balcony overlooking the convention rooms, he wasn't hard to find. Thanks to his elevated boots and Buddha-like topknot, he towered over the typical Dragonball or Mario Bros. characters.

My first question cut to the chase. Why, at a *comic* convention, was he dressed as an 80's rock icon? "To be fair," Eric quickly replied, "there are KISS comic books out there." He was right. Starting with an appearance in a 1977 issue of *Howard the Duck*, KISS has appeared in comic books from multiple publishers including Marvel, Dark Horse, Image, IDW, Platinum, and even Archie comics! While the proposed KISS cartoon series never came to fruition, they did make animated appearances in a couple of *Scooby-Doo* specials, as well as TV shows like *Family Guy* and *Fairly Odd Parents*. Given the number of KISS action and plush figures over the decades, along with other collectibles ranging from buttons and bandanas to licensed tees and lunch boxes, it is safe to say that KISS characters fit within the comic realm.

Eric's costume is impressively authentic. His girlfriend Amy, attending with him but not in costume, gets credit for the makeup. The outfit is comprised of items collected over time; so many that he does not recall where everything was obtained, or in what order. "I'm not even sure how I got this costume to begin with." Some pieces, he points out, are from actual KISS concerts. Has he met the band? "Yes, actually." He points out spots on his chest pieces that have been signed by group members. More impressive, he holds out his arm to show off his tattoos. "I have Gene Simmons' autograph right here," Eric points out. "He signed it with Sharpie. And I also have Paul Stanley right above it."

And how did these pieces – comic cons and KISS fandom – come together? Eric's answer gets to the core of costume and identity: *"It's kind of like a relationship thing with my dad."* He goes on to explain, "When I first started coming to comic con, I came with my dad. He and I started coming as security for vendors." In addition to comic conventions, there was also a shared love for the band. "Me and my dad would go to KISS concerts and everything. It started with KISS conventions, I think, and I would go to KISS conventions dressed up like this, and so I was like 'You know what, let me try going to other conventions dressed up like this.'"

Big Apple Comic Con is Eric's first convention back since the start of coronavirus. In the past, he has attended other events such as Winter Con and Horror Con. He always wears the KISS costume, and is pleased that people have begun to recognize him from one event to the next. "It's a lot of fun. I get a lot of feedback from it." Looking ahead, there are plans to attend more comic related events, and definitely more KISS conventions. "It's just a great experience when we come out here," he explains. "A lot of people are very welcoming and friendly, so it's a nice atmosphere. It's just a lot of fun."

As a firm believer that cosplayers can dress as anyone they choose, regardless of shape, gender, color, and the like, I was a bit reluctant to ask the next question. Why Gene "The Demon" Simmons? In real life, Gene Simmons is a mesomorph (stocky build), but Eric is more of an Ectomorph (lean, slender). Why not dress as Paul "The Starchild" Stanley or Ace "Space" Frehley, who better match his physique? The answer once again goes back to his relationship with his father. "My dad plays guitar; he's more toward Paul Stanley, who is the front man – for anybody who doesn't know – the lead singer, guitarist. My dad plays lead guitar. Gene Simmons is more the bassist. I play bass."

All answers, clearly, go back to Eric's dad – so I asked him to tell me more. "Growing up, I've been listening to KISS music, mostly because of him." He adds with a chuckle, "A lot of people assume it's forced. You know, when they see someone's dad, it's like 'Oh, they're forcing their kids to listen.' Not really. I actually enjoy KISS, and it has a lot to do with how me and my dad get along."

To emphasize the point, Eric repeats, "Me and my dad we get along through KISS. We get along through music." Looking up, he motions to the crowd of people standing around, waiting to get a photo with him: "Music speaks volumes for a lot of people." With that, Eric returns to his fans.

COSTUME CONVERSATION # 2
Kat Sawyer and Lee Montgomery
a.k.a. U.S.S. Tiburon Star Fleet Officers

Married couple Kathleen "Kat" Sawyer and Lee Montgomery are proud members of Star Fleet International, the world's oldest Star Trek fan association. Founded in 1974, the organization has over 6000 members representing more than 220 chapters in over 20 countries. Kat and Lee's chapter is called the U.S.S. Tiburon. (Tiburon is Spanish for shark. "Nothing to do with the show," Lee explains, "but the founders are big fans of sharks – one was in the Navy."). Each chapter has officers. Lee is currently Chief Operations Officer; he keeps track of records and participation points. Kat is the chapter's Counselor, akin to the Deanna Troi character from *Star Trek: The Next Generation*. "My job is to take care of the ensigns – the under 18 kids that join. Getting them stuff to do, to conventions, bring them in."

Starfleet International does not require an affiliation to any particular Star Trek series though, unofficially, the norm for Tiburon is *Deep Space Nine*. The chapter does a lot of philanthropic work. One of the biggest projects is Tribbles for Charity. The group makes the iconic furballs from the original series, and "adopt" them out for a select charity each year. Other events include food drives, toy drives, and serving meals at homeless shelters. The chapter attends conventions with a large booth, including a transporter-ish backdrop ideal for photo ops (see Batman picture from Chapter 1).

As for the uniforms? Lee explains that most items are ordered online. "I try to stay away from anything that is overtly manufactured from, like, Rubies. Rubies costumes are nice, for what they are, but they are a one-day costume." They remind him of the Ben Cooper boxed Halloween costumes from the '70s and '80s. Both agree a lot of it is simply piecing things together, with Lee adding, "Our uniforms are from one place. Our comm badges are from one place. Any of the props we carry - it is all put together from the best of what you have available."

Most fleet-members portray Star Trek characters in general; not trying to recreate a particular person. There are some exceptions in their chapter, with individuals dressing specifically as Data or Dr. Beverly Crusher (*The Next Generation*) or Captain Janeway (*Voyager*). They report that their chapter's Admiral has over 40 different uniforms. Kat has three. Lee has two, but one is in need of repair.

Kat enjoys dressing as characters from alien races, including a cat-like species known as Caitian (from fanlore and an animated series), and a Trill – a humanoid species with spots on their face (from *TNG* and *Deep Space Nine*). Lee is most often a Star Fleet officer, though has been known to dress as a Klingon (a Vulcan-like race from the original series largely revamped for later shows and movies) and a Ferengi (a scheming and highly capitalistic race, associated most with *Deep Space Nine*, and known for their large foreheads and huge rounded ears). "The headpiece for the Ferengi is not as hard as you'd think," said Lee, describing the item he purchased on eBay. "It's just a great big rubber thing. The problem: because it's rubber, it's hollow inside. We bought some art foam, and I filed it down to make it like a helmet. We tape it down with medical adhesive." He now has the makeup process, which originally took about an hour-and-a half to complete, down to about 45 minutes. However, he concludes, "It is hot. It is uncomfortable."

Just as each Star Trek episode begins with the "seek out new life and new civilizations" exposition, the preceding paragraphs were the preview and set-up to the important part of the interview – the process that formed Kat and Lee as a couple, and the healing and helping role that costumes played. They met on an online dating site, and Kat, looking to Lee, says "You wearing a costume is the reason we even met." To which Lee responded with a nod, "That is true." This is their origin story.

When they met, Kat suffered from crippling social anxiety, which impacted most facets of her life. She was hoping to meet someone to help pull her from her shell. Lee had just gotten out of a long relationship and, looking for a human connection, joined a few different dating apps. After an extended period with no responses, he asked a cousin to review his profile. He narrates their discussion. "She looked it over and said 'I know exactly what your problem is. You're a geek. Why is that not on here?' 'Well, it's there. I listed that I like this show and that show.' 'No, no, that's not what I'm saying. *You're a geek*. Why are there not pictures of that? Why is it not showing the level of things that you do?' 'You're joking.' 'No, I'm not. That's something people are going to want to see. You don't hide that.' 'Okay.'

So Lee went through his pictures and posted several from cosplay conventions, including his Ferengi costume. Initially, there was still no response, and he considered dropping the app, when suddenly he received an extremely long message. Kat laughs, "It was a five-page email! If you know me, that's very short!" From there the message exchange began. "We're texting live back and forth," recalls Lee, "and I think that conversation lasted five hours. All because of this one picture that she saw of me as the Ferengi."

"I just sent him an email that said how much Star Trek has meant to me in my life," Kat explains. "My dad and I used to watch *Star Trek* together. Uhura and Troi and Crusher and Seven of Nine; all these women were strong, independent women. They were beautiful, and they could still kick your ass. Well, my mother – I love her, she's my mom

– but she was very much a '50s housewife. Men are right. Women are subservient. Women don't do this thing. I was always on the back burner. My dad – he was just this 'I don't' know how to connect with my daughter' guy. So, he gave me comic books. And through that my dad realized I liked this kind of stuff; 'Let's watch this show.' And it was *Star Trek*. Growing up, that was my dad's and my bonding time, when *Star Trek* was on. My mother, she hated it. And I learned to be who I am and who I wanted to be through these women, and that was part of what I wrote to him in the email. Star Trek has always been a big thing in my life. I basically told him, 'Hey, I want to meet the man who is brave enough to dress as a Ferengi.' Out of all the aliens in the world, a Ferengi!" Lee laughs and adds, "I'll be honest. I don't whether it's bravery or stupidity."

Following this foundational exchange, it was time for the couple to meet. It is here that Kat's social anxiety came into play. "When I first met Lee, I would have panic attacks just going to the grocery store." Their first couple of dates were nonproblematic, quiet, and low-key, but then he added costumes into the mix. "It was our third date," Lee explains. "She called me up and said 'I have this event I want to go to over at the Denver Museum of Nature and Science. It's on magical creatures. Would you mind going with me?'" He told her he would, as long as they both dressed up as wizards. At that, both Kat and Lee in unison detail her response – "'What? No. I don't want to do that!'" The conversation then proceeded rapid-fire as follows:

Lee: "I rode three busses across town, and I brought three backpacks. I brought two trench coats, a great big walking stick, a couple of wands, all this stuff. I said 'Figure out what fits you. Layer.'"

Kat: "This was in June, mind you."

Lee: "We then rode another two busses."

Both: "Got lost."

Kat: "I was really nervous about the whole thing. I'm like 'People are going to look at us weird. Oh my god. They'll think we're these mental patients who have escaped.' But, because the exhibit we were going to was magical creatures, people thought we were actually part of the display. They would come up and talk to us."

Lee: "Yes, they did. Other people were wearing robes from Hogwarts, or Harry Potter-esque, and they were giving us high fives. 'Man, you look awesome.'"

Kat: "Going home, on the bus, people were like 'Are you from a play?' It kind of clicked in my head a little bit then that, okay, if I'm in a costume, I'm a little shielded…because it's not me. It's not Kathleen. It's not Kat."

This first experience with costume helped Kat realize that cosplay both protected her and allowed her to practice those confident qualities modeled by the Star Trek women she so admired. "And then," Kat exclaims, "we had the chance to go to Comic Con." They volunteered to help one of the guests run his booth. Because they were in costume, many assumed they were in charge. Things went great for Kat, until their shift was over. She was supposed to change into her street clothes and meet Lee back at the booth. She describes what happened next: "Well, if you've ever been to a convention, you know it's really hard to find where you need to be. You get lost very, very easily. I'm in a t-shirt and a pair of pants, and trying to figure out how to get back to where I need to be. And there's just so many people coming and going. It was just like a sea, and I had an anxiety attack. I backed myself into a corner, just to breathe. And somebody dressed as the bunny, Frank, from Donnie Darko, came over. I was in full panic. I thought I was starting to hallucinate. He says, 'Can I help you?' And I'm thinking, 'these are imaginary characters; what am I doing? Okay, I'm just going to go with it.' And I told them where I needed to be. They took me back. Frank said, 'Are you safe now? Are you okay?' And I said 'yeah,' and it fully clicked into my head that, when I was in my uniform, I could walk around that convention – because it wasn't me. I had a force field. I had my shields up. Without the costume I didn't have my shield up."

Things have improved greatly for Kat since that episode, not only for conventions but for daily activities and her work as a manager and bartender. "I would have never been able to do what I do for work now if it wasn't for the fact that cosplay helps. Even my work uniform is a form of cosplay, if that makes sense. I put on my black polo, or put on my gray bartender shirt, and I'm not Kat, Lee's wife, the cat's mommy, Bill's daughter. I'm Assistant Manager Kat. I'm the Bartender Kat, and I know how to make my drinks. It helps, being in costume. Just changing your clothes."

"So, yeah, it's helped a lot," Kat concludes. Wrapping up, she shares, "I have a really good friend who is a psychologist, and I've told her this story. It's not a secret. Anybody who knows me eventually will hear the story! And she does use it in one of her talks; one of her panels at conventions. Because she does cosplay, and how cosplay helps through therapy. She's like, 'Yeah, Kat's a perfect example of that.' I'm always a little skittish, a little shy, when I'm out of my uniform. I get in my uniform, I'm Kat, a Star Fleet officer. I don't even worry about it anymore." The moral to the story is clear. Out of uniform, she feels vulnerable. In uniform, if you'll forgive the cheeky paraphrase, she and Lee boldly go where they've never gone before.

COSTUME CONVERSATION # 3
Casey Barrett
a.k.a. Hospital Batman

I watch him when we first arrive at the children's event for a community program. There are a dozen costumed characters milling about: Elsa from *Frozen*, Rocket and Groot from *Guardians of the Galaxy*, Spider-Man, Cinderella, and even our friend Matt, the Colorado Captain. Most are playing games with the kids; shooting baskets, tossing bean bags, or hanging out at the playground equipment. Casey Barrett's character, better known as Hospital Batman, stays in the background. He talks with the kids and poses for pictures but, in true Batman form, he remains somewhat aloof.

After the event, as he changes out of his costume, Casey sits down with me to talk. This is one of twenty or so volunteer events that he does throughout the year in the Denver area. On some occasions, for Marvel-only events, he'll go as Star-Lord (Peter Quill) from *Guardians of the Galaxy*. But mostly he's Batman. Hospital Batman. Some of his fellow heroes also attend cosplay events such as conventions, but for Casey he generally puts on the cowl only for volunteer activities such as Make-A-Wish, MS walks, Destination Imagination, and Tim Tebow's Night to Shine. He also helps a local group, PLANet Giving, that does small wishes for community members. While those examples tell you a little bit of what Casey does as a volunteer, nothing could be more powerful than hearing him explain why.

Casey is the father of two: a 16-year-old high functioning autistic son, and a 10-year-old wheelchair-bound daughter with a genetic disorder that leaves her functioning like a one-month-old. Casey, a licensed CNA, is her caretaker. His third child, a son with a disorder similar to his daughter's, sadly passed away in 2010. Because of these health challenges, Casey labels his family as "frequent fliers to Children's Hospital." Over the years, he recalls many occasions where the hospital had special visitors, ranging from therapy dogs to Miss Colorado. One of the more impactful moments occurred when his daughter was hospitalized for influenza.

"This was 2014 maybe. We took our son to the hospital to see his sister. He didn't really understand. He kind of had a meltdown in the lobby of Children's Hospital. That particular day, Captain Jack Sparrow [from *Pirates of the Caribbean*] walked into the lobby. He [the son] was big into pirates at the time and it completely flipped his day around. That was relief for him but also for me. The character, I've never met him, was fantastic, really got into the role. Costume was great, too; had all the props, the compass and all that stuff. Really got my son into the whole shebang. That was really a big moment for me. For my son, he forgot that his sister was upstairs, forgot we were in the lobby of a hospital. That all just went away in that moment. It really didn't click as what I wanted to do, but the moment clicked the impact of what this does."

A year later, Casey was at a party supply store and saw a Batman Dark Knight costume for around $300. His wife agreed to the purchase but told him to find something else to do with it beyond just Halloween: "If you're going to spend that much on it, get something else out of it." Remembering the Jack Sparrow incident, Casey reached out to the director of volunteers for a local hospital and asked how to get involved. They sat down together and started to talk about the rules. For example, those planning to visit more than three times, "they want you to go through the whole process – the health checks, the blood tests, the background checks, and all that stuff." When all seemed situated, the director said, "I forgot to ask. What's your costume made of? We're a latex-free campus." Ironically, Casey's entire suit was latex! "At this point I was invested emotionally," he told me. "I'm going to make this happen. I started a GoFundMe. I found a company out of Tampa – Gotham City FX – that did a rubber urethane, no latex, custom suit. I raised the money in like three weeks and ordered it." He added that the GoFundMe company did a small promotional piece on his fundraiser, and even donated to the cause.

With urethane suit in hand, Casey was ready to begin. "Coincidentally, the day I got the suit, my daughter had to go in for an overnight EEG study, so I took it with me. Her nurse told me to get dressed in it, so my daughter was actually my first visit." Casey literally beamed as he shared this. "It was just amazing. It really couldn't have been planned any better." He followed that with an equally amazing lobby visit, and he was hooked. "One thing I wanted to make sure is that I was always volunteering," he continued. "I was never going to take money for it. I didn't want to do birthday parties. It was always for kids that needed those kinds of things. At the hospital, none of the kids are there for a good reason."

Casey tried to make a visit at least once a month. As Christmas time approached, he started reaching out to other cosplayers via Facebook and the like, to see if anyone else would join for a visit. That started the relationships that continue to this day, including those that were at today's event. For one of Casey's events, 26 different characters showed up! He also teams up with other groups, especially local Star Wars chapters like the 501st Mountain Garrison, the Rebel Legion, and the Mandalorian Mercs. With the different community groups, Casey likens it to the "six degrees of Kevin Bacon," with everybody knowing somebody, and someone always having a good cause.

He tells me the mother of one of cosplayers runs a small wish organization geared toward children with pediatric cancer. During COVID, Casey and Matt (Colorado Captain) reached out to her. "Everything was on lockdown. Couldn't go anywhere. Couldn't do anything. And that was right about the time all the car parades started popping up here and there. So, Matt said let's do a big one." The organizer identified 34 pediatric families located as far south of Denver as Colorado Springs, and as far north as Fort Collins. "We took Memorial Day weekend and we hit all of them," Casey enthused. "Technically it was 13 cities, 350 miles, in three days – Friday, Saturday, and Sunday. Matt was on his motorcycle. We had a convoy of cars, a lot of open-top Jeeps. It was phenomenal." That parade drove past the home of a woman running a group out of Boulder, CO, called Building a Bedroom, who contacted Casey and Matt. The charity works with families whose homes were lost or damaged in a recent wildfire. For many, the children now had rooms with only a mattress on the floor. The group raises funds (including a major donation from a Denver news station) to purchase bedroom furniture and décor for the kids. Casey and his superhero friends show up for the bedroom reveals. "It's really awesome!"

As someone who also dresses as a Batman version for community events, I wanted to talk a little about the character. "Batman is unique," reflected Casey. "He's got iconic levels at every generation. You put that cowl on and, it's not a shut down, but you hit a level that you just kind of stay at it. There's no other up or down; it's just right there, and that's where you live. Everybody likes to say I brood. Yeah, you just feel that way. You get that tunnel vision in the cowl, and that's where you live. It's weird to feel so powerful but still maintaining a background feel, like you're not trying to be the star. But still, everybody knows it's you immediately. I think you put an expectation on yourself, and what the world expects from you, from a certain costume. It definitely is really easy to find that character when that costume comes on."

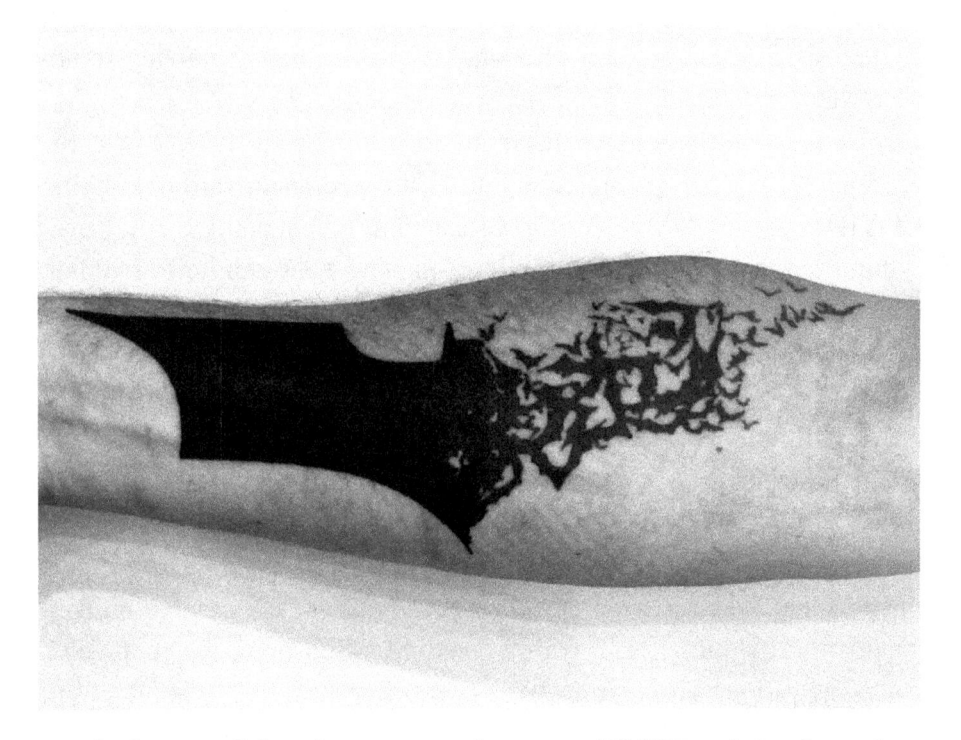

In honor of the character, and as post-COVID celebration when things started opening back up, Casey treated himself to a Batman tattoo: "There are some Batman groups on Facebook and every once in a while, they'll be like, show me your Bat tattoos. And you look through and it's like, 'That's awesome! That's awesome! Uhhhh, did you pay for that? I'm sorry.'" Casey wanted something basic and in black ink only. Ultimately, he picked a bat logo resembling the Dark Knight trilogy version. He almost went with Tim Burton's 1970's version but, since his suit is Dark Knight inspired, "I wanted a reminder of where that started." He landed on an image where the logo was transitioning into flying bats. "When we kind of laid it out, he put the stencil on there and I'm like, 'That's going to look amazing.'"

In addition to gaining a tattoo, Casey has also gained a sidekick. His 16-year-old son not only enjoys seeing dad as Batman, but he also likes to participate. "He actually has done a few charity events with me as Robin," Casey tells me. "We made a suit for him. We bought motorcycle gear, supercross-type stuff, painted it all. I have a friend who has a 3D printer who printed us a really good logo. His grandparents bought him a really awesome mask. He's actually volunteered with me a few times. Yeah, he's gotten into it."

From there, our conversation returns to the suit, and the most iconic piece of the outfit. Batman's cowl. Casey's thoughts on this run deep. "When you're in a mask, it's easy to give in to a character, without feeling like somebody's staring at *you*. For me, personally, I don't feel 'in character' when you can see my whole face. I'm not an actor. I've never tried to be an actor. That's something that goes back to Children's. When I'm in a cowl, you can see these children that are suffering or going through stuff, and nobody can see…" Casey pauses. "'Because it's hard not to react. We did an event where it was a conference for parents of children who were burn victims. So, one conference room on the 2nd floor of Children's was for the parents, and the next room was superheroes hanging out with the kids. It's heartbreaking. But they don't ever get to see my face react to that heartbreak."

Just as one cannot see Casey's face, there is another aspect to this persona that he keeps hidden. Like his comic character namesake, Casey has a secret. He remembers the Captain Jack Sparrow incident, and what it meant for *him* personally – having a *moment* for himself. "For me, it's like 60% for the kids, but 40% for the parents. The parents also forget in that moment that their kid is laying in a hospital bed. It's that moment of just getting lost in the fantasy that comes into the door or the lobby. I've had so many parents who are like, 'Can I just get a picture? My kid's in the ICU.' Or the pediatric cancer ward. Even in those lobby moments, where they're just doing for themselves, they forget they are in the Children's Hospital lobby. Even if it's for 30 seconds, that stress and that worry is just gone for that brief moment."

That is Casey's motivation. Moments. "You know, you get old," he says with conviction. "And you look back and that's what you have. You have moments. That's what everybody remembers." He shares a recent moment with a young boy with cancer who'd been given weeks to months to live. Casey had planned to be at the boy's upcoming birthday party, but felt compelled to attend a neighborhood candlelight vigil held two weeks before. Among the 50-60 people gathered, he was the only costumed character. "The mom went inside and told him that Batman was there, and he said, 'Well, I'm a superhero, too.' 'Yeah, more than anybody out here.'" Casey shared. The boy died the day before his birthday. Casey shakes his head, "The doctor told him he had weeks. Maybe we could hold off to his birthday. I'm so glad I didn't."

My final question for Casey was a tough one. I asked him if doing this helped him with his own grief. "To a degree. There's a part of you that doesn't heal, and I don't think ever will. I don't know if it's healing, but what I do, it's reassuring. There's a positive contribution, and that gets me through, and I think that's kind of enough."

CHAPTER 2

Con(ventions)

Being a geek has become part of the current zeitgeist. Han, 2020, p. 3

In her 2014 self-published book, *Cosplay as Religion*, Holoka argues that cosplay has gone beyond simply being a hobby or form of entertainment, and likens it to a religious sect. While I view her stance as drawing a false comparison, she makes some valid points regarding key elements of cosplay. Like a religion, she argues that cosplay has myths (storylines), sacred items (costumes), sacred space (convention halls), and rituals (contests). She notes that cosplayers eat, sleep, and breathe their characters and, similar to one's integration of religious principles and teachings, cosplayers "take values learned in or from the comic and apply it to their daily lives" (p. 5). Though I'm concerned she's missing the spiritual and supranatural aspects of religion, I appreciate her thought-provoking observations about the role of cosplay in the lives of so many.

Maybe not a religion, then, but definitely a cultural artifact worthy of study. To that end, there is obvious wordplay in this chapter's title, as two dual but related meanings of the word "Conventions" are implied. The first and most obvious are the large cosplay Conventions (most easily referred to as "Cons") which those in cosplay attend. Synonymous words might include gathering, festival, event, or meet-up. The second meaning of conventions are the unwritten rules of social order which we are expected to follow. Synonyms in that case might include words like principles, guidelines, tenets, or norms. This chapter will look at both, including the interplay between the two (which I guess we could call Convention conventions?).

As we saw in Chapter 1, being in costume can contribute to one's confidence and social skills. When individuals have an increased capacity to mingle, what follows is the creation of larger social constructs or communities, each with their own associated rules for conduct. We'll start with the largest social gathering – the Con – and from there look at other systemic configurations of individuals and communities.

Conventions/Cons

There is no doubt that attending a Con is an important, and ever more culturally acceptable, part of any cosplayer's life. "In our field work," argue Seregina and Weijo (2017) "we heard guests call the con a 'homecoming,' 'our own country,' or 'a judgment-free zone,' indicating themes of liberation, liminality, antistructure, and communion" (p. 146). In brief, Cons are a place where we step inside our costume, then step outside our traditional boundaries and enter a world where we feel simultaneously free *and* connected. Duchense (2010) describes Cons as a combination of the free market at work, a 21st century spiritual pilgrimage, and a form of nerd tourism. All those definitions seem to work just fine.

The purpose here is not to highlight any particular Con, but to look at the engagement activity writ large. While there will be differences between a local anime gathering and a mega-event hosted by conglomerate Informa/FanExpo, or between locations rural versus urban, or between pop culture events in which cosplay is a minor part (e.g., toy fairs, comic swaps) and those that are cosplay only events (e.g., the World Cosplay Summit competition in Japan), there will be crossover elements which ring true for all these examples.

For cosplay scholars, understanding this Con phenomenon – and its impact on the cosplayer – is perhaps the largest arena of study. This includes all facets of Con attendance, ranging from simple people-watching at one end to competing in hardcore contests measuring expertise at the other. In the middle we have a broad range of activities; attending panels, shopping the vendors, meeting celebrities, participating in runway walks, or posing for photo shoots at meet-ups and in the hallways. It is actually this middle range – including the performative act of admiring and taking photos of each other's costumes - where most cosplayers land.

Cons are unique from earlier costume practices and theatrical forms due to their "unprecedented modes of mass cultural engagement" (p. 3) and "dependence on source texts from popular new media" (Mountfort et al., 2019, p. 5). Without "popular culture" (comics, animation, TV, movies), cosplay would starve. For the individual, attending a Con in costume gives public proclamation to one's fandom, more than any imagining, viewing, reading, or even interactive social media posts or blogging could ever do. Gunnels (2009) calls this the "immediacy of the physical" [4.1]. She notes that the world of fiction lacks the degree of constructed immediacy found in the performance environment. "Yes, you can imagine that you are Obi-Wan Kenobi as you read a fan text, but wouldn't you rather be him?" Gunnels asks. "Of course, this isn't possible, but cosplay serves as a middle ground" [4.1].

We know that the costume has agency; it empowers the wearer "when it transforms the human body visually, physically, in motion and in the charged context of a shared performance" (Barbieri, 2017, p. 137). Barbieri claims that cosplayers give off a *kinetic empathy*; their movement and action within the costume provides a multisensory connection to the character and storyline which then resonates with the kinetic empathies of the audience. The ebb and flow of posing and picture taking is "a lived process in time, a shared community, a felt experience" (p. 138). Duchense (2010) labels this popular form of display as FTP, or "fandom tribute performance" (p. 21). Whatever you call it, it's a lot of fun.

For example, at a recent Con, while dressed as Kurt Russell's Ego from *Guardians of the Galaxy 2*, I stopped by the red carpet for a scheduled Marvel meet-up. After all the various Spider-Men and Scarlett Witches departed, I posed with a couple young men dressed as Star-Lord/Peter Quill. For those who don't know the story, Ego is Quill's long-lost father. While the reunion is initially a happy one, showcased by the men playing catch with a blue energy ball they conjured with their celestial force, it sours when Quill discovers Ego only wants to exploit his genetic power to take over the universe. By the film's end, Quill and company are forced to battle and kill Ego. On the red carpet, one of the Star-Lord's posed happily alongside me, while the other appeared to vent Quill's anger by aiming his Element Gun at my head (see Image 2.1). I'd brought along with me some blue rubber balls that, when bounced, lit up and sparkled on the inside. Much to the delight of the audience, I then proceeded to play catch with yet another Quill, recreating the father-son movie scene as best we could. Throughout the Con, I gave away dozens of the sparkling balls to children. These shared kinetic performances were a highlight for me, and for many, at the event.

Image 2.1 *Posing as Ego alongside a "vengeful" Star-Lord*
PHOTO CREDIT: Maki Endres

Ultimately, such interactions have a socializing effect. Mountfort et al. describe dressing up of any kind, costume or not, as central to the performance of self. The very act is "fundamental to interpersonal relations, communication and socialization" (p. 3). By playing a role, you train yourself to better understand and interact with others. Pushkareva and Agaltsova explain that, as a cosplayer constructs their persona, they are mastering new images and studying subpersonalities. Every choice made requires the cosplayer to "look at himself from the outside" (2021, p. 7). The empathy that creates then translates into a similar empathy for others.

Now multiply that newfound empathy and socialization by the dozens, the hundreds, and even the thousands of cosplayers that attend various Cons. What a phenomenal and memorable sense of community! Ohanesian likens it to the life-changing experience music fans have when they attend a concert. For youth in particular, these are worlds of entertainment outside the typical boundaries of neighborhoods and schools. "Suddenly, they're surrounded by people who share the interests that make them feel like misfits in day-to-day life" (2015, p. 9). That, too, is the power of the Con.

Crawford and Hancock (2019) provide an articulate expression of the inquiry that is and can be done regarding cosplay and Conventions:

> It is our central argument that cosplay can be best understood as a craft, a subculture, and a performance, all of which are created and recreated in the everyday online and offline lives of cosplayers, but take on greater significance in certain locations, such as at science fiction and fantasy convention and meet-ups. However, in doing so, we hope that this will contribute to our understanding of many other related areas such as craft, creativity, fan culture, identity, leisure, performance, play, practice-led research, subculture, urban spaces, and much more. (p. 1)

Research opportunities are endless. The focus here, of course, is on communicative message exchange about and within cosplayer and costume communities. With that in mind, let's look at some of the community configurations and behavioral expectations – or *conventions* - this creates, beginning with a broader look at some of the more popular cosplay genres.

Genres
A significant majority of cosplay is character portrayal; you are trying to recreate or embody a specific individual from literature, film, or television. Other times, however, a cosplayer may just be looking to embody a stylistic form, or genre. Just as fashion has distinct genres (e.g., Glam, Punk, New-Romantics, Androgyny; see Worsley, 2011), so too does cosplay. Hale defines these as costumes which represent a "general character typology" like robots, ninjas, or pirates (2014, p. 12). Starting with Anime and concluding with Zombies, we can honestly say that genres literally run the gambit from A-Z (though no attempt will be made here to fill in all the missing letters!). The genres discussed below are the top five that popped up during the literature search. Of course, just as fashion genres sometimes overlap (e.g., Androgynous Glam), so too do genres found in cosplay.

Before jumping in, I'll point out that the word genre comes from the Latin *genus*, meaning "type or kind." Similarly, the word *generic* comes from the same root, though it is often associated with being a *non*-type. To be generic is to be very general; not specific. Sometimes, you can have a generic character within a specific genre. For example, in the *Star Wars* universe, you could be someone highly identifiable like Darth Vader or Princess Leia. Or you could be someone generic from *Star Wars*, like a stormtrooper or droid with no identifiable name. Literature professor Tracy Bealer (2022), for example, often cosplays in a *Star Trek* uniform, but not as any specific person. She explains, "Whenever I do cosplay, it's always been kind of inserting myself into the universe as a minor character. I don't know what that says about me psychologically, but aspirationally, I enjoy being like, 'Oh, I'm on the ship, too.' Like I'm not a character you know, but I have an important job." We'll hear more of that when we meet her again in Costume Conversation #8.

Anime Culture

Based predominantly in Asian source material, the word Anime is often used generically to refer to both characters from animated shows and video games (anime) and comics and magazines (manga). World-wide, this is without a doubt the most popular and well-known form of cosplay and will be addressed in more detail in the international Appendix at the end. Even in Western culture, which at times feels dominated by Marvel/DC storylines and Hollywood franchises, anime follows close behind. Teens and young adults, in particular, are drawn to the artistic and sometimes erotic characters, with their bright Eastern-inspired garb, elaborate hairstyles, and intentional poses.

Stemming back to early storylines such as *Godzilla, Ultraman*, and *Gundam*, anime has gone from simple hand-drawn cartoons to complex computer-generated graphics. In the West, audiences are introduced to popular anime shows on channels such as Nick at Nite and Adult Swim (late night programming, respectively, for the Nickelodeon and Cartoon Network channels). Top shows at the time of this writing include *Full Metal Alchemist, My Hero Academia, Dragon Ball Z, One Punch Man, One Piece, Naruto*, and *Avatar: The Last Airbender*. Several of these series also appear in full-length feature films, along with popular movies like *Princess Mononoke* and a variety of *Pokémon* titles. Finally, the current most popular video games featuring animated characters include *Super Smash Brothers, The Legend of Zelda, Super Mario Odyssey, League of Legends*, and *Fortnite*.

One of the more controversial anime-inspired movies was 2017's live action *Ghost in the Shell*. Based off the cartoon series of the same name, white actress Scarlett Johansson was criticized for portraying the cyber-enhanced soldier known as Major who, in the original story, is Japanese (we'll talk more about appropriation in Chapters 3 and 6).

Of all the genres, anime is the most likely to have its own stand-alone Con. A quick search at *AnimeCons.com* reveal the almost two hundred cons hosted worldwide each year, with Eastern-sounding names like Ichiboncon (North Carolina), Ikkicon (Texas), Katsucon

(Maryland), and Sumicon (Nevada). A popular gathering in the southwest United States is called Nan Desu Kan, held each fall at the Gaylord resort and convention center just outside Denver, Colorado. Hosted by the Rocky Mountain Anime Association, the Con celebrates all things Japanese: cooking, dance, culture, gaming, and, of course, anime. Compared to other Con names, which often revolve around food (e.g., katsu = breaded), this title is especially shrewd. It's a play on the Japanese phrase *nan desu ka*; the wording placed at the end of statement which turns it into a question. It is basically a clever way of saying "It's an anime Con, isn't it?"

Fancy/Lolita Culture

Fancy dress is just what it sounds like. Fancy. Ball gowns with lace. Waistcoats with frilled collars and sleeves. Shoes with buckles. Wild (2020) defines fancy dress costume as "a performative form of dress, imaginative and incongruous, worn for a discrete occasion and limited time that disrupts the place of the individual within the social and political relationships of a specific community" (p. 154). Whether it be at a cosplay convention or a masquerade ball, fancy dress – often Victorian in influence and nature – is evidenced by its elegance and sophistication. It is to costumes what *haute couture* is to fashion.

For many, it is an opportunity to fight back against the shabby status quo; "participants attested to a disgust and impatience with the banal sartorial culture of the dumpy middle-aged adolescent: the baggy t-shirt, frumpy jeans, and dirty flip-flops of the American public, who wear this dreadful uniform all over the world: to the theater, museums, restaurants, and even to church. It is a style no one looks good in, yet it afflicts all classes, all ages, and all genders" (Saito and Lunning, 2011, p. 140).

One branch of fancy culture is Lolita attire, characterized by its ruffled skirts and related frills. Connections are made to the 1955 novel *Lolita* by Russian-American novelist Vladimir Nabokov. It tells the story of a middle-aged professor's erotic fascination with a twelve-year-old girl. Though the source material is problematic at best, the character of Lolita is generally described as a precocious girl who, depending on the teller, is either the embodiment of innocence or improperly seductive. The outfits often run that same range; from angelic to scandalous.

Some purists differentiate between Lolita *style*, which tends to be of higher quality, and Lolita *cosplay*, which has the frills but normally is made of cheaper fabrics. Mountfort et al. (2019) argue that "Lolitas do not simply wear a costume but rather symbolically *become* Lolita – in the sense that they embody what Lolita represents within the wider taste community" (p. 242). Ironically, Rahman et al. (2012) say that Lolita culture is *not* cosplay, "because Lolita enthusiasts do not imitate and role-play any specific character" (p. 318). I would argue they are missing the point. When dressing as part of a genre, one merely adopts the style, and does not have to represent any particular person. One can be Lolita-like and not have to be Lolita herself.

At times Fancy culture, particularly the Lolita subgenre, is criticized because there is often a perceived power and gender disparity. For many, the approach is oppressively patriarchal and subjugates women to a trivial and subservient role. Unfortunately, Wild (2020) points out, this sometimes leads to depersonalization by the costume wearer, with explanations like "I didn't know any better." Rather than apologize, he suggests, the wearer should "consider the totality of the fancy dress experience" and frame conclusions about appearance through the lens of self-identity and social identity. "Fancy dress costume can be edifying, entertaining and escapist," Wild concludes. "It is a unique sartorial form that facilitates the exchange of abstract ideas that are inadequately conveyed through conventional discourse" (p. 165). In other words, if it gets us thinking and talking about the roles and portrayals of women, it is doing its job. For example, in Image 2.2, Colorado Anime Fest staff member Caroline Joy "Sakura" Hofmann demonstrates a Lolita-inspired cosplay, selected in memory of a community member and Lolita fan who had passed away. The choice was both thoughtful and thought-filled.

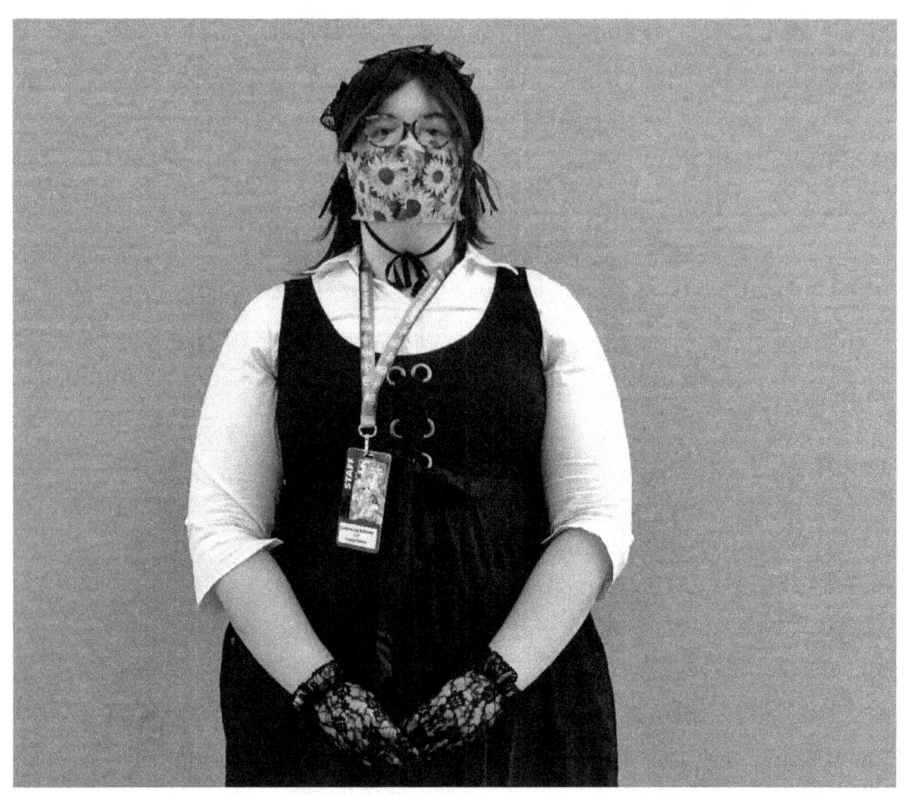

Image 2.2 *Hofmann models Lolita costume*

Furry Culture

Once again, the genre term is somewhat self-explanatory. Members of Furry culture like to dress up in furry costumes. They are not a particular character, per se, but rather some form of animal like a bear, squirrel, or cat. There is a mix of anthropomorphism (human qualities given to non-human entities) and zoomorphism (animal qualities given to humans). A similar group is the Japanese *Gijinka*, who create humanoid animals with personalities, with the goal of causing viewers to feel affection or attraction to them. While beginners may just carry stuffed animals to Cons, full-blown Furries work on and develop their *fursonas* (like "personas," but fuzzy).

Just as four-footed creatures are often skittish, elusive, and difficult to photograph, I found the same to be true of their costumed counterparts. Everyone I spoke with *knew* about the community who likes to dress up in furry animal costumes – and some even claimed to know a Furry or two – but I was not able to finalize any appointments or photo shoots with this hirsute group. No social media announcement, craigslist post, or radio ad could get any to come out of hiding! This should not be surprising, given a 2015 study by Plante et al. (2015) which found that, while "furries describe fandom identification as crucial to their identity," the community often feels stigmatized, and many "fear the negative repercussions of identity disclosure" (p. 361).

An interesting trait that Plant and colleagues measured was "essentialist" beliefs; that is, the degree to which members of particular groups felt a "shared essence" among fellow group members. Essentialist groups share meaningful bonds and differentiate themselves strongly from other factions. The study found that highly identified furries held strong essentialist beliefs when compared to traditional anime fans, and concluded that "highly identified members of stigmatized minority groups strategically adopt biologically essential beliefs about their in-group in response to a distinctiveness threat" (p. 367). Simply put, furries tend to believe they must be cautious in order to survive, and they will hold fast to their group beliefs in order to remain unique and distinct. No wonder they were so hard to find!

Winge (2019) sheds further insight, noting that Furries, sometimes called Fur Kin, often have their own fandom (Furdom/Furrydom) and events. She adds that furry characters may feel like outcasts; they are often treated as controversial within cosplay culture, and are highly fetishized and satirized in mainstream media. Do you recall the 2022 urban legend out of Michigan, where elected officials – speaking against gender-neutral restrooms – accused school districts of allowing Furry-identifying students to use litter boxes? There was no truth to the ridiculous rumor, but it still contributes to the insular reactions within the community itself.

Steampunk Culture

Love the machine, hate the factory.
Steampunk Credo, Esser, 2018, p. 4

Steampunk, according to Winge (2019), is based in an alternative reality where steam engines - not petroleum - rule. It is a reimagined 19th century, interlacing the American West and British Victorian ages. Originally exemplified in classic books by H.G. Wells and Jules Verne, it most recently has become a fiction genre unto itself. (See, for example, William Gibson and Bruce Sterling's *The Difference Engine*, 1990.) Some sources argue that the motif was launched by the 1999 Will Smith movie *Wild, Wild West*, which showcased a number of inventions including a steam-powered weapon shaped like an enormous spider. Others, me included, go back further, noting that the 1960s TV series *Wild, Wild West* (starring Robert Conrad and Ross Martin) introduced us to steam-powered tanks, traps, and even villains, along with a variety of spy gadgets that would make Batman and James Bond jealous. Esser (2018, with integration of Perschon, 2012) provides a thorough detailing of the genre, describing it as Neo-Victorian technofantasy and retro-futurism. Infused with anachronistic, implausible or fantastical technologies, "steampunk's retro-futurist element imagines the alternative futures of *a past that never was* [emphasis added] from the socio-cultural vantage point of the twenty-first century" (p. 1).

Thus, among steampunks, we might find a proper Victorian lady complete with corset, bustle, and granny boots, or a gentleman with top hat, spats, and tails. However, they'll also be adorned with a variety of gizmos and gadgets made of watch parts, leather straps, and brass fittings. Slight variations may exist between practitioners. For example, some may consider themselves *diesel*punk; as diesel fuel and not steam run the engines (for example, as shown in the 2004 movie *Sky Captain and the World of Tomorrow*). There even exists *Nerf*punk, where the various weapons and color schemes are inspired by the soft colorful foam balls and squirt guns. Not only is steampunk (and related offshoots) a genre unto itself, but it also lends itself to a variety of combinations with mainstream characters and styles. Put the word "steampunk" in front of any costumed character name ("steampunk Spider-Man") or related genre ("steampunk pirate"), and suddenly you have created something oddly old-but-new.

Like Fancies and Lolitas, some argue against the value of steampunk, seeing that it harkens back to a colonialist and repressive age (see Winge, 2019). Of course, just because the Victorian era or the Old West were hegemonic is no reason that our re-writings of the past need be. One is allowed to pick those aspects of the era – architecture, fashion, music, literature – and adapt and upgrade as one sees fit. We meet Lady Vo and Chaos in Costume Conversation #5, for example, and they do just that.

Zombie Culture

Long before George A. Romero terrified audiences with his 1968 horror film *Night of the Living Dead*, we were a culture fascinated by reincarnated bodies. Tracing back to Haitian folklore, zombies have appeared in literature since the early 1800s. In early New Orleans, the stories mixed with Catholicism to create voodoo gods and goddesses worshipped to this day. This is another one of those genres which can either stand alone or be easily blended with other pop culture characters. Zombie Batman? Check. Zombie Captain America? Check.

Though Cons will invariably have a zombified hero or two walking around, it is the stand-alone zombie events that are particularly interesting. While participating in a community Zombie walk, a photographer informed pop culture scholar Riley (2015) that "Zombies are camera whores" [2.1]. The point being made was that, like all cosplayers, the individuals who show up for a zombie march do so to be seen. What makes a zombie walk unique is that, in order to participate, you must be a zombie! One can go to a comic Con and not be in costume. In contrast, it would make no sense to saunter along on a zombie walk unless you were wearing tattered clothes, shuffling your feet, and moaning for brains. Riley notes other unique characteristics. For example, Cons are usually in a private space, while zombie walks occur in the public sphere. Also, cosplayers tend to do specific characters, whereas zombie costumes "gain notoriety for their wearers not by their individuality but by contributing to the group ethos, by becoming part of the mosaic of former humanity that now shambles along the streets" [2.4].

At this point, Riley jumps the shark and suggests that this "equalizing" nature of zombie walks might make them useful as a format for political protest. I'm not sure I agree; marching to raise awareness of a social cause while dressed as one of the undead seems destined to backfire. I do agree, however, with an observation by Cosplaymom and her daughter Kiogenic, authors of *Cosplay for Beginners*. They give advice for those times when all your costume planning goes wrong. How can you salvage a costume that didn't turn out the way you wanted? The self-published authors provide a cheery alternative: "You can make a ZOMBIE version of anything!" (2012, p. 37)

Thus far, we've talked a lot about costumes and the *individual* and, in discussing genre, we've also looked at communities and *groups*. At this point, I'd like to spend just a few paragraphs on another cosplayer subset – the couple.

Couples Costumes

Whether they be dressed as specific characters, or simply representing a genre, couples costumes exist when two people want to make it obvious that they *belong* together. Keep in mind that we're talking about *all* types of couples here, from friendship dyads, to familial relations such as siblings or parent/child, to romantic connections like dating or married partners. With that baseline, there are a few different ways that couples manifest themselves in the cosplay world.

The simplest, and most discrete in terms of roles, is the couple created by a cosplayer and their handler. "A handler is someone who accompanies you while you're in costume," Good (2016) explains. Referred to by other terms such as "bag wench" or "cosplay bodyguard," handlers are especially helpful to have if your costume is large, cumbersome, and/or restricts your mobility. Handlers help you set up, carry your personal items, often negotiate photo-ops, and keep you from running into people. Good (2016) offers this advice, "Be kind to handlers! Tell them immediately if you're having any problems or discomfort, so they can help you, but allow them to enjoy the convention, too" (p. 138). Most often the handler is not in costume, allowing them the greatest freedom to accomplish their task (such as that seen with Eric "Gene Simmons" Adams in Costume Conversation #1). The costuming relationship is essentially "cosplayer 100%, handler 0%."

Sometimes, in order to convey the bond, the handler may dress up in some watered-down thematic connection to the main cosplayer's costume. That way, you can see that they belong together, while still allowing primary attention to go to the key character. A fully-winged Maleficent, for example, may be accompanied by a helper adorned as a peasant. The seven-foot-tall Frankenstein might be followed by an assistant in a white lab coat (hunchback hump optional). Here the costuming relationship may be more like "cosplayer 75%, handler 25%." (See, for example, the relationship between Sam Nord and her mother in Costume Conversation #9). For those who want to be identified as the cosplayer's lieutenant, but don't want to bother with a costume, websites like Redbubble.com sell "Cosplay Handler" t-shirts!

The final couple style is where both are in full and connected costumes: "cosplayer 50%, cosplayer 50%." I'm talking specifically about those who try to coordinate their costumes to match, thereby demonstrating their *couple-ness*, and not just *a couple* where both of them happen to be in unrelated costumes. As many will attest, achieving this is harder than it sounds. Trying to find something where both parties have source material costumes of relatively equal status is challenging. (As an older, bearded, white male married to a Japanese female, I speak from first-hand experience!)

The easiest way to do this is along the line of Halloween-esque simple combinations, like prefab couples (Barbie & Ken, Aladdin & Jasmine), or matching categories (both in space gear, Western wear, hippie threads, or cave people furs). Here's also where those "clever" visual costumes come into play. You know, he's wrapped in a crunchy shell, and she's got a flowing yellow gown (Taco + Belle), or he's an electrical plug and she's an outlet. Be careful your creativity doesn't get too abstract. I recall a Halloween party in graduate school where the married hosts were dressed in matching striped prisoner's uniforms, and each was holding a Bible and wearing a cross around their neck. They were "pair'o'cons of virtue." It was years before I figured that one out.

Marketing consultant and artist Kellsie Moore, along with her DJ and fellow model/actor husband David, presented a Con workshop several years ago giving advice on couples' costumes. Both enjoy dressing up, and the prospect of matching costumes was appealing. The biggest problem, they noted, was the aforementioned mismatch in source material. Generally, they found, there are more costume options for men. Costume choices for women tend to be minor characters, "female" versions of male characters, or "sexy" variations on a theme, like sexy nurse, schoolteacher, or nun. "I have nothing against being sexy," explains Kellsie, "but you should have other options" (2023).

The first time they tried to get matching costumes, Kellsie decided she wanted to be Batman. Not "female" or "sexy" Batman. Just Batman, because she loves the character. Unfortunately, there were no traditional Batman costumes that fit her. They did, however, fit David. So, David got to wear the official costume that Kellsie hoped for, while she had to settle for a Batman t-shirt with cape found at Wal-Mart. Still, Kellsie confides, "We felt like we had a couples costume, even though we were the same person!" Sometimes (as shown in Image 2.3), it goes the other way. When the movie *Wonder Woman* came out in 2017, Kellsie felt inspired and decided the Amazon princess would be her next cosplay. She suggested David don the fellow DC-hero Batman costume again, but he was dedicated to the idea of dressing as a couple. He opted for Wonder Woman's 1940's pilot/suitor Steve Trevor. David quickly discovered that, if Kellsie wasn't around to share in the photo op, people didn't have any idea who his character was, or if he was even in a costume at all.

Image 2.3 *Couples costume Wonder Woman and Steve Trevor*

Ironically, despite being difficult to recognize, David's costume was true to the movie's depiction; basically, military style pants and boots with a flight jacket. With that we turn to the final topic of this chapter; one that intersects with all events, genres, and couple/group configurations. Let's examine how accurate one's costume needs to be. (Quick caveat. These views express Western orientations. Differing views from around the world are found in the Appendix.)

Accuracy
In 2022, I attended a Con panel on bullying, featuring Daniel Gibson, co-founder of the CosPositive movement which endorses support for all body types and styles. A key component, he noted, is called Gatekeeping. Paraphrasing Urban Dictionary, Gibson defined gatekeeping as a

My Costume, Myself ◆ 71

negative action occurring when someone takes it upon themselves to decide who does or does not have access or rights in cosplay. He frequently sees gatekeepers attempt to shame others as "fake cosplayers" if they somehow do not fit the expected mold. What intrigued me was that his examples were less about whether someone was the right size, shape, or color for a particular costume but, rather, how complete and accurate the costumes were. He recounted times that novices were ridiculed for having less than stellar costumes, and admonished, "Anyone just getting into cosplay is just as important as the most famous cosplayer, and vice versa."

On this note, Winge (2019) shares a story about a t-shirt design once available in the popular mall store Hot Topic, which read "Cosplay: Do it right or not at all." The not-so-subtle message was that substandard costumes or inaccuracies are not to be tolerated. This suggested a convention that was outside the comfort level for most cosplayers. The store received a lot of negative feedback about the shirt, and it was quickly removed from the shelves. More acceptable seems to be famed cosplayer Yaya Han's (2020) stance that "Your cosplay does not have to be 100 percent accurate" (p. 17) and that "accuracy is in the eye of the beholder" (p. 134).

In fact, most would argue that not only is accuracy in cosplay *not* a mandate, but it is also most often not even *possible*. After attending a Con dressed as Pixar's inhumanly broad-shouldered Mr. Incredible, Anderson concluded that "the artificiality of these bodies places them outside the expectations of biological construction" (2014, p. 26). Burke (2022) agrees, pointing out that "very few people will have the chiseled jawlines, impossibly thin waists, or other unrealistic features of the fictional characters they may want to cosplay" (p. 90). Thus, he argues, rather than aiming for fidelity, the cosplayer might think in terms of equivalent narrative units (e.g., instead of body type, try to convey character more through color or props). Or, he adds, such alterations can actually provide some interesting commentary on pop culture by juxtaposing source expectations with actual performance. Maybe dressing as

Mr. Incredible with less-than-incredible shoulders helps point out our culture's obsession with physique?

Even if we match the body type, Kirkpatrick (2015) points out that we'll never get it right. She says that, in essence, we are translators merely attempting to capture a character's unique nonverbals and speaking style. Cosplay is at best our second language, and we can never become the "first language speaker" of the characters themselves. Nor should we want to. Nichols (2019) says that authenticity and fidelity is a degree of moé. "*Moé* is a complex term; basically shorthand for a fan's pure, spiritual appreciation of the 'self' of the character" [4.7]. All a cosplayer need do is *honor* the essential self of the character, not duplicate it.

In fact, in Western culture, many cosplayers have no desire to exactly replicate their character; they want to bring something of themselves and their own uniqueness into the interpretation. Lamerichs (2011) compares this to cover bands and other forms of impersonation where the performer gives you *their* version, their take, on the existing material. The basic requirement, argues Duchense (2010), is merely that you be recognized as the character. "To that end, a costume can be as simple as a pair of pointy ears, or as elaborate as a fully-rendered suit of armour [*sic*]" (p. 21). If the audience knows who you are, the costume has done its job.

On a lesser note, there is some contention on whether or not a costume should be entirely homemade. Designers Seregina and Weijo (2017) argue that "visible effort and attention to detail are hallmarks of a good costume. The ethos of cosplay calls for crafting as much of the outfit as possible. A true cosplayer would never wear a store-bought costume" (p. 144). Once again, that's a fairly radical view that does not reflect the opinion of the collective. Granted, for cosplay contests which have craftsmanship as a criterion, you want to stay away from purchased items. But a quick glance around any Con, replete with tightly garbed Spider-Men and Deadpools, fully clawed Wolverines, or elaborately head-dressed Hela's, it's obvious that some things are just better when store bought. Why forge a Captain America shield in a body shop when you can purchase a mass-produced one for less money and often with better results?

Thus far, costume norms regarding accuracy are the byproduct of *negative* factors. We cannot be accurate because it is *impossible* to do so. We cannot hand make our entire costume because it is impossible (or improbable, or too expensive) to do so. Hale points out that source text is not only generative because it gives us ideas, but also restrictive in that it tells us how we should *not* look, sound, or act. "It serves as a negative blueprint of sorts, which defines what an accurate imitation is, by virtue of what it isn't" (2014, p. 17). Well, many times, we don't want to follow those negative blueprints. Take heart knowing that costume decisions also spring from the *positive* end of the spectrum; they are not accurate because that is our first choice. Inaccuracy is the look we're going for! Nichols (2021) shares the term *produsage*, originally offered by Axel Bruns, to explain that a cosplayer is both *producer* and *user* of the role. Cosplayers reserve the right to change and adjust the presentation of their characters because that is what fits their needs. "Cosplay doesn't require fans to adhere strictly to a character's depiction in canon," explains Liptak, "The final product is entirely up to the costumer" (2022, p. 103). Accuracy can even detract from what cosplayers are trying to convey.

Oftentimes, cosplayers want to demonstrate their creativity and produce a *mash-up* costume; a costume that merges one or more characters to create something new. We've already shared a couple of ways that characters and genres can be combined. Winge (2019) also shares a popular mash-up she'd seen in several locales – Sailor Bubba! For this, a male (generally husky and hairy) wears an ill-fitting Sailor Moon costume, accentuating his belly and his beard. In discussing sewing patterns, Good uses the term *Frankenpattern* to describe a costume put together from several different patterns (2016, p. 15). Whether patterns are used or not, these Frankensteinish mash-ups are becoming increasingly popular. We might see a mixing of hero and villain (e.g., Bat-Joker, Wonder-Quinn), blended storylines (e.g., Star Wars Elsa, Indiana

Ironman), or a simple combination of genres (e.g., Steam Zombies, Space Pirates). Certainly not accurate, but definitely creative.

Cosplay Light

A subcategory one can use to assess degrees of accuracy is what Casanova et al. (2020) and others describe as *cosplay light* (or, in true reductionist form, *cosplay lite*). Here the cosplayer is primarily in normal street clothes with minor add-ons like pointy ears or a fox tail. Various reasons exist for choosing cosplay light, including time, money, and the ease of creation. Kellsie and David Moore, who we met earlier in their Wonder Woman and Steve Trevor couples costume, opted to scale back when presenting in their Con panel. In addition to cost concerns, they wanted to focus energies on their talk, and so opted for matching Superman t-shirts (see Image 2.4). They selected Superman because "He's a staple." This choice allowed them to "be part of something that we really love and value, without putting in the time and dollars it takes to have a 'legit' costume," Kellsie added. "We still felt welcomed."

Image 2.4 *Cosplay Light*

Professional cosplayer Yaya Han applauds these decisions. "There is no difference between wearing a Captain America T-shirt or dressing up as Captain America," she states. "Both fans are expressing their admiration for the character" (2020, p. 134). Lamerichs points out that cosplay light is perhaps the biggest Convention convention of them all. A majority of people who attend Cons do not attend in full costume or consider themselves cosplayers, per se. However, most put on some kind of adornment for the occasion. Using thematic t-shirts, buttons, hats, and the like, some attempt is made to celebrate the gathering and/or to fit in. "Though this is not cosplay in the narrow sense, in that one is not impersonating a fictional character, it shows there is an intimate relation between even uncostumed fans and their clothing" [4.2].

For many, that t-shirt may be the first step into cosplay. It could be the baseline for something that will evolve in subsequent Cons. (Visit Ken's comments in Costume Conversation #4 for insights into building and improving upon one's costume over time.) Perhaps this is why you see entry-level clothing items from vendors becoming more and more ornate. What used to be a simple one-color screen print on a t-shirt now has elaborate depth and details. Hoodies have eyeholes sewn into the hood, so you can pull it over your head and wear it like a mask. Racks of jackets look more and more like costume pieces from a movie set. Even cosplay light seems to be heading ever upward in terms of appearance.

Whether or not one is aiming for accuracy; whether or not one made their costume or bought it at a store; and whether or not one is doing cosplay light as a first foray into costuming, I appreciate this observation from professional cosplayer Suvi Couture (2022), "There's no good or bad; only growth."

Summary

Whether or not one goes so far as to define cosplay as a religion, you cannot deny that the elements of cosplay create a certain type of community. Most often, those elements are found at Conventions/Cons, where participants hone their social skills by communicating with popular culture texts and with each other. That social engagement creates conventions, or guidelines, for a variety of subset communities. Among those are stylistic genres (including Anime, Fancy/Lolita, Furry, Steampunk, and Zombie cultures), as well as the specific subgroup of costumes for couples. Interspersing all of this is an ongoing dialogue on conventions regarding costume accuracy and construction, including such purposefully inaccurate manifestations as mash-ups and cosplay light. In the three "Costume Conversations" that follow, all couples, we see direct character interpretations and two distinct genres.

Costume Conversation # 4
Ken Barrett and Brianna Cecil-Barrett
a.k.a. Lord of the Rings Wedding Theme

"I think of myself as a dungeon master first," says Ken, referencing the interactive role-playing game Dungeons and Dragons, "because I am a D&D story writer." He loves his job at an Amazon warehouse, "But truly my passion goes into my hobbies." Brianna's job and hobby are more closely entwined: "I have an Associate's degree in Baking and Pastry Arts, so I'm a professionally trained pastry chef." Her goal is to someday open her own shop but, as she explains, the food industry became a little toxic over the past few years, "So I just bake for fun on the side now."

As we chat in preparation for their photo shoot, I thank them again for agreeing to recreate for me their *Lord of the Rings (LOTR)* themed wedding outfits. Their original ceremony was held at a Renaissance Festival, where the costumes fit right in. Prior to meeting, both were fans of the festivals. Ken was a regular and Brianna had been there once on her own. "I wanted to go as a kid, but it was too expensive for my mom to take us to the one in Wisconsin. A single mom with three daughters; that's pretty expensive." When they became a couple, they attended more often. After their engagement came the discussion of wedding plans. One day, while shopping at EntertainMART, they found Ken's *LOTR* sword. From there, the wedding theme and location pieces fell into place.

She is wearing a reproduction, custom made in England, of the dress worn by royal Elf Galadriel (played by Cate Blanchett). Ken's outfit is more generic, based off a combination of garments worn by human warriors Aragorn (Viggo Mortenson) and Boromir (Sean Bean). Ken explains, "I've read the books – she will tell you how annoyingly I've read these books and go over them. I love Aragorn for the fact that he went through all these trials and tribulations to make sure that, by the end of the books, everything came to peace. And for Boromir, it's a tragic story that shows redemption. It's something that I think we're sorely lacking."

While much thought was put into their outfits, more time and energy went into the decisions about their rings. Brianna's ring faithfully replicates Galadriel's ring, Nenya, one of the Three Rings of Power.

Ken's ring, called the Ring of Barahir, is worn by Aragorn in the trilogy. It is a family heirloom passed down from his ancestor Barahir, given for saving the life of Elf Finrod Felagund, and representing the bond between Aragorn's family and the elves. While costume suppliers sell the ring, they are inexpensive knockoffs. To ensure quality, they had Ken's ring custom made.

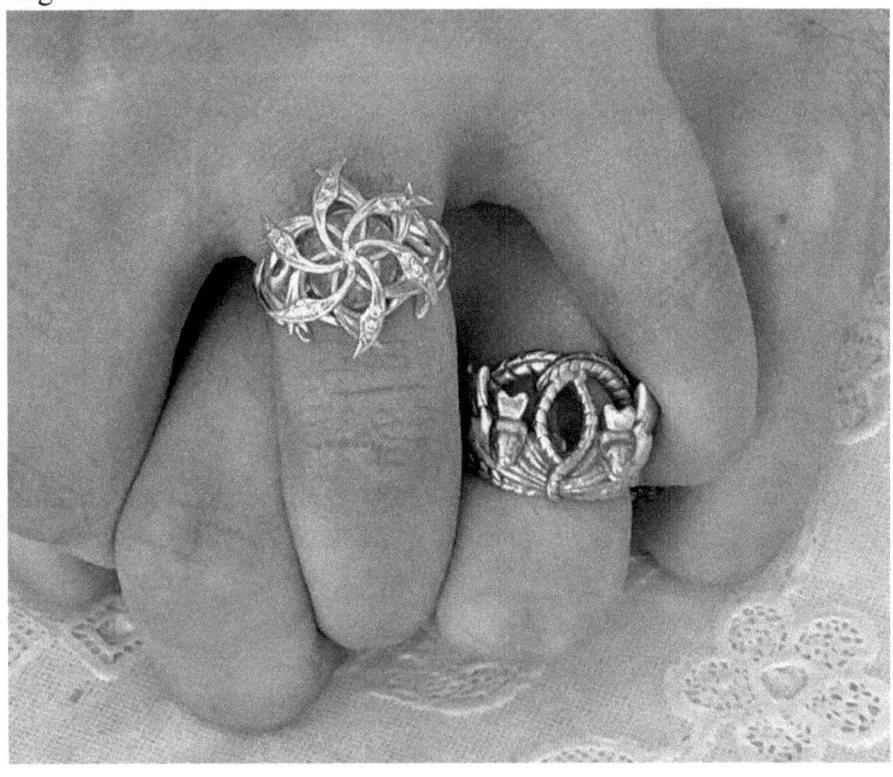

After hearing the stories about their wedding, I asked them where their love story began. He's from a military family; born in California, but has lived in Turkey, Germany, and Korea. She's from Grafton, Wisconsin. How did they meet? "This is one of my favorite stories to tell," Brianna answers quickly, "We met online. *Okay Cupid*." Ken nods, smiling. He knows what's coming. "I messaged him," Brianna continues, "I was like, 'He's not that great looking, but we have a lot in common. So why not?' I remember thinking that. In my defense, his picture wasn't that great compared to his in-person." Ken continues to smile.

The things they had in common included a variety of pop culture phenomena like *Star Wars* and anime. "And then he didn't message me back! Okay, I'd fully given up. I'm just going to accept my fate as a crazy cat lady. I had two cats. And then he messaged me a few months later." Ken interjects that he was temporarily in another relationship, and it wasn't cool to court two women at once.

Brianna continues. "We messaged each other, and then I was going out of town for my aunt's funeral. Her funeral was at Halloween because that was her favorite time of the year. I inherited all her Halloween cookie cutters. We were making cookies with her cookie cutters, and I jokingly invited him over. 'Hey, you want to come decorate cookies for my aunt's funeral?' We hadn't met yet in person. He's like, 'Yeah, send me the address!'" Brianna goes on to explain that she was *not* going to have the first time they met, with both her mother and an ex-boyfriend (now just friend) present, while making cookies for her aunt's Halloween funeral. No way. But her friend stole her phone and texted Ken the address. Ken sits back; he knows how the story ends. "So, the first time I met him, he showed up in a Sailor Moon belt and had a light saber on his hip. And the first thing I thought was, 'He's the one!'" Smooth, Ken. Very smooth.

While both are big fans of *Lord of the Rings* and of the Renaissance Festival vibe, and both enjoy going to comic cons, they don't coordinate any of their other cosplay outfits. Ken's other costumes include Revan from the *Star Wars* expanded universe, and an in-progress suit of armor complete with chainmail. His future costume goal would be an Officer Corps member from the tabletop game *Warhammer 40,000*. Brianna has done Sailor Moon and Bastila, from *Star Wars' Knights of the Old Republic*, but her favorite is Belle from *Beauty and the Beast*: "I have Belle's big yellow dress at home. When I go to comic con, I always have a bag of books, and I give out free books to kids I come upon." She is currently practicing Belle's signature from Disneyworld examples, so that next con she can sign books for the children as well. Brianna also enjoys 1940s-50s pinup styles. In those outfits, she volunteers her time as a member of Battlin' Betties, a group which raises awareness of PTSD and suicide rates for veterans and first responders. She recently attended an Honor Flight, where she met a World War II veteran who had lied about his age and enlisted at the age of 15.

Not only do their styles differ, so too do some of their opinions about costume expectations. Knowing that the book would focus on issues of race (see next chapter), I asked Brianna if she'd be comfortable dressing as Disney princesses of color, such as Jasmine, Mulan, or Tianna from *Princess and the Frog*. "I think for little kids it's okay," Brianna explains. "For them it's just their favorite character. They don't understand the history. They don't understand why people would be upset. It's just 'I want to be Mulan.' Mulan's this kick-butt awesome girl. Saves China. Jasmine's just a pretty princess who helped defeat Jafar. Or Moana. She met Maui and all these characters. But for adults, it's a different scenario. I feel like I would love to portray Mulan, but at the end of the day, I'm not that type; I can't portray Mulan."

Ken offers his perspective. "I see where you're coming from, and I have a far different opinion about that. Cosplay is open to everyone. I don't care what ethnicity, what you look like, it is for everyone, so that you can portray your favorite character. To say that we are just going to culturally lock them into one specific thing defeats the purpose of the community. To say you can't be Mulan because you're XYZ does not fly for me. It is a costume that empowers you. And if that's what it takes for you to get into cosplay, and to feel accepted there, that is okay. I know that modern politics have gotten a little bit edgy into that. For me, it will always be, as long as you're respecting the character, I'm perfectly fine with whatever you do. I know where you're coming from."

The dialogue continues in diplomatic fashion. Brianna: "I understand both sides of the spectrum. I always thought it'd be fun to cosplay as Akita from *Atlantis*. I don't want to be offensive to someone else's culture, I don't want to be offensive." "That's the biggest thing," Ken concludes, "is just respecting it."

Stepping away from the question of culture, I ask them what advice they would give to people wanting to create new costumes and new characters. Both discuss the need to consider logistic factors, anticipating things that might go wrong, like glue on costumes that might melt in the heat. Most recently, after returning home bruised from a Con, Ken realized his armor needs padding underneath. Additionally, Brianna recommends taking your audience into consideration. "If you get a Belle costume that goes up past your knee, to me, that's not cosplay. If you're going to do Belle, you can do her blue dress, her green dress, her pink dress. And it can be store-bought, as long as you're trying to portray that specific character. But if you're going to just wear that sexy Belle dress, that's not what kids want to see." With exasperation, she adds, "It's Belle! My gosh!'"

Ken then provides great advice for the novice. "Start your costume at a basic level, if you can't afford it, and move up. You can always improve on it in some way, shape, or form. If you just put a t-shirt on, I would say put a little more effort in. Get a cape, even if it's just a sheet. You're just starting out. You're getting the concept put together. Cosplay is starting at the very bottom – 'Here's my concept, here's what I can get together before convention' – and then moving up a little bit at a time. Don't be afraid to budget your costume. You don't need to be spending or bankrupting yourself to get it to professional levels. You're doing it for fun. 'I can't spend $2000 right away. I can spend $300 this year, $600 this year.' Budget it out until you get to the costume you want. That's exactly why, when I see the guy that made 8-foot-tall space marine armor; he didn't make that in a day. He probably started with just a helmet. That's my two cents. If you're just doing a t-shirt, try a little bit more."

The biggest piece of advice is yet to come. Why do it? What are the benefits of dressing up? How does it make you feel? Ken starts. "I would say the most beneficial part is that you can go out, and no matter how you're dressed, you can feel like you belong in that setting. When I go to comic con, doesn't matter what people are dressed like, how good their costume is, everyone's going to at least try to give you, 'Hey, you're doing good. Here's how you can improve a little bit on it.' You know, give the encouragement - 'You're doing great. Can I get a picture with you? You start seeing the creativity behind a few costumes, too. It just gives that sense of community."

Brianna agrees, and adds, "I like bringing smiles to people's faces. If someone's having a bad day, I can brighten their day just by dressing differently than other people. That makes me happy." To make that happen, she continues, you have to take a few chances. "I was afraid to do Belle. I was afraid that because I wear glasses that kids wouldn't like me. I was afraid when I first did it, because I had my natural hair and not a wig; I was afraid because I couldn't get my hair perfect, kids wouldn't like me. Or people would say that's a terrible version." All her fears, however, were put to rest. Children love her Belle costume. Her neighbors love the Betty dresses. All her feedback has been positive. Brianna concludes, "Don't be afraid to branch out and try something new."

"I feel like I'm in my second skin," Ken adds, mentioning that they purposefully came to the interview in costume, rather than changing when they arrived. "I love these to death. If I could wear them more, I would. Honestly, it's one of the most relieving feelings. I put this on? No one's going to question it? Fantastic!"

COSTUME CONVERSATION # 5
Voniè and Chase Stillson
a.k.a. Lady Vo and Chaos Crossfire

As Vonié and Chase *Stillson*, their story is fairly straightforward. They met in their early 20s and realized they both enjoyed things like Halloween, Renaissance festivals, and comic books. Married now for seventeen years, they have two teens – a boy and a girl. Vonié is a licensed professional counselor and board-certified dance therapist. She is the owner and clinical director of Equilibrium Counseling Services and utilizes "geek therapy" (helping people to connect with the popular culture topics they are passionate about) in her practice. Chase is a machine repair technician, working for a 150-year-old company that builds equipment for generating power. He "fixes the machines that make the machines."

In their costumed reality, the story is more dramatic. In that world – a Victorian-esque civilization devoted to STEAM (Science, Technology, Engineering, Arts, and Mathematics) - they and their two children are the family *Crossfire*. They live on the Airship Iron Opal; the world's largest and only iron dirigible (similar in nature to the Civil War Ironclad battleships except, thanks to a gas called ether [100 times lighter than helium], their ship flies). The gigantic, armored balloon was built with a deck on top for shooting down enemy planes. The war ended, however, before the ship launched, so the Crossfires bought it from the government, turned the top deck into a longue with a pool, and converted it to a floating cruise liner. The Iron Opal, named after the fiery black opals found in the ship's top windows, is large enough so that other smaller airships can dock and come aboard.

Known as Lady Vo, Vonié started as Captain of the ship. As their ranks grew, and other families with other ships joined them from around the country, she became Admiral of the Conundrum Fleet. Chase, known as Chaos ("because I'm either creating it or fixing it") is the Airship's head engineer. No uniforms required, but members identify by wearing a metal Airship Iron Opal pin – designed and manufactured by Chaos himself.

As with many great fictions, there are elements of truth dispersed throughout the tale, such as Chaos/Chase's metal fabrication skills. They had been introduced to steampunk culture when living in the south and, upon moving to northern Colorado, wanted to create something for their family of four to enjoy. They took lessons from experience. For example, in their previous group, some of the characters created fun and interesting names that, unfortunately, were hard to remember or pronounce. "Part of why my steampunk name is Lady Vo is most people can't pronounce my actual name, especially when they see it written," Voniè explained. (Note: It's pronounced "vo-nay.") All such decisions were carefully crafted. "It's acting with intention," Chase added, "And people that really deep into steampunk, who have been doing it for lots of years, and have really amazing outfits, and have spent a long time committing to a given character; those people have a tendency to do their characters with intention."

So, they had a name for their family. Their daughter adopted a steampunk Tinkerbell persona, while their son began an ongoing journey of playing with different personalities and traits. Not long after, other family members followed. For example, Chase's mother is known as the Duchess and, in their story, she is the one who bankrolled the airship purchase. Voniè's mother, a recreational therapist back in Mississippi who teaches the value of play, also participates from afar. Yet another piece of fact that inspires the fiction, she represents part of the expanded universe of airships that turned the singular Iron Opal into an ever-growing fleet. To this, they've added numerous local members who have moved away, but still want to remain connected – literally and figuratively – to the mother ship. "Just because they've moved away doesn't mean they've stopped being a part of our group, and being connected to who we are," Voniè tells me. With that, they have members spanning the country, coast to coast. Their oldest member, who visits when she can and stays with the Stillson/Crossfire family, hails from Minnesota.

Keep in mind, not all steampunk groups are the same. Some, like comparable *Star Wars* and *Star Trek* fan organizations, have rules which chapter members must follow. For example, the nearby Denver Victorian Steampunk Society, an offshoot of the Denver Victorian Society, has stringent guidelines about costuming and accuracy. While the

Crossfires respect historical reenactment groups, such as the Society for Creative Anachronism, the passengers and crew on the Iron Opal participate simply because it is fun. Unlike their exacting day jobs, leading a steampunk lifestyle allows them to explore their creativity without worrying about specs and checking off boxes. "No, we're not that formal at all," Voniè explains, "For us, if it's not fun, it's not worth doing." "Let's go play," Chase adds, "Let's go do something where rules don't matter." Despite this flexibility, the Stillsons are clear that this group is *their* creation, and they have the final word. The tightest restriction they place on the group is how their members will treat other people:

Chase: "If you're wearing an Iron Opal pin, you will behave yourself."

Voniè: "You can feel what you feel, but you're not going to treat people ugly."

Other than that prime commandment, not only can you be flexible with rules in their parallel universe, but you can also rewrite history. Voniè shares, "The fun part about steampunk is, we can cherry pick what we want and don't want to keep from different areas, and then bring it into present day. It's the history that never was. It's not reenactment, so we don't have to worry about being historically accurate, but we can be historically and science-fictionally inspired." The Stillsons especially appreciate historical revisions that are socially aware. "If you could rewrite it and change it," Voniè asks, "how would you? Especially from a civil rights, social justice lens. That's so beautiful to see younglings talk about, if they saw wrongs, how would they change them?"

This open and inquisitive spirit draws a variety of people to their ship's doors. Voniè explains, "Anyone can be a passenger on our ship. It's people who follow our Facebook page, or people who interact with us at cons. For someone to become a crew member, they have to let it be known that they would like to become crew, and everyone who is a crew member gets to know them. It's an all-or-none vote." To this Chase adds, "For us, the big thing is that steampunk is a title that people can bestow upon themselves. There's no steampunk court that rules that. The only thing that we really have control over is if someone becomes crew with us or not. And just because someone doesn't become crew doesn't mean they're bad or not a good steampunker. It just means that their style didn't fit with our style."

Despite this minimal rite of passage, their family has grown and become quite diverse. Chase tells me, "And they range the political spectrum. We have die-hard Democrats, die-hard Republicans, and they don't always get along with each other…just like your family members, right?" "But," chimes in Voniè immediately, "they know they have to play nice, or I will holler." In addition to cons, the group – often traveling in the Stillson's 15-passenger van - participates in local community events, art and craft festivals, and social get-togethers at people's homes during Thanksgiving and Christmas, where they "break out the pretty china." One couple in fact, known as Dragon and Lady Dragon, met on the Iron Opal. Now married (Voniè officiated the wedding), the Dragons have since become parents to two little steampunk Power Rangers.

Not surprisingly, Voniè tells me, "We've had members of our crew tell us this ship has literally saved their lives." There is diversity beyond just age and geographic locale, and a variety of individuals claim the airship as home. Some members are physically challenged. The Crossfire family enjoys being creative with accommodations. For example, one crew member has a variety of developmental delays and physical health conditions, including seizures. From a safety standpoint, the metal membership pins might prove a hazard. For this crew member, their official "pin" is made from felt.

A number of members belong to the LGBTQA+ community. Voniè tells me the story of a crew member who used the steampunk community as a place to explore his gender identity, and learned to start being his true self. "There were a few members of our crew, and our passengers," she continued, "who have been exploring what their identity is, what their gender is, and trying to become comfortable with showing their true self to the outside world. Our stance is, this is who you are. Thank you for letting us see you."

From there conversation turns to the line between cosplay and lifestyle, and the extent to which steampunk is part of their daily lives. We are sitting in Voniè's office, adorned with things like a steamer trunk and geek-inspired artworks. Chase points out that their home was constructed in 1914. "The thing I put my keys on when I walk in the door is a little wrought iron table that has piping coming out of the top of it for my hats to sit on, with a gauge on the top of it. My chandelier has a clock built into it." While Chase often rides a motorcycle, his other mode of transportation is a steam-powered penny farthing (those Victorian style bicycles with the huge front wheel).

But ultimately, they realize, it's more than just the social trappings that keeps them coming back. There is something about the style that is both comforting and empowering. Voniè shares that a big part of her personal journey was becoming comfortable with her body shape. "We have resources from more than just our neck up. We are whole bodies of resources." She tells a story from a few years before: while attending a comic con in the South, a friend from high school, who hadn't seen her in years, recognized her laugh and turned to find her, "But it took them a minute to recognize me physically. To see me in a corset, and something that was showing my shape, was something that was so different than anything I did before. Then, I wore the biggest, widest blue jeans you'd ever want to see, and the biggest t-shirts. To be comfortable to wear something that showed my shape was a huge piece of moving forward and becoming comfortable in my own skin." And, she adds, there are other benefits to wearing a corset. "It's the prettiest back brace you'll ever wear."

Chase's journey involved reconciling this passion with the sometimes-conservative perspectives in his profession. "To be clear, I'm a mechanic. There's lots of mechanics, in a very masculine, very macho, very cut-and-dried 'this is normal, that's not normal' kind of world. This, according to most mechanics, is not normal behavior. They go, 'You dress up in funny clothes and do what for fun?' And I'm like, 'Yep. Get over it. Or don't.' And I was not always like that," he admits. "It was probably ten years ago when we really started doing cosplay, where I just decided I'm done trying to figure out how to fit in the little box that my job gives me. It recharges my batteries. I could never have told you, until I ended up with her, I would never in a million years have guessed that this is what would charge up my batteries. Some people go hiking, some people jump out of airplanes, some people will go snowboarding. We dress up and socialize."

COSTUME CONVERSATION # 6
Elaine and Ember Waterman
a.k.a. Blackbeard and Jim from *Our Flag Means Death*

Thomas G. Endres, PhD ♦ 92

Based lightly on a true story, the HBO Max comedy series *Our Flag Means Death* tells the story of real-life British aristocrat Stede Bonnet (Rhys Darby) who, in the early 1700s, walked away from his wealth to become a gentleman pirate. During his often ill-fated journey he meets and falls in love with the notorious Blackbeard the Pirate (Taika Waititi). In one touching scene, the two men are separated by fate. Broken-hearted, Blackbeard shaves off his namesake facial hair, puts on Stede's pink floral bathrobe, and gives way to his feelings.

Among Bonnet's crew is a fake-bearded but deadly pirate known only as Jim. Played by real-life nonbinary actor Vico Ortiz, one episode reveals that Jim, identified as female at birth, is gender fluid. To their relief, the fellow pirates don't seem to care, and Jim can remove the false whiskers. All the crew seems worried about is whether or not they can still call them Jim.

It is against this backdrop that we meet Elaine Waterman and her non-binary teen Ember. With Elaine in floral robe and beard-free, and Ember a dead ringer for Jim, the pirate story is a great cosplay scenario which allows this articulate mother and her child to explore and celebrate Ember's journey. Such a creative approach to understanding life through art is all in a day's work for Elaine. She is Executive Director of the Firehouse Art Center in Longmont, CO, and a professional artist in her own right. "If anyone were to ask me what my medium is, I would say I am a generalist. I've basically dabbled in every kind of art medium there is. I went to school for 3D art, so sculpture and stuff like that. Graduated with a Fine Arts degree as well as English Literature and Art History degree. I moved to New York City and ended up going into fashion design. I went to F.I.T [Fashion Institute of Technology] and worked at Macy's and Bloomingdale's, fashion design department there, as well as at Marvel."

In addition to sufficient art training, Elaine also had a key ingredient to becoming a top-notch cosplayer. Growing up, she really loved Halloween. "Halloween was my favorite holiday, and it wasn't until my kiddo Ember and I started cosplaying together that I got connected with the cosplay community. I really actually didn't know that people got together and dressed up days other than Halloween. It was amazing, because we spent all this time making our Halloween costumes because we loved it, and getting involved with the cosplay community gave us the chance to make more magic throughout the year."

Given her years in New York City, I was a little surprised that she wasn't exposed to cosplay and comic conventions. "Did not even know that people would get dressed up in their little fandoms," she admits. "I had no idea that there were my people around that liked dressing up and doing stuff." Her first Con was in Denver. "I was essentially on Facebook and found out they were doing a Marvel photo shoot. Ember dressed up as Captain America and I dressed up as Black Widow. These were completely store-bought costumes; I don't think we made anything. We just wanted to go and have fun." After that experience, they began to make the Denver Con a regular outing. Realizing now that people often make their own costumes, Elaine got to work. Early costumes had her as Marceline (from *Marceline the Vampire Queen*, Cartoon Network) while Ember was Marceline's human friend Finn. Later, Ember was a peashooter from the *Plants versus Zombies* video game, while Elaine, fittingly, was a zombie.

Has it always been the two of them together? And are the costumes always a thematic match? "Most of the cons I've been to have been with Ember, but I've done a couple of things by myself, too." During a short spell living in California, the cosplay hobby continued. "I was fully into it at that point," enthused Elaine. "Loved making stuff. Sculpting. All sorts of craziness. Did some pretty elaborate costumes there." She did attend one Con, the Anime Expo in LA, by herself. She learned a few things about costuming at that event. For example, it was really hot, and parts of her costume were melting and falling off. Her conclusion? "It was fun."

Other than that rare solo-outing, it is most often a mother-child event, and Elaine usually puts the most effort into Ember's costumes. Her favorite costume created for Ember was Drift from *Fortnite*. The favorite for herself? "As far as mine, probably Yoshimitsu from *Soulcalibur*. That was the samurai warrior with the skull face. That one was pretty elaborate."

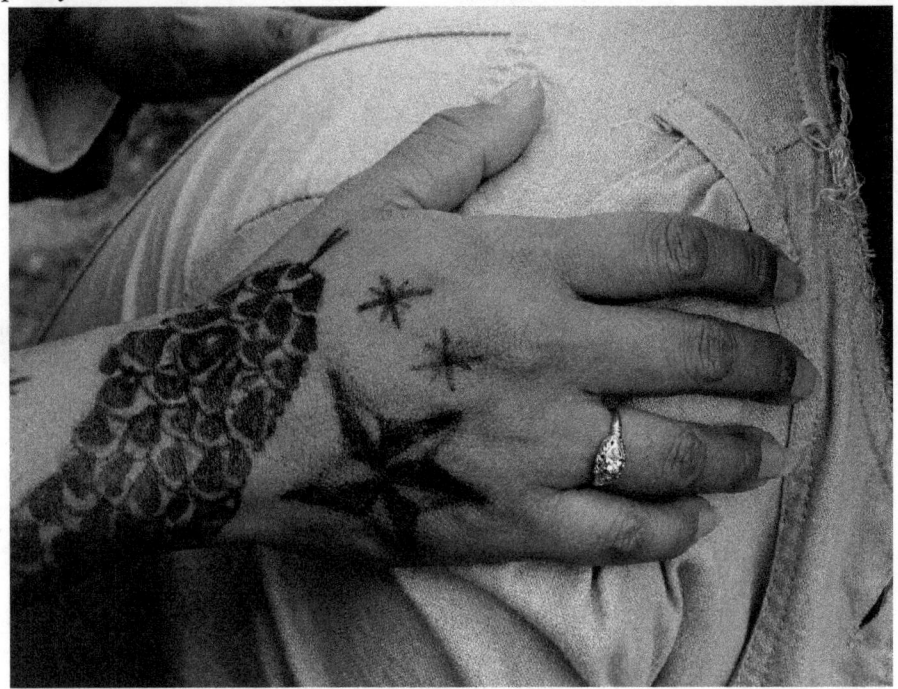

With this background established, I moved deeper with the questions. I was most interested in how dressing up in costumes makes her feel. "I really love that you get to inhabit a different kind of persona, while bringing parts of your own personality into it." That led me to wonder whether she views costumes as an alternative personality, someone you are not; or are they instead an extension of your existing self? "I think both of the statements are true. When I cosplay Marceline, a lot of it is you love that character, but *what* do you love about that character? It involves aspects of their personality that you wish to bring into your life. I guess, psychologically, you could make a huge argument that these people that you're playing, their strongest characteristics are probably something you want to emulate in your life that you don't get a chance to. I definitely can see that it's kind of breaking out and getting to do something that you're not able to do, but I really feel that it picks up on stuff that's already inside you."

Elaine shares that, since she got into cosplay later than most, she is on the older end of the spectrum. She admits that a lot of costuming these days for women is super sexy, and she tends not to do a lot of that. Still, that doesn't stop her from doing certain characters "in a corset and small skirt," as opposed to being the literal character. "And that's fun, too. I feel like it definitely gives me a lot of confidence when I'm in costume." Sexy motif or not, the type of costume she enjoys most is the one that requires face paint or make-up. "Whenever I take pictures and post them, everyone is like, 'That totally doesn't look like you. You look completely different.' It's a really interesting thing."

Discussing questions of gender, and of showing her face, we turn to examine the current pink floral robe. Obviously, Blackbeard's storyline character is a male. Is she playing it literal, or is she giving an interpretation of a *female* Blackbeard? "No, no. I don't think that I play female versions of the character. If I want to do an accurate cosplay, I will *crossplay* and be that person, how they express *their* gender identity. This character has so much put into it as far as historical accuracy, I felt like it needed to be something that was as represented on screen. That went into my decision of whether I wanted to be Blackbeard as a female, or Blackbeard, or just Edward." Edward, incidentally, is Blackbeard's given name – and what he calls himself when he is clean-shaven and vulnerable. Currently, Elaine feels she is portraying Edward. "Which is great. I do have the stuff to make the beard. At some point I'm going to do a different cosplay where he's fully Blackbeard."

Moving on from gender, I ask if she has similar viewpoints about race and culture. Does one need to be cultural match? "That's interesting, obviously, as a Filipino person. I do tend to try to find characters that have similar skin tones, not because of any feeling that I shouldn't play those characters, but that I give a better representation." She does recognize that Asian-American representation in the media is often problematic (e.g., the aforementioned Scarlett Johansson as the Japanese Major). She often selects those characters with a darker skin tone because she best embodies the depiction. "Not to say that if I ever wanted to do – I'm trying to think if I have any blonde characters – I would feel fine playing those as well. I don't think I've ever stayed away from a character. Obviously, Marceline is a vampire, so I've had to change my skin tone for that."

Are there any unwritten rules regarding race? "I guess you're referring to blackface or darkening your skin tone? I feel like there are definitely rules, and I feel like everyone will tell you." For Elaine, she is okay with mixed-race representations, as long as it's done respectfully. "I think Disney characters are a little problematic," she adds, "because they are so generalized and stereotyped. Like Mulan is an Asian person and this is how you dress up as this character. I feel like, as an Asian-American, as long as it's done respectfully, and it's not done in a way that is stereotypical or disrespectful, I feel like that's fine. Before all of the representation and issues like that, when I was younger, I probably dressed up as Pocahontas. I think there is a lot more awareness, just a lot more situational awareness. As long as you make the decisions knowing the historical stories of the people you're playing – you have to do your research if you're going to do something like that."

She shares specifically a Dias de los Muertos (Day of the Dead) celebration that takes place every year in her hometown. "A lot of people that really love the celebration are not of Latinx descent. I feel there is such a great feeling of respect and sharing of cultures that you can kind of tell when it's done disrespectfully and when it's done out of celebration."

All of this goes full circle, and comes back to her portrayal of Edward/Blackbeard, and Ember's portrayal of Jim. Once again, Elaine has thought the issue through and provides an insightful conclusion to our interview. "The characters have so much to do with costume and identity. In *Our Flag Means Death*, Jim is a non-binary character and, in the show, their pronouns are used correctly. The fact that the show is about queer characters and non-binary characters, I feel like the outfits they use are really very thoughtfully chosen. Edward is upset because Stede has left, and so he's exploring a more gentle, feminine side. The clothing allows him to do that. Jim spends a lot of the time having the other pirates think that they are a man, and the clothing allowed them to do that. As far as costume and identity, your clothing allows you to express who you are. Whether that's gender identity or just self-expression, I think it's a really important link. Just like you can change your clothing, it gives you a stronger connection to who you are." That, it seems, is a fantastic point to wrap this up. "Changing your clothing and changing your costume doesn't mean you're changing yourself; it just gives you a better understanding of who you are."

CHAPTER 3
Identity and Representation

There are no ethnic, racial, spiritual, or geographic limitations or expectations when choosing a character to Cosplay.
~Winge, 2019, p. 12

The headline read: "A Black TikToker was accused of appropriating a Japanese character. Then she was banned." VICE World News (Montgomery, 2021) tells the story of Mia Rios, a 23-year-old black cosplayer from California, who posted TikTok photos dressed as her favorite character - Asuka Langley Soryu from the popular Japanese anime *Evangelion*. Immediately, negative comments surfaced accusing her of culturally appropriating and fetishizing the character. One user blatantly said they didn't like African Americans. Another user, claiming to be Japanese, accused her of sexualizing Japanese people. Rios told the reporter that, as a black woman in cosplay, she was made to feel like a "gross, disgusting, ugly monster." One user, angry that she had "ruined" the character, suggested that Rios kill herself.

The greatest thing about cosplay is the ability to expand and transform yourself through costume, and then share your journey with a like-minded and supportive community. Usually. Sadly, the most narrow-minded viewpoints come from within the community itself. Nobody ridicules and ostracizes cosplayers more than other cosplayers.

I'll be honest. This phenomenon was my motivation for writing this book. The more I attended Cons with my daughters, the more I viewed it as a colorful utopia. There were families hanging out together. People with disabilities were fully embraced and included. There was every color, size, and shape of person imaginable. And the "nerdy" kids, the ones who would have been pushed around when I was in high school, were proudly on display center stage. Only later did I start to hear the rumblings about nay-sayers, back-stabbers, and downright bullies. In this chapter, we'll address those sensitive identity issues like age, race, gender, body/ability, and religion, with the goal of establishing guidelines and keeping the bullies at bay. As Winge (2019) notes, there will always be "negative critiques from some peer Cosplayers when ethnic, gender, racial, and size lines are crossed or challenged" (p. 12). If this book can help reduce just some of that negatively, it is worth all the effort.

Age

As a cosplayer in my sixties, this issue of identity is at the forefront of my mind. It is not, however, on the radar for most cosplayers. I've never met anyone who cares if a young person dresses as someone older, or vice versa. What little research that exists speaks mainly to the cognitive differences between the generations, and how that might impact our cosplay abilities. Harrington (2018), for example, reports that creativity "rises rapidly as a career begins, peaks about 20 years into a career (typically late 30s to mid 40s) then slowly declines with age." By age 80, our creativity is allegedly half what it was in our peak (p. 235; citing Simonton, 2016). Admitting it is a generalization, he concludes that "the age-creativity curve appears to persist across cultures and throughout history" (p. 235).

Harrington's goal is that "fan scholars" (those who research and study fandom topics like blogging, fanfic, and cosplay) not forget about older fans and older artists. He argues that, for older fans, creativity may be more expressed through talk and process, and less so on product. Scholars need to recognize the unique characteristics of "creative ageing" (p. 238), since the psychology and emotionality of the 70 or 80 year old is not the same as 20 or 30 year old fans. "If gerontology has shifted towards a focus on the creative potentials of ageing, it is in our interest as media/cultural studies scholars to engage in that dialogue, keeping in mind both productive and 'non-productive' creative expression as well as both cognitive and emotional dimensions of creativity" (p. 239).

Begrudgingly, he's probably right. I haven't aged out of my love for costumes, and have yet to enter the "you kids stay off of my lawn" phase. But, as someone who teaches popular culture courses to twenty-somethings, I see the difference in our likes, understandings, and interpretations. Harrington suggests that, in addition to emphasizing the health benefits of "crossword puzzles and Sudoku," ageing fans who are enmeshed in television, movies, and even comic books "offer an alternative path towards healthy and happy ageing that encompasses multiple forms of creative expression" (p. 240). I will simply add that cosplay can and should still be in the mix. Other than historical reenactments (see Costume Conversation #11), we should never "age out" of enjoying character portrayals.

Race

Unlike ageing, the identity issue of race is a major one in Western culture (see the Appendix for an international view). In the same VICE World News report (Montgomery, 2021) that started this chapter, Anuli Duru, a black female cosplayer and artist from New York City, reports being told she shouldn't dress as certain characters due to her darker skin or her curvaceous body. "I don't know how to put that lightly, but we can't really get away with just wanting to dress up like a character without receiving some sort of hate, backlash, sexualized comments, or just a weird gaze upon us." Why is race such a hot button?

When it comes to cosplayers of color dressing as lighter-skin characters, the hostility they receive is nothing short of prejudice and racism. "Cosplayers of color are often forced into an uncomfortable space, one where they are confined to either a limited number of characters who look like them who have appeared over the years, or stepping outside their racial group and into a different one, tasked with reimagining the character at the same time" (Liptak, 2022, p. 100). In other words, other than the limited pool of characters like Luke Cage, Samuel L. Jackson's version of Nick Fury, or the population of Wakanda, black cosplayers do not have a lot to choose from. In the last chapter, we saw that white female Kellsie was willing to be Batman even though the character is male. In the same vein, a black cosplayer should be equally allowed to dress as Batman even though the character is white (see "Litt Knight" interpretation in Image 3.1). Loving Batman is the only criterion you need.

Image 3.1 *From l to r: Don Hudson II (Litt Knight), Tanya Layman (Catwoman ala 1960s Eartha Kitt), Orlando (Batman)*

Of course, it's never as easy as just saying loving the character is enough. "For people of color to traverse racial boundaries by cosplaying as white characters is to traverse literature and media that seeks to make us invisible," declares Kirkpatrick (2019, [1.2]). Again, we are talking about a long history of exclusionary practices. Characters like Batman and Superman could easily have been heroes of color, but how would that have been received when they first hit the comic book stores in the 1930s? Fortunately, things are better now, but we have yet to obtain a critical mass of characters of color. They still remain the exception.

Famed cosplayer Yaya Han, a Chinese woman who has struggled to find characters that match her skin tone, and received scorn from others for her choices, is aware of the challenge. "However, any racist remarks I have received are nothing compared to the vitriol that black cosplayers have to face on a daily basis" (p. 147). She states that a main reason people cosplay is to "be whoever we want while still feeling content in our own skin. Black cosplayers do not have that luxury" (p. 147). She argues that, as with many activities and organizations, black people are underrepresented. "The invisibility of black cosplayers mirrors the experience of black people in the real world" (p. 147).

For those cosplayers of color who adopt light-skinned characters, Kirkpatrick offers insightful praise. Even if they have no intent on making a social statement – "they just want to cosplay a beloved character" – their decision "becomes revisionist as they create an original version of the character" [6.1]. Despite getting pushback from narrow-minded fans, he concludes, they are an inspiration to *blerds* (black nerds). "In the brave display of their transgressive superhero bodies, they materialize a better today and hint at an alternative tomorrow" [3.6].

While it should be perfectly acceptable for a cosplayer of color to embody whatever character they want, white cosplayers need to consider impacts due to long-standing systemic inequities. Liptak (2022) concedes that "performing arts has a long and unfortunate history when it comes to race." Early minstrel shows, for example, utilized white performers in black makeup to play racist caricatures of African Americans. While that practice is now a thing of the past, he argues, "every year brings up some viral moment where a college student or overzealous costumer decides to color their face in a similar fashion" (p. 99). Understandably, Liptak's view is that, even if the person is trying to present an accurate portrayal, the social impact and history of the practice outweighs their good intention.

Blackface

There is a big, ugly, and open wound on the face of cosplay. It oozes and stings and has never healed...this wound is inflicted on a large and marginalized group that crosses all ages and genders. I'm talking about racism and blackface in cosplay. Yaya Han, 2020, p. 145

The former minstrel show tactic of using black grease makeup to create exaggerated stereotypes of people of color, generally known as blackface, is to be avoided at all costs. Continuing from her description above, Han explains that, in addition to minstrel shows, blackface was used by slave owners and slave trade supporters to mock the black population. She laments that it still appears occasionally in comedy shows in Asia. Her condemnation of the practice is unequivocal. "The historical implications of blackface are severe enough to render the practice immoral and place it alongside the N-word and the Nazi salute as things you cannot do because they are considered morally wrong" (p. 148).

Race and Gender combined

In her excellent article on Black Femme (black women, female identified nonbinary individuals, trans women, womyn, or womxn, and related terms), who identity as Black and of Afrodiasporic descent, Thomas (2021) explains the goal of cosplay or mas (masquerade) is "the undoing of rule," that is, undoing the colonial interventions in pop cultural canons. For her, comics, TV, and films create a social reality which perpetuates sexist, homophobic, and racist ways of knowing. "Black women cosplayers often confront insult, misrecognition, and judgements on their costumed looks that are deemed incomplete because, for example, they do not match up to a comic book character's race or body type" (p. 328). She encourages the breaking of norms; for example, a curvy black woman as Poison Ivy or a petite Black woman as Michelle Pfeiffer's Catwoman. "Cognitive biases in cosplay reflect societal norms carrying over into imaginative realms" (p. 341). To be hypervigilant about accuracy regarding gender or color contradicts the purpose of the activity. After all, Thomas argues (referencing the Myrtle R. Douglas story from Chapter 1), cosplay was started by a woman dressed in a costume from the future. Where would we be if we didn't break a few rules?

Gender

Cosplay, as a practice, offers a unique opportunity to both explore and present appearances that may or may not confirm to participants' birth-assigned gender or the original or canonical gender of characters in television, movies, or video games. Nichols, 2019, p. 275

Skin tone aside, few areas have received as much attention in cosplay studies as the topic of gender. Of course, the term gender is broad and covers a lot of areas. For most, it refers to one's psychological orientation more so than the sex one is assigned at birth. It is a social construction more than a physical one. That is how we will approach it here, and I will point out when and if I mean something different. We will look at these questions from a few different angles, including gender of the cosplayer, crossing gender boundaries, and sexual identity and orientation.

Gender of cosplayers

Before we start confounding variables and switching labels, let's look at a good old-fashioned study of cisgendered differences; that is, differences between those whose gender identity matches their assigned sex at birth. Simply put, between biological males and biological females. In 2018, Rosenberg and Letamendi conducted a survey of 929 cosplayers. They wanted to find out if either sex was more or less extroverted/introverted than the other. Interesting question. In the general population, studies have found, women tend to be more extraverted than men. (Keep in mind, the stereotypical understanding of introversion and extroversion is a little off. Many think it means that introverts are shy and extraverts are outgoing. That's a piece of it, but the more important distinction is that introverts get exhausted when interacting with others and need private time to recharge, while extraverts get energized by others; it feeds them.) Thus, the general "big picture" assumption here is that men are more likely to run out of energy at a social event, while women are more likely to gain power and vitality from the activity.

When it comes to cosplayers, Rosenberg and Letamendi found no difference between the sexes. All fell within the "normal" range between the two extremes. While this may sound insignificant, it has some fascinating implications. It suggests that female cosplayers tend to be more *introverted* than the general female population, while male cosplayers tend to be more *extraverted* than the general male population. There seems to be something about cosplay that attracts those in the middle ranges. They suggest that women are more accountable to fashion, make-up, and objectifying standards. Those women less extraverted than the norm seek out a safer space to be viewed. Men, on the other hand, are not used to such objectification in the real world. Guys might need to be more extraverted than the norm to feel comfortable dressing up in costume.

Beyond that, most of the studies that have been done on sex-based definitions of gender (women and men) focus on the female cosplayer. Not surprisingly, the intent is to deal with power imbalances and objectification of women. Kotani and LaMarre (2007), for example, provide the unique view that generic portrayals of robots, pets, dolls, or alien entities are often merely metaphors "used to speak of the social position of women, to describe their confinement within a patriarchal system" (p. 50). For them, the movie *The Stepford Wives* (they were talking about the 2004 version with Nicole Kidman, but the 1975 version works here as well), in which women are portrayed as "artificial fabrications," simply increases the myth that femininity and attractiveness are tied to these otherworldly trappings. This could lead to the truly objectifying view that real women are, well, dolls.

Similarly, Birkedal (2019) examines how cosplay provides a space to understand and yet resist the "violent, gendered discourses inherent in so many popular culture narratives" (p. 189). She did this by dressing as Marvel's superspy Black Widow, Natasha Romanoff, who often feels she is a monster because, as part of the Soviet protocol for her training, she was made barren. From the *Stepford Wives* orientation above, you might think Birkedal's reaction would be horror at being reduced to such an artifact. Instead, she observed, "It feels *delicious*" (p. 200). She recognized she was on display, but empathized with a character who was perhaps a "nightmare" inside, but "dressed like a daydream." She realized, ultimately, that Natasha is both, which contribute to her character's strength and resilience. "In that recognition," Birkedal concluded, "there is incredible power" (p. 200).

Nichols would view this as a healthy response. In discussing women's participation in cosplay, she argues that it provides an opportunity to explore "a variety of elements" within their identities. "Cosplay is a venue in which they may be coy, sweet, strong, badass, vulnerable, violent, outgoing, introverted or intelligent, all in the same weekend" (2019, p. 276).

Beyond that, in both the research and in actual practice, cosplay and gender boundaries begin to blur. Winge (2019) begins by pointing that the cosplayer's "corporeal body presents challenges in maintaining a perceived gender or expected physiques within the hyper-gendered costumed body" (p. 160). In other words, the over-sexualized and/or excessively muscular body types we see in the source material cannot be duplicated in real life. Regardless of our sex or our gender, we cannot be the "man" or "woman" we see in the comic book pages. "Moreover," she adds, "as Cosplayers achieve agency through roleplaying their chosen characters, designations such as gender are becoming more complicated in the ways it is revealed or denied on the corporeal body" (p. 160). Here, I believe she is saying that not only does gender get blurred because of the impossible bodies we attempt to imitate, it also blurs due to the purposeful and empowering decisions cosplayers make on how they choose to represent those bodies.

To rewrite the presentation of sex-based bodies is a healthy decision. Buetow (2020) applauds this form of expression. "Members of both sexes tend to form groups in which they wear costumes and fashion accessories in order to actualize fiction and draw on cisgendered or transgendered aspects of their inner selves." As we've been seeing all along in this book, cosplay is a wonderful vehicle for experimenting with and expanding upon aspects of one's personality. And, for most of us, how we perceive our gender is an integral part of that personality. "Their joyful activity of costumed role-playing provides respite from the distress produced by health challenges; evokes inner strengths in creative ways; and transforms and reconstructs their personal identity" (p. 433). We will see several examples of that transformation in the Costume Conversations that follow this chapter.

Two caveats

Before digging deeper into complicated gender perspectives, I'll quickly share the views of two studies which put a slightly different spin on the topic. The first is a 1997 article by Freitas et al., who remind us to not only look at an outfit or costume to determine who someone *is*, but to also interpret what it says regarding who they are *not*. Thus, a costume sends messages about both "identity" and "identity not." For example, you may have in your closet a selection of outfits you consider your "least favorite clothes." You might keep them for a reason - such as dress clothes for funerals or interviews, or grubby clothes for working in the yard - but you don't view them as a good example of who you feel you are. Those are your "identity not" clothes. As for gender, "that which is masculine is often constructed by means of its distance from that which is feminine. Masculinity becomes femininity *not*, rather than a straightforward, positive construction of a dominant normality" (p. 328). Here's an extreme example. In the Marvel universe, there is a character named Mahkizmo (yes, it purposefully sounds like *machismo*), who rules a planet in which women are enslaved. A male cosplayer who picks this character to avoid any implication or accusation that his "dressing up" is a feminine thing to do, is picking it for its *not* characteristics. Some men do this, argue Freitas and colleagues, to avoid seeming interested in fashion and potentially being perceived as homosexual.

"Gender and sexuality become intertwined in the realm of masculinity *not*" (p. 329), they observed. Their study dug deeper, including interviews with gay men and lesbians who, in a similar way, avoided any such stereotypical outfits because they did not want to become "visual caricatures" (p. 329). They realize the male/female, gay/straight binary distinctions are too simplistic. "The question is not simply what do clothes mean or not mean. Rather, how do we use them to negotiate border spaces – spaces we need to conceptualize as tenuous, fragile, barbed, or elastic, rather than as fixed and dichotomous" (p. 334). Our takeaway from this is to simply remember that costumes can say a lot about one's gender and orientations. What we choose to wear, and what we especially choose to *not* wear, sends messages about how we feel in our own skin.

The second caveat comes from the work of Gn (2011), who downplays the impact of cosplay and gender politics. "Unlike other social groups that may stress the need to politicize an essentialist idea of deviance, conscious gender politics remains a rarity within the cosplay community" (p. 585), he argues. Given the amount of research done, and the importance placed upon gender identity from those interviewed in this book, that seems a naïve statement. However, Gn argues that gender in cosplay is simulacra, or "copies without an original referent." In essence, for something to be simulacra, it needs to create a product or image that portrays a reality, despite the fact that such reality probably doesn't and never did exist. Think about the popular trend these days of having a "ranch wedding." Bride and grooms go to great lengths to have plenty of shabby chic signage placed everywhere, adding twinkling lights to fence posts, and serving champagne in Mason jars. It's beautiful, but it's a simulation; weddings in the Old West weren't nearly that fancy (or expensive)!

"This means that through the consumptive act in cosplay, the image becomes a disembodied sign that acquires its own material force" (Gn, 2011, p. 587). Thus, if one is portraying a character in a gender-blurred fashion, he says it is less an expression of gender identity or a conscious desire to be deviant, and more motivated simply by their "intense attraction towards the character" (p. 587). Yes, changing the gender or gender characteristics in source material may seem to subvert hetero-normative standards, he says, but concludes "it does not operate within a single field of difference" (p. 589). In other words, it doesn't matter. Beyond that, he points out the gender issue gets blurred with non-human variables like being elves or aliens. Since elves and aliens are not real, then male elves or female aliens are likewise not real, and we shouldn't worry about the gender portrayal, since it cannot be understood in human terms. Again, I'm worried he is missing the point and the power of gender identity.

Whether or not we agree with either Freitas et al. (identity *not* makes a difference) or Gn (gender politics in cosplay are minimal), both reports give us food for thought. It is the stance of this book, however, that gender decisions and portrayals matter, often make a statement, and go a long way toward making a cosplayer feel at peace with their picture of themselves.

Crossplay

The most popular way to blur gender lines is via *crossplay*, sometimes referred to as gender-bending, in which the character and the cosplayer mix and match gender portrayals. As such, we might see a female Wolverine or a male Supergirl. This is not new. Most know that, in Shakespeare's time, all characters, male or female, were played by men. But that's more of a misogynistic historical hiccup, and not really crossplay as we define it. More relevant might be early androgynous fashions, like the flat-chested, boyish look popular in the 1920s. As Worsley explains, "It was a decadent time for survivors of both the war and the great flu pandemic of 1918. The ratio of young women to men was three to one. Some girls were simply never going to find a man, so why should they not enjoy life with a male kind of freedom – easy-to-wear clothes and hairstyles, a job, cigarettes, cocktails, sex, and dancing all night?" We saw a similar occurrence in the 1960s, as models like Twiggy promoted the boyish look. Changing course, the 1970s promoted long hair, floral shirts, and bell-bottomed jeans for all, regardless of sex.

Incidentally, I encountered at least one caustic interpretation for these style trends. Giddon (1985) shares a 1953 study which "offered the psychoanalytic interpretation, offensive to some people, that some male designers are homosexuals who are afraid of or hate women and who thus seek revenge by making women look like boys" (p. 227). I must admit, in all my discussions with cosplayers and how/why they dress as the opposite gender, no one said it's because they hate men or women and are trying to sabotage sexual politics! We can only hope people have better reasons than that.

For example, *Rule 63* – an internet creation that can be found via any search engine – states that, for any fictional character found in source material, there exists a universe with a gender-swapped version. Our planet tells the story of an island filled with Amazonian women, in which the Princess Diana is trained; she later to join the ranks of the world as the heroine Wonder Woman. Rule 63 would say there's a universe with an island of Amazonian men. The prince, let's call him Dan, dons a star-spangled outfit to become Wonder Man. I like this explanation!

Yaya Han (2020) offers that women in particular are drawn to genderbending because so much of the culture is created by men about men. As such, when men crossplay, it is quite often done as satire and humor within the ranks. When women (and men not doing it to be funny) gender-bend, she claims, it allows one to be "queer-positive and celebrate gender fluidity;" and that the experience is both empowering and freeing (p. 118). Winge (2019) agrees, but points out a challenge encountered by females who portray male characters. By reversing the associated visual messages, one could – intentionally or not - "eroticize the Cosplayer wearing the costume" (p. 101). Think about that. A woman who, with serious intent, dresses up as Wolverine in order to access and explore his animal angst and visceral power. To have a male cosplayer look at that and think, "Hmm, that's kind of hot," starts to diminish the portrayal. This gets complicated even farther if the woman consciously eroticizes the costume, i.e. dresses up as "sexy" Wolverine.

Perhaps the most rigorous investigation into crossplay was conducted by Tompkins (2019), who begins with the observation that gender is a social construction regulated by societal discourse, and it specifies what is and is not permissible for each binary sex category. Crossplay is not controlled by that discourse and is "typically not undertaken as a form of parody or gender-exaggeration but rather aims for an authentic transformation of a mundane, gendered body into a cross-gender body of a mediated character" [1.2]. As such, she considers this a healthy subversion of heteronormative bodily and gendered practices. Most important, crossplay may "provide a relatively safe way for individuals to experiment with their bodies, gender performativity, and identity" [3.3].

Based upon cultural assumptions, though outdated they may be, masculinity is associated with authority and power. Despite advances, we still exist in a patriarchal society. As such, Tompkins observes, "when a self-identified woman dresses as a male character, this act may arouse less scrutiny than when a self-identified man dresses as a female character" [3.5]. She suggests that going from female-to-male is seen as "moving up the gender hierarchy." As a result, she discovered, women tend to feel empowered by crossplay, but men feel disempowered.

Thomas (2015) encountered similar apprehensions associated with crossplay. She reported a significant level of anxiety in the way crossplayers repeatedly emphasized the fact that their choice of costume had nothing to do with their sexual orientation. It seemed like a defensive response to the sometimes "prejudiced and homophobic discourse that surrounds crossplay." This was particularly true with male crossplayers. They did not want to act feminine, and they were quick to stress that "crossplay was only about fun and it did not mean they were homosexual or transgendered." Some argued that only a "real man" can be comfortable putting on women's clothes, while others differentiated between a cross-dresser - viewed as a lifestyle for all occasions - and a crossplayer, who does so only in special circumstances (p. 32). "Crossplay does have subversive possibilities," Thomas concludes, "although many participants themselves do not recognize these practices as a threat to the established order of gender binaries" (p. 34).

So, is crossplay political? The answer is…it depends. For some, it is important exploration, and for others it is just another costume. That latter group aligns more with Gn's claim above; it is not about gender politics; the cosplayer simply has an attachment to a character. Even the expansive Tompkins study concludes that, in a majority of cases, people choose to crossplay simply because they like the clothing associated with the costume.

That would be the case for Carleen Rose, who cosplays as Captain America. Her husband Kenny Bush, in true couples costume form, joins her as Cap's best buddy, Bucky "Winter Soldier" Barnes. Carleen (2022) explains, "I've seen some really amazing gender-bent cosplay on social media, but when I was putting together my Captain America cosplay, it didn't truly occur to me that I was gender-bending. Kenny and I wanted to do a couples cosplay, but we didn't want to limit our ideas to actual couples." Kenny adds, "I had no particular reaction to Carleen's choice in character, I felt we were just choosing something fun to do together that was away from the normal choices and obvious. I feel anyone can gender-bend a character that they feel embraces them or a character that speaks to them. That is the essence of cosplay."

I asked Carleen who she felt she was portraying. Was she a female Captain America, or just simply Captain America – who happened to be modeled by a female? For her it was the latter, the actual male character, though she clarified, "It wasn't an exact replica of Captain America, more like the essence of the character, which to me is the purpose of cosplay. I had a modern suit with the World War II shield. I didn't do it intentionally, but it's like I created my own multiverse version of Captain America." So, in this case, we have a female cosplayer portraying her interpretation of male character, while her male husband portrayed that character's male compatriot. Their rationale is consistent with Gn and Tompkins' observations that decisions are often based on attachment to the character. It is also consistent with Tompkins and Thomas's conclusions that it is easier for females to cosplay as males than vice versa.

Image 3.2 *Captain America (crossplay) and Winter Soldier*

Based on my observations, this perspective accounts for a significant portion of crossplay I've encountered at many events. Crossplay examples seem to be straightforward female-to-male depictions of male characters. The few male-to-female conversions I've seen, like a bearded Wonder Woman, are done for humorous effect. This commonality, however, should not be assumed to explain all cases. There are still those "subversive" instances (Thomas, 2015; Tompkins, 2019), where a statement is being made about gender, power, orientation, and presentation; especially in select communities.

LGBTQ+

After attending numerous cosplay and fan events, Clyde (2021) said of the settings, "I have discovered what I call a queer ethos, in which gender fluidity and same-sex romance serve as signifiers of an authentic self, pure love, and a practice of radical inclusivity" (pp. 1050-51). She goes on to commend all participants, even those who do not consider themselves part of the LGBTQ+ community, for their inclusivity and open-mindedness, claiming they hold their own "nominally normative sexuality" in a "noncommittal limbo," identifying as "basically straight" or "coincidentally cisgendered" (p. 1050-1051). That is, they don't make a big deal of their heterosexuality. In her interviews with long-time cosplayers and "older informants" she often heard comments like "the whole fandom is queer now." The remarks were made in a light-hearted and joking fashion, indicating an understanding that the cosplay culture "has grown into a fertile field in which to explore one's gender identity and flout social norms" (p. 1051).

The biggest concern Clyde encountered was in an interview with a non-binary cosplayer who expressed frustration that "gender identities" still reside with and are controlled by the observer rather than the observed. In other words, if I were to dress in a fashion that made a statement about my gender-identity or sexual orientation, but it was only viewed through a narrow and cisgendered lens, then the meaning lies in the eyes of the beholder. The non-binary cosplayer she spoke with was concerned this could objectify "an otherwise self-gendered subject," provide others with a space for mistaken assumptions, and force the non-binary individual into "a categorized box" (p. 1051). As a communication scholar, I empathize with her interviewee, but add this is the danger of *all* communication. Meaning ultimately lies in people and their own perceptions. The great thing about cosplay's inclusive flair is that – despite mistaken assumptions – the floor is open for conversation and mutual understanding.

This inclusive setting is recognized by Liptak (2022), who notes that cosplay allows one to present themselves as they choose, regardless of the gender or orientation of the character they portray. "Cosplay can be a conduit for fans to explore their gender identity or operate under another name, and it provides a relatively safe environment for them to experiment with those depictions." He admits that it is not perfect, and that trans and non-binary cosplayers are not completely free from discrimination or harassment, but at least "it is an environment in which changing one's appearance is the norm" (p. 103). If you want to test drive an unexplored facet of your personality, a Con is the ideal environment.

The 2017 documentary, *Cosplay Culture*, interviews renown cosplayer Jake Girard of Suki Cosplay, and follows his trans journey as he transitioned from female to male. Jake mainly portrays Kakashi Hatake from *Naruto* manga. His initial crossplay efforts, as a female dressed like a male, began to give him insights into his own identity. "By personifying a male character, it allowed me to figure out that, when I was a man…I felt like I was alive. 'Oh, yes, this is a real feeling, yes, that's it.' But it was hard to put words on that feeling. I realized it's what I wanted." Jake admits that, eventually, he would have come to this realization outside of cosplay, but the opportunity to dress up in like Kakashi provided both clarity and comfort. "When I came into the cosplaying community, it was a very open culture. I used conventions a lot to experiment how I was feeling." Jake explains that he'd had questions about his identity ever since he was a teen, but he didn't understand all the feelings. Now, with the help of cosplay, a weight has been lifted from his shoulders. "It really changed my life, all my life. My personal and professional life." We get to hear a similar story from Jonathan in Costume Conversation #8 at the end of this chapter.

Body Size

One of the most pervasive forms of harassment in the cosplay community is body shaming. Yaya Han, 2020, p. 139

As I indicated at the beginning of this chapter, one of the things I find most appealing about cosplay at Cons was the acceptance of people regardless of shape and size. Ours is still a narrow-minded culture, however, and those under or over normative weight ranges often remain a target for ridicule. Most cosplayers behave and are respectful but, as the saying goes, "haters gonna hate." Winge (2019) comments that body shaming negatively impacts the cosplay subculture in significant ways. "In most instances, both female and male Cosplayers evaluate primarily female Cosplayers more harshly than their male counterparts" (p. 144). The most disturbing part of that evaluation is that females are a disproportionate target. Winge mentions several satirical memes and comics which suggest that large men can portray characters without criticism, but women are held to higher and different physical standards. She concludes, "There is a distinct difference how females 'of size' (i.e., larger body types) are treated compared to males with similar body types" (p. 145).

Fortunately, noted cosplayer Yaya Han – whose body type falls within the socially desirable range - is not silent on the issue. She condemns any form of body shaming; most particularly what it referred to as "fat shaming." "Plus-size cosplayers are routinely accused of ruining a character," she notes, pointing out that they already face many barriers, from character selection to finding patterns and accessories (boots, gloves) in their size. "Imagine working your way through all these barriers only to be met with ridicule" (2020, p. 140).

My experience has been that much of the commentary, both inside cosplay and out, is justified by the shamer due to "health" reasons. They claim to only be advocating healthy eating habits and lifestyles for the sake of the other. Such poorly veiled excuses are inexcusable. We can certainly care about the health and well-being of our fellow travelers on this planet without resorting to ridicule.

Ability/Disability

I've also noted, with pleasure, the number of differently abled participants in cosplay. Individuals with physical and developmental disabilities, ranging from autism and other forms of neurodivergence, to missing limbs and reliance on wheelchairs, frequently find Cons a supportive place. I'm especially intrigued by character choices, and whether or not one's levels of ability come into play in the decision-making. For example, I have seen wheelchair users specifically select source characters who are also wheelchair bound, such as Marvel's Professor Xavier from the *X-Men* or Oracle (the former Batgirl) from the DC realm. Other times, the characters selected are definitely able-bodied, which could lead to feelings of liberation. And sometimes the costumes are just downright creative. I recall a recent Con where a young girl in a wheelchair was traveling around in a very realistic Dalek (the rolling robotic enemies of Dr. Who) costume.

Despite the prevalence, however, very little research exists on the topic. Kirkpatrick (2019) offers the term "cosability" to refer to those cosplayers with disabilities, though I see no evidence that the term is catching on. The most detailed inquiry I found came from Winge (2019), who provided thoughtful commentary on whether you should costume service animals. Some conventions forbid it, while others have yet to develop any policy. The majority agreement speaks against it, as it creates confusion about an animal who is working. While they're on the job, one should not treat a service animal as a cute little pet to be cuddled and scratched. That becomes increasingly difficult if they dressed as an adorable Ewok or the like.

Instead of relying on outside resources, it seemed best to communicate directly to those cosplayers who are differently abled. See, for example Sam (Costume Conversation #9) and Ches "Newman" Bond, Sr. (Costume Conversation #16). Via email, hearing impaired cosplayer Jenny Shumaker explained that she prefers to dress as silent (or mostly silent) characters. "It helps as it's difficult for me to portray characters through speech in the talking cadences one would expect a character to have," she explains, adding, "With silent characters, I consider it a bonus to focus on communicating with body language alone."

At a recent Con, I had the opportunity to speak with Quianna "Ace" Camire. Ace was dressed as Elizabeth Liones, a princess of the Liones Kingdom in the anime/manga *Seven Deadly Sins*. Ace has been doing cosplay for a few years and makes costume choices solely based on whether or not he likes the character. The floral adornments on the chair's wheels are not part of the costume. They are always there and are done to add color. "Makes me feel more comfortable going out in a wheelchair," Ace explained. The purpose is to express positivity about life, rather than being mad about it. (See image 3.3)

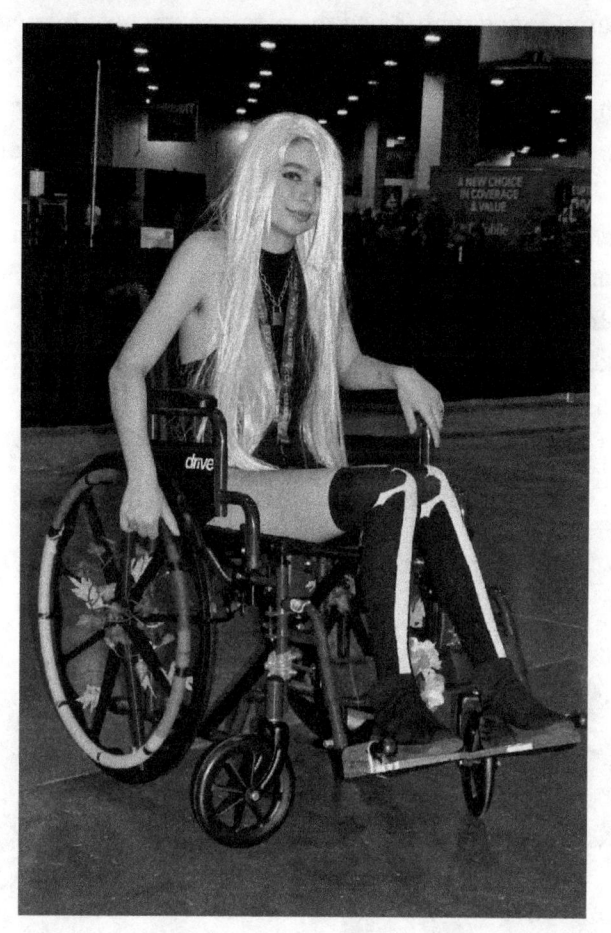

Image 3.3 *Ace Camire as Princess Liones*

"I love cosplay," Ace continues. "I have fun with it and it's what I love to do." For a while, Ace had a fairly large social media presence as a cosplayer, but shied away from that after receiving negative feedback. I was curious if disability was a factor. "I don't really display disability so much online, because there's a lot of hate that goes around about it." So, it was less about ability are more about human nature. Again, haters gonna hate. "I just don't want to deal with the repercussions of people being rude or just annoying. I didn't really express a lot on the internet but, when I did, there was a lot of pushback," Ace concludes. "I didn't want to deal with people." Nor should he have to.

At the same convention, I had the pleasure of speaking with Angèle Khan. Though she had previously attended medieval festivals, this was her first comic Con, and she was having a wonderful time. She is dressed as Kairi, friend of protagonist Sora, from the video game *Kingdom Hearts II*. The game is a popular one, incorporating many Disney characters from Mickey Mouse and Donald Duck to Fa Mulan and Captain Jack Sparrow. "I've played that game since I was seven, and always loved that game and loved that character," Angèle tells me. "She's also a redhead like me, so I don't have to dye my hair." (See image 3.4)

Image 3.4 *Angèle Khan as Kairi*

It didn't take long to teach me a lesson that things are not always as they seem. I stopped Angèle because she was in a wheelchair, not realizing she is fully mobile. Her disability is ocular albinism, a retinal disorder that causes impaired vision. Angèle, a graduate of the Colorado School for the Deaf and Blind, is in a wheelchair today due to a leg injury; though she admits it helps to have friends navigate her through the massive gathering. "Sometimes I bring my cane, or I bring help to be guided so I don't get lost in a crowd." Unlike Ace, she has never encountered any resistance to being differently abled. Still, difficulties do pop up. For example, she'd called ahead to the Con to check about wheelchair rental and was told they were available at the local UPS store. The problem? We were talking on a Sunday, and the UPS store was closed. Fortunately, her father made some calls and was able to find a replacement. And that, she claims, makes the day worth it. "I feel good. I feel excited. It's just cool when people compliment, or they know who the character is." Thus, not so different after all.

Religion
While this isn't the most discussed variable in cosplay research, there is no denying that religion is a critical component to many individuals' sense of identity and is therefore worth addressing. At times, religion and popular culture appear at odds with one another. Crome (2019) for example, addresses Christian uses of fandom, such as fan fiction recasting Hogwarts as a Christian school. Such acts often receive criticism from both inside and outside faith communities. Insiders call it blasphemous, while outsiders accuse the writer of proselytizing or introducing right wing revisionism. In reality, the cosplayer or fan, most likely, is not trying to convert non-believers or, conversely, replace traditional religious belief with secular views. They are just hoping to tie together diverse perspectives in their lives which they value.

Crome goes on to argue that some fandom can provide a metaphor for faith. It doesn't take too much imagination, for example, to equate *Star Trek* to an organized religion. He describes an example where a

Southern U.S. minister delivered sermons dressed as Matt Smith's Eleventh Doctor from *Doctor Who*. The entrance and interior of the church was decorated to resemble Doctor Who's flying and time-traveling police phone box, the TARDIS ("It's bigger on the inside."). He also notes that C.S. Lewis' *Narnia* stories used Christian allusion and allegory. "Rather than seeing fandom as potentially in opposition or as a replacement to religious belief, it would be more fruitful to examine the ways in which different aspects of media usage and fandom feed into the lived religious experience of individuals." In that vein, I recall a vivid sermon by my parish priest where he wielded a broadsword and spoke of King Arthur. Likewise, a former student turned pastor recently delivered a sermon wearing the jewel-encrusted gauntlet used by Thanos in Marvel's *Infinity War* and *Endgame*. Fandom and faith are not incompatible.

Hijabs

Perhaps the most challenging integration of faith belongs to Muslim cosplayers. In particular, female followers of Islam are required to keep their hair covered in public by wearing a hijab ("veil"). Less common in cosplay but still doable are those who wear a niqab (face covering) or burka (full head covering with mesh over eyes). El Jurdi, Moufahim, and Dekel (2022) interviewed 25 hijab cosplayers and, acknowledging that the body is a site for negotiating identity, suggest three levels of authenticity that must be reconciled. First, one strives for authenticity as a cosplayer. This *social dimension* requires that the individual be recognized as a participant in the community. The *personal dimension* is an authenticity obligation to properly represent the character. And finally, and most important, is the *religious dimension* and the authentic presentation of one's religious identity. These dimensions are interactive and flexible, they argue, and allow a fan to negotiate a space as a legitimate cosplayer, delivering an acceptable character performance, as practiced from a religious point of view. That's a long way of saying "With thought, it can be done." For example, one quick way to make the pieces fit is simply to select a scarf to match the character's hair color.

Maitha, a Muslim woman who wears a hijab and an abaya (black cloak) is able to make cosplay work. She purposefully selects male characters who wear modest, loose-fitting clothes (e.g., Clark Kent, Captain Jack from Dr. Who) as female characters are often too sexualized. "Maitha indicated that she used cosplaying as a platform for dismantling negative stereotypical views of Arab women as restricted from participating in such activities. She explained that spectators who stopped to converse with her often asked if such an activity was culturally permissible" (Aljanahi and Alsheikh, 2021. p. 214). Similarly, while interviewing a Muslim woman, Yamato (2020) discovered her goal was to select a character to extend who she was as a Muslim female. It was less about escapism and more about making public her internal beliefs. Raising public awareness, as we shall see, is often a goal for the female Muslim cosplayer.

Dachs and Harman (2020), using the acronym HCP to refer to the hijabi cosplayer, provide details about the Hijabi Cosplay Gallery (HCG), an online community with 15,000 members in Malaysia, Indonesia, and Singapore. Advice given includes reminders to avoid characters that are too sexy, or are related to non-Muslim mythologies (e.g., angels, demons). Dachs and Harman also report that Muslim cosplayers feel like ambassadors for their religious views. "HCP are not passive recipients of meanings from the popular culture, market or Islamic faith. Rather they are proactive negotiators that assemble signs and symbols to create their self-identity. Thus, the costumes they wear represent the outcome of a successful negotiation between their multiple social stakeholders" (p. 46).

This is definitely the case for Rawan Bardmi, who I had the pleasure to meet at a recent Con. Originally from Jordan, she has lived in the United States since she was three years old. She has attended Cons for almost a decade, and this day she was adorned in a Hogwarts robe, carrying a wand, and wearing a scarf with the Deathly Hallows symbol (she also has tri-colored and patterned Hogwarts scarves to choose from). She's attending with a new Muslim friend; they met at a faith community event and knew they'd get along, because one of them was in a Star Wars t-shirt!

When asked, which comes first, the hijab or the costume, she told me she picks the character first, and then figures out how to meet the headwear requirements. She's thinking about doing a Gamora costume, from *Guardians of the Galaxy*, but it is problematic because she would probably do a wig rather than a black scarf. "Technically, my hair is covered, even though it's a wig. I wouldn't do that (wear a wig) as a day-to-day, but for the event I could." (See Image 3.5)

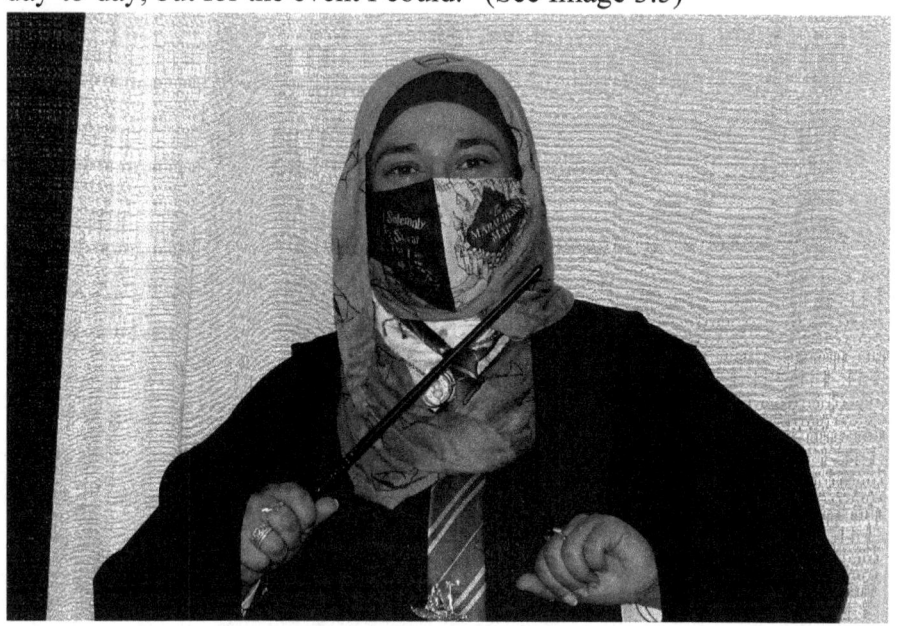

Image 3.5 *Rawan Bardmi integrates a hijab with her Hogwarts robe*

Considering some of the negativity mentioned above, regarding body size or disability, I asked Rawan if she encountered any hostility at Cons due to her religion. Fortunately, her answer was "No." "I've had people come up, out of their way, to call out my hijab or say how nice it was. I had a couple people take pictures. Never anything negative. This is really nice." Likewise, I asked, do she or her friend ever experience disapproval from fellow Muslims? Again, the answer is "No," she explains with a smile, "Because we're both such cool nerds." As noted in the research cited above, Rawan feels like an ambassador for her faith. She is happy to bring awareness and understanding to others. "Sometimes people shy away from an event like this, or wearing a costume, because a lot of – especially – superheroes might be scantily clad. I think it's important that you can show up and be part of the community, even if you look a little different, or try to find a way to blend in the religious aspects, and still have fun."

Changing Attitudes
Life is not perfect in cosplay culture but, all things considered, it is an open and supportive community. More and more Cons are embracing the *cospositive* movement, which embraces participants of all demographics and identities. Winge (2019) comments that cosplayers of color are, for the most part, able to play any character regardless of race, while other cosplayers "are discouraged (via peer pressure and harassment) from playing a character that is illustrated (or described) with darker skin" (p. 146). Well, we should drop the harassment piece, but there's probably nothing wrong with peer pressure simply to remind people of long-standing racial inequities. All that's needed here is an understanding of power variables and a little sensitivity. Liptak (2022) laments that slut-shaming or sexual harassment, "an internalized misogyny that seeks to control women's behavior" (p. 111), still exists – but that's sadly true worldwide. It is not endemic to Cons. We still have a way to go, but things in cosplay seem to be heading in the right direction.

Summary
While superheroes might have a secret identity, the cosplayer of today need not keep their identities hidden. The cosplay community is by and large an inclusive one. Stories of hate and harassment still exist, but the trajectory of cospositivity moves ever upward. As long as you've been thoughtful about portrayals, you can cosplay as whoever you want. No matter how old you are, the color of your skin, the gender that you are -

or want to be - or wish to portray, whatever your body size, your level of ability or disability, or the faith that you practice, you will be welcomed here. Yes, haters gonna hate but, with any luck, those negative voices will diminish as the collective cheers of support grow in celebration of the multiple identities present. Hopefully, this book assists the culture in leveling up to a new playing field of equity, diversity, and inclusion.

COSTUME CONVERSATION # 7
Gracie Villa
a.k.a. Jaskier from The Witcher

My Costume, Myself ♦ 127

Rapid City, South Dakota. It is pouring rain. Despite the fact that it is her birthday, Gracie Villa is kind enough to dress up for photos and sit for an interview. We meet in the lobby of the historic Hotel Alex Johnson downtown. She is dressed as Jaskier, the male bard from the Netflix series *The Witcher*. I learn she was born in Fairbanks, Alaska, but has lived in Rapid City and the small surrounding towns since she was three. She entered the military after high school and was stationed in Arizona and Missouri, but came back and has remained in the state ever since. The mother of four started doing cosplay with friends as an extension of high school theater, and now is bringing her children along to conventions.

Having been born in South Dakota myself, I'd been waiting months to ask her my first question. *Where* do you go to cosplay? After all, the state of South Dakota, which covers over 77,000 square miles, has a population less than 900,000. Compared to my interviews with New Yorkers (8.5 million people in 306 square miles), one can only assume the opportunities are few and far between. "It is not easy, I can tell you that much," Gracie exclaims. For ten years she attended an event in Rapid City called SoDak Con. That faded away and was replaced by the Black Hills Con. On the other end of the state, in Sioux Falls, one can attend the Siouxper Con. Beyond that, one needs to attend Planet Comicon in Kansas City, smaller cons in Iowa or Nebraska, or a few larger events like Nan Desu Kan in Denver. "Beyond that," she tells me, "there's *nooooothing*!" Gracie actually sees this as an advantage. Many in the region don't have money to travel outstate, so, "When a convention pops up in Sioux Falls, or a convention pops up in Rapid City, they're like, 'Wait, that's only 30 miles from me. Oh, that's only like two hours away. I can do this!'"

If cosplay events are a challenge to find, imagine how difficult it can be to exercise her true passion – drag. Gracie is an avid drag *king* (female who does male impersonation). "About three years ago, the Center for Equality here in Rapid City hosted a Baby Ball, which is, 'You've never done drag before. Come give it a try.' There's no judgement. I didn't realize it was a competition until afterward. I sang 'I Want

You to Want Me' and ended up winning 'Mr. Black Hills 2018.'" From that, she was invited to perform in other South Dakota towns like Sioux Falls and Aberdeen, and at Pride events in locales like Gillette, Wyoming. "Which," she informs me, "was a really surprising place for a Pride." Within a year, Gracie was adopted by a nationally known drag "family" surnamed Rose. Her drag mom, Treasure Rose, has won pageants all over the United States. Her drag father, Sterling Rose, also does pageants: "He has the big glowing, glittery cape and the epaulettes that go out for twenty miles."

"Doing drag is super-duper empowering, but it's completely different than cosplay. It's just a whole other animal. You can get away wearing a cosplay costume and not *being* the character, whereas with drag, I get up on stage I am no longer Grace Villa; I am James Gemini Rose." Gracie does physical comedy. In one number, she does a reverse striptease, and goes from boxer shorts to fully dressed dancing to the song "Pants" by Here Come the Mummies. "It's all puns and plays on words, about a guy getting ready for a date, but all of the words used are semi-suggestive. That was my whole number and people just got the biggest laughs out of it. And that's all I really want. If I'm there, and the audience is having fun, that's all I really want out of a drag show." Gracie then fills me in on some of the finer points about drag outfits. She wears a binder (currently worn with her Jaskier costume) to flatten her breasts, and a packer to fill out her shorts. "Drag queens tuck and drag kings pack."

While she loves doing both cosplay and drag, she recognizes significant differences between the two. "Cosplay is something I do for fun. Drag is more of a serious matter at times. It's all the weight that comes behind it. Drag kings are a lot newer than drag queens, so I feel like drag kings have something they need to prove. My partner, who is also a drag king, and I ended up having to talk to a director of Pride. On their flyers they put 'drag queen' on everything, and we're like, it's not just them. We're here, too. That happens quite a bit." One of the reasons drag kings get overlooked, she explains, is that their outfits generally are not as flashy as those worn by drag queens. "It's been said that it's almost like kings are cheating. They can get away with wearing closer to street clothes. If that's what your persona is, that's what you have to go with. You can do a suit, but it's never going to be as glitz and glamorous as the queen wearing the $2,000 Hollywood-walk dress." That's why Gracie focuses on her comedy, knowing that the humor in her show – more so than her outfit – is what people will remember.

I learn from Gracie that RuPaul doesn't allow drag kings on her show, perpetuating the myth that drag is limited to female impersonation. Other misunderstandings come from people who confuse or overlap drag with other lifestyle variables "A drag queen puts on a dress. 'Oh, you're a cross dresser. You're a transvestite.' No, drag and cross dressing are completely different things. Drag and being trans are *completely* different things. Just because I dress like a dude does not mean I want to *be* a dude. It means I enjoy performing drag." Additional complications arise in drag culture when gender identities go beyond the binary division that men are drag queens and women are drag kings. Some women, known as hyperqueens, insist on performing as a female. There are differing opinions on whether a non-binary performer should dress as a king or a queen. The same with mid-process trans-performers.

"They have their top surgery, but they still feel like they should be competing as a drag king." Some venues have gotten on board. "My partner is actually competing at a pageant called 'What the Fuck' pageant," Gracie told me, where you can present and perform however you wish.

Fortunately for drag king Gracie, both the drag and cosplay communities have reacted positively to her gender play, though one group is more exacting than the other. "I find both groups to be very accepting. It's a little bit harder in drag shows. It's a lot more on-the-surface accepting to do male cosplay than to do male drag. Everyone in the cosplay community realizes it's temporary, like I'm not going to stay as Jaskier once I go back to my hotel room. Whereas, when you're doing drag, it's a little more permanent. Until I am done with the Pride performances, the whole weekend I am not me. I am James Gemini Rose. I need to put away the feminine for that entire time. Whereas, if you're running around as Jaskier, and I giggle – and my giggle is high pitched – no one goes, 'Oh, you're out of character.' If I were to do something like that in the drag community, it kind of ruins the illusion. But with cosplay, that 'temporary' makes people a lot more accepting."

Both activities, Gracie believes, are excellent environments to explore gender boundaries. She knows that drag was easier for her since she'd already been accustomed to male cosplay. But in cosplay, Gracie also enjoys wearing the frilly Lolita costumes. How does she decide? "It's honestly what I feel like in the morning. I wake up, 'Okay, am I going to be more feminine today, or am I going to be more masculine? Am I going to wear cargo shorts and a button up t-shirt and my binder, or am I going to wear a dress and a button up blouse? I look at the convention as a whole and decide before I leave, but then I usually end up switching and/or packing extra, just in case." On that topic, Gracie admits that, on the gender identity scale, she is a bit of a chameleon. "I don't identify as non-binary, to just throw that out there; it really depends on who I'm with. My partner exhibits a lot more masculine, and I feel a lot more comfortable being feminine around them. I have some friends that are a lot more feminine so, partially because I'm a mom and usually I'm one of the older ones in the group – I usually end up taking on the more masculine role of protector."

At this point, we move on from gender issues, because I want to get Gracie's opinion on other topics, like race. Lack of tolerance, for her, is "the biggest thing that drives me nuts." She shares the story of an African American friend who cosplayed as Hinata from the anime *Naruto*. "One of the troll-y, horrible comments she got is that 'Hinata isn't black.' Her answer, I love it, was 'Well, she's gonna be black today.' Cosplay is for everybody!" She shares another story of an out-of-state cosplayer she met at a recent Black Hills Con. A short, stout, Filipino man, he arrived dressed as Sailor Moon, complete with *fuku* (combat outfits worn by the Sailor Senshi), and red boots with matching nails. He told Gracie the level of acceptance he got "out here in the middle of nowhere Midwest" was better than he received at larger city conventions, and is making it a point to return. They became online friends once he found that Gracie was also Filipino (though she adds, "Yep, I'm the whitest Filipino person you'll ever see.").

That acceptance, to Gracie, is the essence of contemporary cosplay. "Don't be a gatekeeper. Gatekeeping is stupid. It's outdated. If you're gatekeeping, if you're sitting there tearing apart that poor girl that isn't a skinny enough Faye Valentine (from *Cowboy Bebop*), then you should not be at the convention. Who knows, that could be the world's best cosplayer but, because of the negative comments, they're going to go home and decide they're never going to a convention again. You have responsibility for your words. Cosplay is for *everybody*. That kid that's dressed up as Baby Yoda to the old lady and old man dressed up as Popeye and Olive Oyl – shush – if you can't say anything nice, don't say anything at all. Just shush. Let them go and have fun."

Clearly, Gracie is an articulate cosplay advocate. As we've heard from others, she wants to support in particular those just starting out, knowing that they have room for growth. "You have never seen anyone brighten up so quick as when you find a cosplayer that you know is just trying. Like they just got there. They're wearing a brown bathrobe as good as they can for a Jedi robe, and you give them a compliment? Sunshine. And the next year they might come back with something better. They might take more time; they might invest more."

With that, I asked Gracie if she had anything else to add. She did. "One of the biggest things with me is Cosplay Is Not Consent. Cosplay Is Not Consent. I cannot say it enough. I have met way too many female cosplayers that don't want to wear the frilly little Lolitas, or don't want to wear the Faye Valentines, or even Daenerys from *Game of Thrones*. There was a girl who dressed as Daenerys and these guys were reaching out and brushing their hands against her sides. She's like 'I am never going to wear this cosplay again.' That just breaks my heart, because, you know, she has a daughter; she's going to relay that experience to that girl, and then that girl's not going to want to wear the frillies. When I was younger, part of the reason why I started doing male characters was because I had heard all those stories. Then I realized I really enjoyed doing male cosplay and I stuck with it. It's only now that I'm an adult that I feel a lot more comfortable going back into the feminine cosplays, and wearing the frillies, and wearing the Lolitas, and the high skirts. Cosplay is not consent. Always ask before you take pictures. You never know what someone is running from, or trying to protect themselves from. It's like all the consent that you have to sign to take pictures of your children. Do the same at a convention. Always ask. And if they say no, don't be a butt about it."

She sums it up. "Cosplay is for everyone. Cosplay is not consent. Don't be a troll about it. Don't be a jerk."

COSTUME CONVERSATION # 8
Jonathan Alexandratos
a.k.a. Non-binary Star Fleet officer

Non-binary storyteller Jonathan Alexandratos and their partner, Tracy Bealer, are no strangers to comic cons and fandom. Together they upgraded the former *Rocky Mountain Conference on Comics and Graphic Novels* into the *Page 23 Literary Conference* (so named because the average comic book has 22 pages, and literary scholarship is what follows). For a number of years, the conference – held within a Con – regularly drew popular culture scholars from around the country. Both currently teach literature and culture courses at their respective universities in New York, where Jonathan is also a playwright and renowned authority on vintage toys. In addition to appearing as guest in such media productions as *Trek Untold: The Star Trek Podcast that goes Beyond the Stars* and the documentary *Billion Dollar Babies: The True Story of the Cabbage Patch Kids*, Jonathan is also editor of an anthology (to which Tracy contributed) titled *Articulating the Action Figure: Essays on the Toys and Their Messages*. They are currently working on a book mapping the evolution and artifacts of Happy Meals. My point is, when it comes to things pop culture and fandom related, Jonathan is not only the interviewee; they are the expert.

To begin, I ask Jonathan to explain their costume. It starts with a red *Star Trek: The Next Generation (TNG)* skant (a short-sleeve tunic akin to a mini-dress), black pleather pants, gold go-go boots, and a "non-binary bunny communicator pin." The outfit is important to them because "it plays with gender in a way that I think is really fun and important and validating." Jonathan recalls seeing the skant in *TNG*'s first episode, "Encounter at Farpoint." "My reaction to that as kid was, 'Oh my god, it's a guy wearing a dress.' Right? And later in my life I started to unpack that response. I was reading things about the *Star Trek* skant specifically, and how it's unisex. That was actually a liberating view - a utopian future where people are able to wear clothing that may clash with the cis heteronormativity of now. We can maybe make that utopia now, if we just start to empower people to wear what they want to wear, whether or not it goes with socially constructed gender norms. So, I wanted to start wearing the skant for that reason. That let me wear what

I am on the inside, which is someone who gets a lot of joy from expressing their gender in a way that they were not raised to, but in a way that feels very natural. And, also, the Trekkie side comes with that, which is also very important to me, because *Star Trek* embodies the future I would like to live; in the utopia and the freedom people have there, that we might be missing in today's world."

Many of Jonathan's other cosplay costumes include gender play, such as a simple blue Star Fleet tunic (worn by science officers) from *TNG*, paired with matching blue lipstick. "Another one that I've gone all in on is a white, alien, ranger costume. If you're familiar with the third season of *Mighty Morphin Power Rangers* in the '90s, there's this little sort of end note which they called the *Mighty Morphin Alien Rangers;* basically, some footage from a different Japanese show which they overdubbed in English. During that period, the Ninja White character from the *Super Sentai* (the Japanese original) was a female character in Japan. When they brought her into the U.S. show, the Zord robot she pilots was assigned to the White Ranger, who was like the most masculine character of all time. So, what you get is this macho guy who would get into this Zord that would do all these delightfully feminine movements. I like that juxtaposition. That was cool to me. I got the whole body suit. It's wonderful. I get to put my body into a character that is a female character that was also used or translated into a masculine way. There's all sorts of gender confusion there that I love."

Interestingly, it was cosplay that led Jonathan to a deeper understanding of their non-binary orientation. Starting small by dressing as Marvel detective *Jessica Jones* (somewhat unisex jeans and black leather jacket), their first obvious crossplay was to dress as Eleven, the young girl with telekinetic powers from *Stranger Things*. "It really was a big revelation for me, how much I enjoyed it. I kind of wished I could dress like this all the time, and then the thought dawned on me, 'Well, why don't you?' So I wrote an article for Core.com which talked about cosplay, and how cosplay made me realize I'm non-binary. Cosplay becomes a safe environment – a relatively safe environment – for gender exploration. Because you can always sort of laugh it off. If someone's being a dick to you just say 'Yeah, yeah, it's just a character. Whatever.' You don't have to have that authentic moment if it's unsafe to have it. That was very liberating and very revelatory to have that moment through cosplay. This area of the spectrum that lets you take a masculine body and put it into elements that are coded more feminine. For me, that feels right. That feels like home."

"From there," Jonathan continues, "it was just the question of, how do I incorporate that into my day-to-day? Costume is like the reference, and the day-to-day is like, 'Well, I can't be that *extra*, so I'll just take little bits of that; little wisps, little pieces of the cosplay, and just carry that with me, and use that for strength and courage." For example, Jonathan does a streaming show called "Toys 101," which they describe as "a solo show explaining my journey through queerness via the toys that I have." The costume they have on today is a regular outfit on the show. "It works in that environment – a theatrical environment – so I used the word 'costume.' However, that being said, it isn't that different from what I wear on a day-to-day basis. I like incorporating elements of Star Trek, elements of being non-binary, elements of pushing gender norms, and this costume actually gives me a lot of courage to do that." They point out that, if you find a place of comfort in full costume as they are now, smaller representations in public - "little pieces of jewelry, little pieces of clothing," - are not so scary. "I think what people forget, especially in bodies that are assigned male at birth, pushing into feminine clothing can be a very scary experience. That probably could be true across the gender spectrum, but I can definitely speak for that slice. I think the more courage one has, if you're in that kind of body, the better."

I want to talk to Jonathan more about their experience with public perception, but I'm not quite ready yet to leave the cosplay Con environment. I want to hear more about where they believe cosplay and issues of identity meet. Jonathan answers, "I think that gender and cosplay intersect with race and class and body type in different ways for different folks. I think that for black folks there are a different set of challenges. I think that for fat folks there are a different set of challenges. For folks who are not necessarily the wealthiest; that can also impact the ways in which cosplay is read and accepted." At this point Tracy adds, "And disabled." "Disability, yeah. That's a big one," Jonathan agrees. So, I ask, in the Con environment, who belongs? "The only gate I'm interested in keeping is the one that keeps fascists out. Other than that, I think we're good. The line we should be really interested in drawing is who's here to love and who's here to hate, and if you're there to hate, then that is the element we should really push back against." "What about blackface?" asks Tracy. "I think it's territory where we have to be very careful," Jonathan responds. "Definitely no black face. I won't say they don't belong, but I bump on that. I wouldn't want to cosplay as someone from Wakanda because that feels like a site designed for the empowerment of a specific group of people, that I am not in, and I have privilege outside of. For me to appropriate that would be contributing to a history of appropriation that is not okay."

Jonathan reminds us that we need to ask, "Who holds more privilege? In what ways does that person hold more privilege, and then how can that be dispersed in a way that's fair and equitable?" On that note, since other interviewees have commented on newbie cosplayers and novice or substandard costumes, I ask Jonathan's opinion in that arena. Again, the answer is grounded in a caring attitude. "People who are there lovingly, and who are in let's say a Superman t-shirt, and they're like 'Hey, I'm cosplaying Superman,' I'd be like 'Great!' When you see that, I don't know anything about that person's situation. That could be a person who just happens to love Superman t-shirts, great. That could be a person who sees the prices on Superman costumes and can't afford that, great. That could be a person who for whatever other reason, that could be allergies, or some other reason, just can't or doesn't want to wear a full-on Superman spandex but still wants to be a part of this community. I think we have to really show that person a lot of love. Because, why not? If they're truly a fan, they want to participate, they want to join in for the right reasons, yeah, let them. I don't think we need to get into the territory of saying 'Oh, you're not as good as us.' That's not helpful."

Now we can turn to public perception. I wonder aloud if "people in general" are as loving and supportive as the cosplay community aspires to be. Jonathan tells me they hear two voices in their head. "Voices from the past. You're brought up to believe that you just shouldn't be doing that (combining gender styles), so it feels very transgressive in that sense. But also then, the voices in society that are in front of you, and most of them are very supportive." Looking to their partner, Jonathan adds - "Tracy is very supportive" – and continues, "But, yeah, you do encounter sometimes folks who are less okay with it. In this city, in the 1960s, you had to be wearing elements of the clothing for your assigned gender, or else you could get arrested. So, it's hard to separate all of society from that history right away. And 2022 is still not very far off from the 1960s, so it's there."

I quickly understand Jonathan's comment about Tracy's supportive nature, as she pitches in. "I never thought of it as anything other than really exciting and cool. Jonathan picks such cool characters that I also like. Jonathan's sense of style is impeccable. To see it re-imagined through some of my favorite franchises is fun for me. I was just excited to see what was coming next. It's fun to see Jonathan get celebrated for what they're doing, and they just always look great."

With support like that, Jonathan has come to terms with those voices from the past, and is confident in the face of other resistance. Most important, they understand the need for advocacy. "With younger folks I've talked to, especially younger non-binary folks, in many cases I'm the first adult they have seen that has validated non-binary identities. And that means a lot to them, at least as far as what I'm told." Recently, they were giving at a talk at Queens College on a non-gender related topic, and offhandedly made a small point about non-binary identity. Afterward, they were approached by a non-binary high school student who told them it was the first time they'd ever heard a teacher validate their experience. "That's good," Jonathan explains. "Because now, that person has a significantly reduced chance of suicide, that person has a significantly reduced chance of negative self-talk, and all those things that can happen when you're growing, when you're a teenager, and you're trying to figure out where you place yourself in this world of adults. And that gives me a lot of happiness to think about that."

"Wear what makes you feel good," Jonathan concludes, and, citing *Star Trek* once again as their personal resource, they end with a recommendation for anyone using clothing and costume to explore identity, "Wherever you can find your sources of courage, use those."

COSTUME CONVERSATION # 9
Samantha Nord
a.k.a. Lady Deadpool and Lady Loki

My Costume, Myself ♦ 141

The first time I encountered Sam, she was rushing past me at a Con. Dressed as Wonder Woman, complete with sparkly bustier, her costume emphasized the fact that her arms are not fully developed. Her aura was one of confidence and class, with no sign of discomfort that she is differently abled, and I knew I had to interview her for this project. When we finally got together months later, she proved to me that my initial impression was correct. Poised and articulate, we had a wonderful conversation while she modeled two outfits for me – Lady Loki and Lady Deadpool. Here is her story.

Sam has Holt-Oram Syndrome. Because the congenital disorder often includes both limb disfigurations and corresponding heart ailments, it is more commonly referred to as Heart Hand Syndrome. A rare disorder, occurring in less than 1 in 100,000 births, Sam is frequently left feeling alone with her health issues. "Having short arms is not a common disability. There's no place for somebody like me in the Paralympics. There's one support group that I heard about in the UK, because my ancestor from the 1500s was an English sailor who had Holt-Oram. My mom has a variation of it, and my uncle has another variation of it, and theirs aren't as obvious. And my grandfather had it. But outside of my family, I've only met two other people that were born with short arms, and neither of them were born with a heart condition, so they probably just have what was originally called Club Hands."

The rarity of the disorder means that Sam lives in a world not designed to assist with her needs. "There are accommodations that I use in the bathroom that are not common in the United States. I only recently found out that bidets are a lifesaver for me, but because of U.S. soldiers in World War 1 and 2 going into French brothels, they associate bidets with prostitution, and so they became demonized in the United States, as dirty and unclean. And the reality is that most of the rest of the world washes with water. They've been installed in homes for a hundred years or more. People are finally starting to get it, but they're not common over here, and I had no idea how much that would be helpful and useful for me, and how much pain and trauma that would have saved me as a little kid growing up."

"That's just one example that the world isn't built for me," Sam continues. "These are more common disabilities. You have things like Braille on elevators and doorways, and accessible buttons, and ramps on sidewalks, for people that are blind or in a wheelchair. The deaf have whole communities and arguably their own culture because they have their own language. I could potentially have a service dog but there isn't any existing framework for what that service dog would look like or how they would need to be trained. So, I don't have a service dog, although one might probably be helpful."

These impediments, however, have not stopped Sam from striving to her full potential. If given the choice, she prefers to be outdoors. For high school, she attended the Rocky Mountain School of Expeditionary Learning. "Expeditionary schools take you camping 2-3 times a year as a class and, when you're a little older, some or all of those trips are backpacking. Your whole life is on your back for a week or more. I really got to love just being outside as part of my life." Now in graduate school, she has a focus in archeology. She spent two years in the UK and was able to work on a dig on Salisbury Plain (300 sq. mile plateau in southern England; home to Stonehenge). "The work that I've most enjoyed is working as an archeology technician with the Forest Service."

Sam hopes to work with the Forest Service again, but currently is in her "second favorite job" working for the Denver Art Museum. Not only does she love being around museums and art, but she is also an artist herself. "I've painted and drawn my entire life," she tells me. Both of her grandmothers were active hobby painters, and Sam follows suit. "What I like to create when I do original work tends to be surrealist drawings or paintings. That stuff should be online under my handle *LithicSpiral*, which is archeology inspired: lithic for the Latin stone, and then spiral for stone partnerings which you find all over the world. I started and still maintain a portfolio on *DeviantArt.com* under that handle, and I occasionally remember to post things on Instagram."

And, in the midst of all this, how does cosplay fit in? "The other part of my life is getting really into geek stuff, like comics or cartoons.

Mostly I gravitated toward Marvel cartoons as a kid, specifically the X-Men. Probably because I'm a marginalized person in more than just being female, but also being disabled, having similar persons with similar struggles portrayed was always really powerful." Her favorite character from X-Men was Rogue, a teen girl who drains the life energy from others should she touch them with her bare hand. "I had a lot of chronic pain, so I didn't like being touched as a kid. The concept that her character 'can't touch' other people, even though it was inverted from my situation, who didn't like to be hugged a lot or jostled. I liked that narrative flip: 'Oh, she hurts other people by touching them.' I don't know that I was entirely cognitively aware of that until I became an adult."

While X-Men comics were her first love, they were not her first cosplay. "What did I do first? The first costume I did – post-pubescent – was probably a cat. That was my first word. I've always had cats as pets, or lived with cats as housemates, which I think is a more accurate term for cats. But," she clarifies, "I don't consider myself a Furry; that's not a part of my world." Beyond that, Sam's family went to the Renaissance Fair every year, so she would dress generically as a peasant, lord, or lady. "That's where I got my start in costuming."

Then, around ten years ago, Sam discovered an online store called *ThinkGeek* (bought out by *GameStop* in 2019), which sold higher-quality costume pieces based on characters from shows. "That's where I started getting into the idea of dressing up like other characters. Then I started trying to find costumes that I could wear as my everyday wardrobe that were also like the character." She started in the *Star Wars* realm, buying items like Darth Vader and Luke Skywalker light sabers. Though she makes some of her costume-wear, she still finds items she likes at *GameStop*, *Hot Topic*, and *Her Universe*.

In addition to the two characters she prepared for today, she also has multiple *Star Wars* costumes, and pieces for others, such as the dress for Mononoke-san from *Princess Mononoke*: "Which is my favorite film, actually." Some of the pieces are acquired for her mother, who often attends Cons as her handler. "Because I need her help a lot of times at cons, it's fun if we are wearing what would be 'couples costumes,' but not really couples. Last comic con, I was Wonder Woman, and my mom was Hippolyta, her mother. And I have Leia and Rey." Right now, she is working on a General Leia costume for her mom.

At this time, her primary costumes are the two she brought along: Lady Loki and Lady Deadpool. Sam brought along the action figures for both characters, demonstrating that this is not gender-bending; both characters exist in female form. They are also the costumes that most align with her identity as a person with a disability. She explains that one "gets a more positive reception at cons if you are fitting the canon of the character." Lady Loki, she reminds me, is simply Loki. "Loki's character is gender-fluid, both in the comics and the historical mythologies. And they're a shapeshifter, so having short arms shouldn't be an issue. For some people it might be, but it shouldn't be, because the character *could* conceivably have short arms." She also likes the shifting Loki persona because, a few years ago, her father came out as transgender. "And that's part of the appeal of Loki. Loki is a bigger symbol for the LBGTQ community than the character is really given credit for at this time. Maybe with the new Loki TV show, and the multiple different Lokis, people finally get it. The character is gender-fluid, and the Norse god is gender-fluid, and I think that's huge for anybody with a different gender identity."

As for Lady Deadpool, her reasoning is equally convincing. "Deadpool is a fantastic representative or symbol for the disabled community. It's easier to fit the canon of a character like Deadpool, who regenerates, when you have anatomically different features, like in my case, shorter arms." Please notice in the full-color photo of Sam as Lady Deadpool, she is wearing a pair of severed arms at her waist. Thus, you are given the distinct impression that her arms are now regenerating back out of her shoulders. Brilliant! "The Deadpool characters represent disability in a very unique way. They are disabled with the ability to be fully capable. You are presenting that full capability and the disability at the same time. The fact that they are regenerating characters means that, if you are missing limbs, or you're in a wheelchair, it still fits the character – because the character could be healing from an injury or from a battle. For me, I guess, I like being perceived and accepted in that way. It's a kind of win when it happens. And I got that positive response the first time I put on Lady Deadpool. I feel like I fit the canon of the character well enough to be accepted by anybody that's into geek or nerd stuff." Sam pauses after this sentence, and then adds the most moving words I heard in any of my interviews. "I kind of felt like I fit somewhere, in a way like I'd never felt like I fit anywhere else."

From there, we talk about acceptance. Has she seen any negativity? "I have not directly, but I do follow some cosplayers on social media, and some of them are black, or overweight, or both, and they get a lot of negative comments when they post their cosplay photos online. I do have lighter skin, so I think people are less likely to criticize me for that, and I do have a disability. I've noticed that people don't like to directly criticize people with visible physical disabilities, even if they're thinking it." Though not personally a target for her size or skin color, the anthropologist in Sam definitely has an opinion about exclusion. "I have a soapbox about race. Basically, it doesn't exist. Ethnicities can exist, obviously; there are different cultural backgrounds and cultural identities. But saying that we as a human species have separate races, like dogs have separate breeds, is just obnoxiously ridiculous. There's no evidence for it anywhere. If you analyze the facial features of enough human beings in a given area, you won't find any commonalities to differentiate them from humans in another area. Our genetics don't vary enough across the world to declare that there's race."

That said, Sam recognizes that people are becoming more open-minded about character representations. She tells me she'd been unable to join some of the formal *Star Trek* or *Star Wars* fan groups, because she doesn't look enough like the characters; doesn't fit the descriptive requirements. "As somebody with a physical disability, particularly the one that I have, I don't qualify for the military. I don't qualify for *our* actual military, so how would I qualify for *space* military?" Now, the reins seem to be loosening, and multiverse storylines out of DC and Marvel are making exceptions more of the rule.

Speaking of DC, before I leave Sam for the day, I ask about the Wonder Woman outfit I first saw her in. Unlike the Ladies Loki and Deadpool, the character does not shape shift or regenerate. With a wry smile, she says, "Female empowerment. I'm not just a disabled person, I'm a woman. When Wonder Woman came out, it was a huge blockbuster, with a big action female lead. Cosplaying as Wonder Woman is huge. It makes you feel powerful. She's become this universal symbol for female empowerment in every sector. As a woman, how can you not cosplay Wonder Woman?" When it comes to costume and identity, Sam has figured it out.

Part II
And Beyond

Vestis Virum Facit *(clothes make the man)* Erasmus, *Adagia* 3.1.60

The apparel oft proclaims the man. Polonius, in William Shakespeare's *The Tragedy of Hamlet,* Act 1, Scene 3

We all dress to accommodate social and environmental factors and to reflect our personal aesthetics and identities. Shukla, 2015, p. 1

CHAPTER 4
Professional and Work Costumes
Clothes make a statement. Costumes tell a story.
~Mason Cooley, American Aphorist

Welcome to the non-cosplay half of the book. That statement is more complicated than you might think. In the previous chapters, we have already seen both overlap and contradiction between the various topics. Some costume wearers (for example, steampunk) don't believe they are cosplayers because they don't attend comic conventions. Some Con attendees believe they are in costume because they are wearing the same t-shirt with a logo that they would wear any day to the park. And ultimately, at some level, *all* costume wearing is costume play – hence *cosplay* – right? The first half of this book examined the most common understanding of cosplay; those people who dress up to go to comic and related fandom conventions, with maybe the occasional foray into cosplay for a cause. This second half of the book looks at costume use outside those arenas. As this chapter title indicates, we'll be looking more at professional and work costumes in the next few pages, but first, let me try to draw a few working definitions to get us through.

In research, we call these "operational definitions." Basically, when trying to define XYZ, an operational definition is a way of saying, *"in this particular case*, this is what I mean by XYZ." It doesn't make it true. It just gives us all a common point of reference to carry on the conversation. You encountered one such definition in Chapter 1, with our operational definition of costume itself: *A costume is a conscious decision about clothing, recognizable as outside the everyday norm, that an individual wears in specific or public locales, in order to make a statement or send a message.* With that in mind, I offer some of the following distinctions between clothing and costume categories (See a summary table in Figure 4.1).

A Continuum of Costume Categories

I view these distinctions as running along a continuum from very specific in terms of purpose and locale, to the very general and open-ended. By specific, I mean there is something about the task or environment that requires the individual to dress in a particular fashion. At the other end of the continuum is the everyday use of clothing, with very few restrictions beyond "No Shirt, No Shoes, No Service." As you'll see, this book focuses on the *middle* of the spectrum. The outside edges, given the operational definition of this book, are not costumes. Let's examine the whole continuum, starting at the specific end, with uniforms.

Uniforms

Outfits that are required within a profession or activity, ranging from football and marching band uniforms at a high school sporting event, to the regulation garments worn by our fighting forces in various branches of the military, fit some – but not all – of our definition of costume. Yes, the clothing is definitely outside of the norm and is most often worn in public, but they are not costumes as defined by this book, because they are not the unique conscious choices made by individuals. The very word itself indicates that a uniform is not a costume, because it is – well – *uniformly* worn by a collective assigned to look *the same.*

That said, there is no denying that uniforms can evoke the same or more response from the viewing public. Leathers (1997) explains that, while all clothing can communicate one's degree of power or powerlessness, "This is particularly true of uniforms" (p. 150). He notes that uniforms appear frequently in countries where a high priority is placed on differentiating people based on status; "In Rome, for example, the large number of different uniforms worn by different kinds of law enforcement officers is almost overwhelming" (p. 150). He summarizes multiple studies showing that individuals in uniform tend to have desirable personal qualities attributed to them, such as attractiveness, competence, reliability, and intelligence. While certainly worthy of further inspection, that is not the intent of this book.

Cosiform? Uniplay?

You're right. I did just make those words up. I'm not trying to create new vocabulary but, as I was trying to think of the transition between uniforms and costumes (even in the interviews you'll read over the next couple of chapters), I needed some language to keep my thoughts distinct. While these two make-believe terms seem to be mere portmanteaus of "uniform" and "costume," I'll provide separate definitions that excludes one from this book's focus, while marginally including the other.

Cosiform. This combination of words begins with focus on the word *costume*. The outfit is indeed a costume, worn to portray a character in a particular context. But the wearer is *assigned* to the outfit; it is not an autonomous or intentional decision or creation. Take for example those who perform in theater productions. When my wife and I were in New York City to interview and photograph Jonathan, Tracy, and the costumed characters on Times Square, we took time to see two Broadway shows, *MJ: The Musical* (based on the life of Michael Jackson) and *Harry Potter and the Cursed Child*. Both were outstanding productions, enhanced even more so by the caliber of the costumes worn on stage. But those costumes were as much uniforms as anything else. They were not independent and interchangeable. Harry Potter would no more show up in a sequined jacket and one glove as Michael Jackson would moonwalk across the stage in a Hogwarts robe.

A Continuum of Costume Categories	
Uniform	Required for a specific task or environment; the same for all; no individual interpretation.
Cosiform	A costume, but required for a specific task, e.g. theater. Individual does not choose.
Uniplay	A required uniform but, within boundaries, individual adornment is allowed.
Cosplay	Costume play for a specific environment or event, e.g. a Con, fundraiser. Individual choice.
Costume	Identifiable character wear selected by the individual. Recognized as a costume. All occasion.
Genre	Clothing representing a collective storyline; individual choice within genre boundaries.
Hobby Wear	Clothing normative to an activity. Generally, not viewed as a costume in public perception.
Formal Wear	Clothing worn for special occasions. Recognizable but not viewed as a costume.
General Wear	Everyday clothing choices worn in public. Normative. Not viewed as a costume.

Figure 4.1: A continuum of costume categories ranging from specific (location, task) to general. Darker shades are those falling within focus of this book.

(Vertical axis: Specific ↔ General)

In the same way, I made choices about this book based upon how and why a costume was selected and where it was worn, even if it's the same costume. Let's say a person is hired by one of the Walt Disney Theme Parks. After attending Disney classes and finding out about the character rules, they are assigned to play Mickey Mouse. They put on the professionally produced Mickey outfit, the same one supplied to all the Disney parks worldwide, and proceed to portray the character originally known as Steamboat Willie. No embellishments or interpretation is allowed. That person is *not* included in this book, whereas a person who chooses by buy an off-brand Mickey costume and stand in Times Square for tips (see Image 4.1) *is* included. I recognize that both are in a costume, but the Disney one I'd label a *cosiform*, which falls outside the realm of individual and conscious choice about who you portray, what you wear, when you wear it, and where.

Image 4.1 *Costumed Characters in Times Square. Pictured l to r: Veronica Perez (Elmo); Ana Perez (Minnie); Wilma Segarra (Mickey)*

Uniplay. On the flip side of this coin, starting with the word *uniform*, are those assigned outfits to which one has made personal embellishments. In the first chapter, an example was given of the Best Buy employee who augments their blue work shirt with matching hair and nails. This is a conscious choice outside the norm. Because they are *play*ing with their uniform, it enters a gray zone that starts to get at the focus of the book. Again, the distinction is indeed slim, but would include the football player with neon shoestrings, pads, and a helmet adorned with non-regulation stickers, or the college graduate who has built an elaborate LEGO display on top of their mortarboard.

One career in which uniforms are often personalized and adorned is in Roller Derby. Though teams are required to follow certain regulations, such as the Uniform code from the World Skate International Rules of Roller Derby (www.worldskate.org/roller-derby/about/regulations.html). Most of the rules pertain to safety codes (regulation skates, pads, mouthguards) and standards (size, placement) for numbers so you can tell which player is which. Text, advertising, or logos need to be at least two inches away from the official numbers, and no two players can have the same number. Jammers (the ones who can score points) must wear a helmet cover matching the team colors. Jewelry is allowed as long as the referee doesn't view it as dangerous. If so, it needs to be removed or taped over.

Beyond that, roller derby competitors are free to adorn their uniforms as they see fit. Maddie (who skates for Rocky Mountain Roller Derby under the name Audubondage), told me that, as long as you comply with the rules, "anything goes as long as you aren't going to harm yourself or another player" (2023). She adds that referees check everyone over before a bout begins. Though not printed in the rules, officials can also remove any "symbols of hate or oppression of a minority group" that is on a uniform. Much of the adornment is done via makeup, Maddie explains, such as the skater known as "Scald Eagle" who, not surprisingly, does her makeup to look like the bird of prey. At the very least, skaters use a lot of glitter, "or something intense to look intimidating to the other team (heavy eyeliner, claw marks across the face, stripes under the eyes)." Of course, this is all done in fun, especially for theme nights, such as a Halloween bout between vampires versus zombies. One unfortunate thing I learned was that some of the costumes are being toned down, not because of the rules, but rather due to audience members "over sexualizing athletes who wanted to be taken seriously." Like cosplay Cons, it is always the rude minority who takes away from the fun.

Cosplay/Costume/Genre. These three center categories from the attached Figure 4.1 are the crux of this book, and have already been discussed in great detail in the previous three chapters. The distinctions between them are minimal, with costume, and our working definition from Chapter 1, at the center of the three. All meet the criteria of conscious and individual decisions outside of the norm. They are all clearly recognized by both insiders and outsiders as being *costumes*. On the more specific end of the trio is cosplay which, as noted earlier, more and more comes to mean costume play for a specific event like a Con or fundraiser. On the more general end of the spectrum are genre costumes, which do not portray specific costumed characters. As you recall, Chapter 2 provides numerous examples from A-Z.

Hobby Wear. Here is the gray area on the general end of the spectrum. I'm referring to those clothing choices which seem common to individuals who partake in certain activities. Hunters. Martial Artists. Hikers. Gym-goers. Bikers (both the motorcycle and bicycle variety). As you read each of these words, did a mental image pop into your head of what that person might be wearing? We might not always be able to tell the difference between an Urban Cowboy and a rural one, but we can make a pretty good guess as to what they both have on.

I remember once being in a pair of blue jeans, boots, and a denim shirt. I told my daughters I could be any of one several different styles simply by what I chose to put on my head. An orange fluorescent ball cap and I'm a hunter. A 10-gallon Stetson and I'm a cowboy. A doo-rag bandana and I'm a biker (the motorcycle kind). Rarely would these people say they are in costume. And they would all probably feel comfortable walking around Target or Wal-Mart in their selected attire. But it is recognizable, and in most environments, it does stand out. This is perhaps the real-world version of cosplay light.

As I typed this, I was reminded of observations encountered in my earlier book, *Sturgis Stories*. In my various interviews, individuals explained to me that riding motorcycles provided them with a sense of *independence*; they stood out from the crowd. Yet, ironically, most of them happened to be dressed *alike*. Blue jeans, black leather vests, doo-rags, and occasionally black leather chaps, were definitely the norm. In her Foreward to the book, Ann Ferrar (author of *Hear Me Roar*) pointed out that the "superficial similarities" of "thousands of bearded men in black T-shirts" has "become a source of humor" (2002, p. 6). It is good humor, to be sure. Everybody understands the importance of the "costume" to the culture.

Formal Wear. This small sliver of a category is pretty self-explanatory. Tuxedoes. Ball gowns. Bridal gowns and bridesmaid dresses. It is not what you would wear every day, and it is a conscious choice, but given the strict societal norms that govern such attire, you would hardly call it a costume (unless, coupled with a sequined mask, you were attending a masquerade ball).

General Wear. On the most general, least-specific, end of the continuum we find the everyday clothing that each of us wears. Yes, some people dress more formally than others. Some follow a particular fashion style or trend. Some have designer leanings. In contrast, wearing hoodies and sweatpants, my students often look as if they confuse clothing and pajamas. It is all conscious choice and it is all public setting, but none of it is outside of the norm.

Bottom line. This book looks at that Table's middle section of *cosplay/costume/genre*, with occasional glimpses into *uniplay* on the specific end and *hobby wear* on the other. Before we leave that table, however, remember that *all* those categories along the continuum are constantly being judged and evaluated. It is not just cosplayers who are subject to scrutiny and criticism. Such judgment is human nature. Summarizing Leathers (1997) once again, the clothing we wear is a strong determinant of the impression we make on others, especially regarding credibility, likability, interpersonal attractiveness, and dominance. He shares several interesting studies which found, contrary to popular belief, that dressing to appear credible or dominant (e.g., wearing the "power suit") can negatively impact likability and interpersonal attractiveness. Let's see how this unfolds in costumes worn in work situations.

A Caveat: Non-costume Work
Before we dig too deeply into costumes worn at work, let's take a quick detour and look at a perspective for getting ahead in your *non*-costumed professional life by thinking *of* cosplay. New York literature professor Tracy Bealer (2022) explained earlier in the book that her costume choices tend to be of complementary minor characters in a storyline universe; she'd rather be an unnamed person on the *Star Trek* crew than a specific and identifiable character. "I love universes that are so expansive, you can just be somebody that nobody's heard of and still feel perfectly at home." She likes her costume to say, "I'm not a character you know, but I have an important job." With that orientation in mind, she's found a way to translate this into work performance. "I heard the term 'competency porn' recently," she clarified. "It's people who really enjoy watching others who are good at their jobs. I think that's a large part of what attracts me to *Star Trek*, and I like to imagine myself as being that competent. For me, imagining myself in a universe where I just admire the character so much can be a way of encouraging those qualities in myself." She reluctantly admitted to having moments of struggle while working on a book project. I can relate. "What has really helped is to imagine myself working on it in Ten-Forward, the bar from *The Next Generation*." Sometimes she'll even play atmospheric noises from the ship. "I imagine myself in a world where everybody is really committed to doing their job and doing their job well. If I can imagine myself in that space, maybe it will help me to also be motivated to do my job and do my job well." Concluding that this is more soundscape cosplay than costumed cosplay, she recommends this strategy as a way

of connecting with the universe you want to be a part of and communicating that to both self and others. This combination of popular culture and positive visualization could prove to be an effective tool for many. Maybe I don't have to dress as Han Solo or General Leia to feel confident getting up in front of an audience. But I can visualize myself as such, or hum a John Williams soundtrack as I take the stage, and that imagery may evoke the feelings needed.

Professional Cosplayers
When you hear the words "costume" and "work" put together, you probably don't think of the visualization technique Tracy outlined. More likely you think of becoming a *professional* cosplayer; someone who is paid to dress up, promote products, and attend Cons. As indicated in the Preface, professional cosplayers were purposefully *not* interviewed for this book, as I wanted to capture the stories from people who otherwise don't have a platform. Still, we can talk here about whether or not one can make a career out of cosplay.

Scott (2015) calls these people "fantreprenuers" – those members of a fandom who have found a way to monetize their work. Easier to remember (and spell) is Haborak's label of the "star cosplayer." "Unlike the Kardashians," she explains, "who present curated versions of themselves as themselves, star cosplayers present curated versions of themselves as the characters they portray" [7.1]. A quick Google search will take you to the social media sites of whichever cosplayers happen to be the shining star at the moment. (My search the day I typed this chapter listed the following as the top cosplayers in the United States: Holly Conrad, Adrianne Curry, Anna Faith, Kat Gunn, Yaya Han, Linda Le, AJ Lee, Jay Maynard, Olivia Munn, Jessica Nigri, Liz Katz, Brinke Stevens, and Meg Turney.) Haborak expresses concern that these cosplay professionals are more concerned about establishing an identity brand than they are about establishing community. Calling it an "online charade," she accuses them of using media like Instagram to "accrue social capital."

Of course, it is not just cosplayers who do this. For many professions, social media presence is the hill upon which status-hopefuls live or die. This is especially true in the realm of popular culture. Media exposure is often what makes it *popular*. Turning specially again to costumes, Haborak concludes, "the star cosplayer conveys a lifestyle: identity becomes a brand in this ever-evolving American dream, a quest for cultural capital. This networked identity influences the audience to worship the elite cosplayer, now deified as a celebrity" [7.10].

While this view may be somewhat cynical, Haborak is not alone. Mountfort et al. (2019) have a similar view of what they define as "Commercial" cosplay: "This form of commercial application may be seen as evidence of 'fake' cosplayers selling their souls and disrupting the magic boundary between the play world and real world by tainting their play with market-driven practices, thereby negating the power of the players and disrupting the open and improvisational ethos of play" (p. 127).

If it appears I am trying to disparage professional cosplayers, I am not. For every "fake" cosplayer out there making it rich off their characterizations, I'm sure there are two or more sincere ones who are grateful they've been able to capitalize on a passion. Wouldn't we all love to do that? And, quite honestly, it is not like there are that many making it big. Porter (2015) interviewed a handful of professional cosplayers, such as Yaya Han, and asked if it was easy to make a living as a cosplayer. Riki LeCoety, a.k.a. Riddle, a Canadian-born professional based out of Atlanta, answered, "It depends on the type of living. Do you want to eat ramen every day? Then yeah." The same question was asked of FanExpo coordinator James Armstrong. Adding another term to our vocabulary, the pointed out that those who become "CosFamous" are overwhelmingly female. Only about 10 percent of fans, he guessed, are interested in male cosplayers. If you do that aforementioned Google search for famous cosplayers, you will indeed see that most are female. Of the baker's dozen my search uncovered two paragraphs above, only one was male (8%). And a significant number of those fall into provocative or erotic portrayals. Madison Avenue taught us long ago that "Sex

Sells." Why should fantreprenuers a.k.a. star cosplayers a.k.a. CosFamous be any different?

Busking

Outside of Cons, the most common form of work involving costumes is via busking, or street performances. Not all busking is costume centered. You may be walking through Grand Central Station, a Washington D.C. subway tunnel, outside a cathedral in New Orleans, or any one of thousands of public spaces, and encounter somebody entertaining for tips. They may be playing the guitar, blowing into a saxophone, singing into a microphone, or banging on upside-down five-gallon buckets. It is been said that such widely recognized actors as Robin Williams, Pierce Brosnan, and Steve Martin were discovered performing on the street.

Of those in costume, some may have an act or a shtick that accompanies their performance. Singing, comedy, juggling, or – my personal favorite – standing statue-still, not moving a muscle, until somebody drops coins into their bucket. Most often, however, costumed buskers just walk around the streets, posing for photographs, and accepting tips.

Who to Portray?

When deciding to wear a costume to generate tips, are some costume styles more effective than others? No research has been done on this, but an educated guess would tell us "Pick someone popular!" No doubt yet-another Spider-Man (I witnessed four at once on Times Square) is going to get a better reception than Captain Action (a relatively obscure comic book and action figure from the sixties, about a man named Clive Arnos who discovers magical coins which allow him to have the powers of and impersonate other more well-known heroes). Social media presence is a power tool for fictional characters as well.

Given the proliferation of superhero movies in the past decade, selecting a character from Marvel or DC seems a safe bet. Brownie and Graydon (2016), in an analysis of comic artwork, argue that the superhero costume "remains one of the most singularly compelling signatures of a genre that is fast approaching its eightieth year of existence and one which has become a pervasive colossus of modern pop culture." One of the reasons the super suits are so enticing, they add, "aside from their brazen primary color schemes, is the way they are worn with such total confidence" (p. 1). Of course, they're not talking about street performers; they are talking about the fictional heroes as drawn by the artists. Still, the busker could take a lesson from their analysis of Superman:

> There is no trace of self-consciousness despite the inherent absurdity of his costume, only absolute moral certainty and unwavering commitment to heroism. The implication is clear: the kind of person who would wear such an outfit is someone who knows exactly who they are and what they stand for. The costume is an intoxicating demonstration of personal and ideological confidence that suffocates the potential for ridicule, especially when displayed in conjunction with awesome, superhuman feats. (p. 1)

So, while a busker might not be able to do "superhuman feats," they should at least aim for "no trace of self-consciousness" while standing there in spandex, latex, and sweat.

Confessions of a Superhero

In 2007, Matthew Ogens directed a documentary titled *Confessions of a Superhero*, which followed the lives of four buskers in Hollywood: Christopher Lloyd Dennis (Superman), Maximus Allen (Batman), Jennifer Garrett (Wonder Woman), and Joe McQueen (Hulk). There are a few upbeat moments, but ultimately the documentary portrays busking as a fairly dismal lifestyle. Garrett (Wonder Woman) was doing this while simultaneously trying out for movies. "Sure, a doctor saves lives, but is he remembered," she asks the camera. "Is he there for all times? People are still talking about Marilyn Monroe. People are still talking about Elvis Presley. People in the entertainment business are always here." Garrett has since gotten minor roles in B movies.

Also cast in a low-budget film or two was McQueen, whose Hulk character got the least amount of airtime in the documentary. There is one memorable scene where he shows up on the sidewalks later than usual, having passed out because the temperature inside his Hulk costume could reach 130 degrees F°. The film presents Allen's Batman, in costume, talking with a therapist about his anger issues. Later we see him being hauled off by the police for accosting people on the street. A Google search shows he was last seen busking in the streets of Las Vegas.

Most of the documentary focuses on Christopher Lloyd Dennis who, due to a striking resemblance to the late actor Christopher Reeve, plays the movie version of *Superman* from the 1980s. Claiming to be the son of screen actress Sandy Dennis (something her family and estate deny), Dennis is an avid Superman collector, living in an apartment covered floor to ceiling in Man of Steel merchandise. He speaks the most about the lifestyle, and seems the most intent on displaying the "absolute moral certainty" mentioned by Brownie and Graydon. He explains the busking rules to the viewing audience, such as not approaching tourists on the street (they must approach you) and not charging for photos (tips only). Despite showing up on occasion in "man on the street" segments of the Jimmy Kimmel show, Dennis never really got his big break. Again, a Google search finds that meth was Dennis's kryptonite. Sadly, he was found dead in a Van Nuys, California, clothing donation bin on November 2, 2019. The assumption is he was high, looking for a place to warm up, and suffocated amongst the clothes. A follow up documentary, tentatively titled *American Superman*, is allegedly in production at the time of this writing.

In short, the documentary – and the history that followed – is a tragic portrayal of street busking. Still, it is worthwhile viewing for those wishing a behind-the-scenes look at the life of the costumed street performer.

Times Square

Our own visit to Times Square in New York City reinforced some of the negative aspects. Earlier in the chapter you saw the picture of Mickey Mouse, along with compatriots Minnie Mouse and Elmo from *Sesame Street*. Inside those costumes are Ana, Wilma, and Veronica;

three young Latin American immigrants who are a little unsure about talking to me. I assure them I will treat them, their story, and their picture with respect, and tip each of them for their participation. Unfortunately, not all tourists, or locals, treat them well. Each has had people swear at them, push or grab them, or try to knock their costume heads off. When they do take off the full-head masks for a breather, they've received racist comments once people see the color of their skin. There are plenty of police patrolling Times Square, so I ask if they are of any assistance. I'm told it depends on the officer. Some look out for them but, for the most part, they feel on their own.

Things are not quite as bad for Mirelbis Peña, as her Bumblebee costume (from *Transformers*) is fairly large and imposing (see picture in color section). Her biggest challenge, not speaking much English, is talking with tourists. And obviously she cannot collect tips with those giant robot hands. Fortunately, she has a handler, whose name we did not catch, who does the negotiation and the collection of funds. Nowhere in the interview did we get the impression they were having any fun.

Hollywood Boulevard
Life is different in Los Angeles. The buskers on Hollywood Boulevard, walking up and down the Walk of Fame near Grauman's Chinese Theater, do not seem nearly as tormented as their New York counterparts. In fact, on this sidewalk, where the late Christopher "Superman" Dennis trod, the buskers seem to dominate the space. The first pair we came upon was a Spider-Man brandishing two Deadpool-esque swords walking along with a Micky Mouse from Fantasia. I explained the book project to them and asked if they'd be willing to pose for a picture. They would, for $40. Apiece. Out of curiosity more than anything, I asked if they were allowed to set a price or if, according to state law, they could only accept tips. Spider-Man started yelling at me, telling me that he pays taxes and that his business card says he can charge whatever he wants. As my wife and I walked away, he followed us, hollering that he makes $600,000 annually. Next.

Given the number of characters wondering around, I was wondering if I could get a group shot. We checked in with another Spider-Man, but he worked alone and did not want to be photographed with other characters. Okay, next. We moved on to Minnie Mouse (Marie Cerrantes) and Catwoman (Jackeline Lopez), who work and walk together for companionship and safety. They were pleasant to talk to, worked only for tips when offered (yes, I tipped), and posed for a shot (see Image 4.2).

Image 4.2 *Cerrantes (Minnie) and Lopez (Catwoman) on Hollywood Boulevard*

By the way, this was summer in LA, and the sun was beating down on the sidewalk. It was no doubt *hot* in those costumes. Looking across the street, there were no tourists on that side, but there was shade. Standing there out of the heat were two men; one dressed as a Minion (presumably one-eyed Stuart from the *Despicable Me* movies) and the other as Zach Galifianakis's character Alan Garner from the *Hangover* movies. We crossed the street to get out of the sun and talk to these laidback buskers who seemed more interested in staying cool than raising capital (see photo in color section).

As we were heading that way, the Minion's costume appeared to deflate and sag. Before we reached them, Zach/Alan lent him a hand and he was inflated and ready for us when we arrived. Turns out the suit's air pump battery had died and needed to be replaced. Inside the suit was Johnny Shakespeare, also known in social media as "One Song Johnny" and, according to his posts, he is "thegreatestactoronearth." He loves his costume, as the pump which keeps it inflated also acts as a mini air conditioner.

In real life, Zach/Alan is an actor and writer named Tim Bachard. He and Johnny don't work together officially, but they like to stay on the cool side of the street and chat. In their conversations, they discovered a unique connection. Johnny asserts that he is a descendent of the great bard William Shakespeare. Tim tells us that he is related to 11th century Scottish king Mac Bethad mac Findláich. Born around the year 1005, and serving as King of the Scots from roughly 1040-1057, he is known in English simply as Macbeth. The men confirm my suspicion that they are only allowed to work for tips. Tim says he averages $50 an hour, but that doesn't mean every hour is the same. The range, they tell me, can be from $0 to $600. Looking across the street, they agree that some of the performers on that side are jerks.

Spotlight Story – Lenny Hoops

Because these latter three chapters have less outside research, it provides an opportunity to expand upon select stories; not as fully as the Costume Conversations at the end of each chapter, but more than just a passing quotation or two. For our first spotlight story, we head to the Santa Monica Pier in California.

Located due west from downtown Los Angeles, the coastline's first concrete pier was constructed in 1909 as a pathway to transfer the city's treated sewage out to the sea. That practice did not last long, fortunately, and once discovered to be an ideal fishing locale, an amusement park and public facilities were built throughout the early 1900s. Multiple improvements and upgrades were added through the decades, and it is now the home to numerous restaurants, rides, shops, and street performers (www.santamonicapier.org). Incidentally, in 1936, America's 2,488-mile Mother Road - Route 66 - which starts in downtown Chicago, reached the pier, earning it the unofficial title of "End of the Trail" (www.route66roadtrip.com).

In order to busk on the pier, one must purchase an annual license. Due to competition for spots on the weekends, permits are handed out via lottery in the morning. You are not allowed to perform in the same spot for more than two hours, and must move to a spot at least 120 feet away from where you were initially performing.

While most performers are of the musical variety – solo or group acts – the presentations are relatively subdued; people strumming guitars or playing electronic keyboards. Not so with Lenny "Lenny the Great" Hoops. You hear his raspy voice traveling down the boardwalk before you see him. "Ladies and Gentlemen," it booms, "I have decided to stop drinking and smoking. What I'm going to do is I'm gonna drink first, then I'll smoke later."

When you come upon him, you see a black man of indiscriminate age, wearing a white tuxedo and white tennis shoes. He has just put on a long red cape and a red, white, and blue sequined top hat (see photo in color section). Something about this seems familiar. Not exact, but familiar. Suddenly the recorded music swells, and he bursts into a flawless rendition of "Living in America," the song that James Brown sang before the Apollo Creed and Ivan Drago fight in *Rocky IV*.

We pull up a nearby table and watch Lenny entertain the crowd. James Brown evolves into Ray Charles mixed with Louie Armstrong in equally stellar versions of classic hits like "New York, New York," "Mack the Knife," and "Hit the Road, Jack." In between he engages in friendly and not always politically correct banter with the crowd. To the men, "Take that girl and get her something to eat. Ain't nothing gonna happen on an empty stomach." For the ladies, "Hold onto him, girl. Don't let him get away 'til you get the rest of that money."

Behind him sits a small table with a stack of CDs, and a rolling cart (just the right size to transport everything on those 120 feet journeys down the pier every two hours) covered with costume pieces. Hats, sunglasses, capes, and a silver trumpet all wait their turn. After about 20 minutes, Lenny takes a break and comes to join us at the table.

We discover he is a young and spry 61-years-old. "I grew up in the South. Spent time in the military. Kept me fit and all of that." We compliment him on his banter with the crowd; he is quick on his feet. "Used to do a lot of stand up. Way back in the 80s and 90s. Def Comedy Jam. Showtime at the Apollo. Geraldo Rivera show. Joan Lunden show. Comic View." Eventually he got a four-year gig traveling as an entertainer with the circus. "That's how to see America," he tells us. That's also where he started collecting the costume pieces: "Had a lot of sequins, a lot of costumes, a lot of all that shit." Now that he is done traveling, and needs to travel light on the pier, he has sold off much of his inventory. "All the other costumes, I had to sell them to a costume shop. They gave me a couple of thousand bucks." He still likes to travel to New York and entertain, so he keeps a storage unit with costume pieces there, so he doesn't have to haul his stuff back and forth across the country.

Given his background and love for New York, how did he end up in Santa Monica? "Well, I used to live in New York years ago, and it was too damn cold. I said I'm coming out this way. I went to see my cousin who needed a bone marrow transplant. I wasn't a match for it, but I ended up staying and working. Took me a couple of years to get my own place. Then the place burned down, so they had to give us a new place. Now, I live six blocks from here. Elevator in the building. Great view of the ocean. So, I'm living the time of my life. Why not Santa Monica?"

Of course, the main reason we are talking is I want to know more about the costumes. Lenny definitely has an opinion on that. "I explain to some of the other entertainers out here. You have to come out here looking like you're an entertainer. You can't come out in your jeans and your tennis shoes. They *do* judge the book by the cover." He elaborates. "It's fashion. Music and fashion, they always go together. You wouldn't go see Dianna Ross if she was just wearing her regular old shit at the concert. She's changing costumes four, five times. Sequins, this, that. Listen, she wants to WOW you with the costumes. That's what it's about."

And how does he feel when he is in costume? "Wonderful! It's all about the costume. Think about it. You look good, you feel good. When women put on their high stilettos, they feel beautiful. They look good. How can they not? That's what it's about. If clothes does that for you, yes."

"And who doesn't love looking at fabulous things?" Lenny concludes. "Men and women, come on now. You go in a store you see shoes, or even underwear. Right now, people are picky about their underwear!" Lenny laughs, shaking his head at both the excess and the beauty of our fascination with outfits. "People are picky about

> their socks, man! Hats." Looking to the crowd, he admonishes them "Accessorize!"
>
> It's time for Lenny to get back to work. He thoughtfully gives us a couple complimentary copies of his CDs. We promise to send him a free copy of the book once it is published. We wish him well, telling him to keep up the good work. He nods, promising, "Just gonna be what I am."

Two more potential topics are left for this chapter: gatherings like Renaissance festivals and fairs, and historical reenactments. Both also have a home in the next chapter on lifestyle choices. That is, both of these arenas have paid positions that people do as their job, and both have a large number of passersby and volunteers who merely dabble. Since two of the Costume Conversations that follow are with paid workers in historical reenactments, we'll address that one here.

Historical Reenactment

Costumed people can be found at landmarks (e.g., military forts, founding communities, cultural centers) across the country, explaining and recreating history to all who visit. Most well-known, perhaps, is the Civil War reenactment of the Battle of Gettysburg that has taken place each summer in Pennsylvania for roughly 160 years. When this event is combined with similar presentations around the country, it is estimated that over 50,000 people are involved with Civil War reenactment each year (Shukla, 2015).

Liptak (2022) explains that "historic interpretation needs to bring the past to life. It should be more than the recitation of fact – it's multidisciplinary and thought-provoking" (p. 138). He adds that, by "re-creating period garments, historians gain some insight into the lives of the people who inhabited those clothes" (p. 140). More important, for the visitor, "It's one thing to read about a battle in a history book and another to feel the concussive blast of a cannon or see a member of the museum staff sweating in the summer heat" (p. 141).

Shukla (2015) agrees, adding that "historical costumes enable their wearers and beholders to travel in time, to imagine or inhabit the past" (117). Taking it even deeper, Fudimova (2021) argues that "historical reenactment is an effective tool for studying the material and spiritual evolution of mankind" (p. 1). Clearly, this is more than just "dressing up and pretending to be someone from the past." For many, being a "living historian" is a deeply enriching, educational, and even transcendent experience.

Shukla (2015) explains that those who heed the call devote considerable amounts of both time and money to acquiring detailed historic information and then attempt to achieve an accurate accounting via costume. "The challenge is to look like the real person, and to think as he would have thought, in order to accomplish an accurate impression" (p. 148). As we've seen throughout this book, putting on a costume can empower the wearer and help them to embody positive characteristics of the one they are portraying. This appears to deepen with a historically accurate outfit. "Accuracy of uniform can welcome the reenactor into the life and thoughts of his persona and can carry him back in time, perhaps to experience a 'magic moment,' that fleeting, intense feeling of being dropped into another era, a rare instant that relies on authenticity" (p. 148).

When creating such a costume, be wary of the FARB; a negative term for anyone or any element which is not historically accurate. There are different opinions on what the FARB acronym stands for: some say it means *"far be* it from me to criticize" or "fast and ruthless buying," (Shukla, 2015, p. 138), but it refers to all errors in costuming, such as smoking filtered cigarettes or wearing a modern-day wristwatch. I recall a scene in one of my mother's favorite movies, *Somewhere in Time* (1980), where a contemporary gentleman (Christopher Reeve) falls in love with the photograph of an actress from 1912 (Jane Seymour). He learns to mentally transport himself back in time so they can finally meet. The catch is, his masquerade must be perfect. His clothing, his style, all have to match the period to which he is transported. All is well until he reaches into the pocket of his vintage suit and pulls out a penny stamped 1979. The spell is broken, as is the man who returns to his own time. (Not sure if this is a happy ending or not, but the man then starves himself to death and meets up with his love in the afterlife.)

Okay, not all FARBs are as drastic as the one from that film. And not all who interpret history are equally serious. Shukla describes the true die-hard, or "hard-core" historical interpreter as the one who lives, eats, sleeps, and breathes as authentically as the individual they are trying to portray. This could include sleeping outdoors on the ground and, if necessary, eating semi-rotten meat. Somewhere more toward the middle is the "motel militia" who stay in nearby air-conditioned motels and only show up for the reenactment fights (p. 139). Wherever you fit in the continuum, Shukla adds that the experience works better if you physically resemble the person you are impersonating.

There are thousands of history books, Shukla points out, but none capture the richness or are as rewarding as history retold in live performance. "Camaraderie, sociability, personal pleasure, and self-education are among the reasons why these men spend thousands of dollars and hundreds of hours in hot wool uniforms on battlefields, portraying the men who fought and died in the Civil War" (2015, p. 151). But there are other purposes for Civil War reenacting, she adds; "functions that are dependent on achieving an authentic persona and accurate interpretation: heritage, ideology, and education" (p. 151). Foremost among these, she concludes, is the goal of public education. To teach a new generation where we came from and how we have evolved, before those memories and lessons disappear.

We will meet some of these individuals in Costume Conversations 11 and 12.

Summary

Moving on from comic conventions and events, the focus has turned to other venues for costume practice. Looking at a clothing continuum from Uniforms through General Wear, we looked quickly at the influence of costume visualization for work settings and the experience of the professional cosplayer who has monetized on their hobby. The heaviest focus here was on busking, or street performing, with research and interviews conducted from Times Square in New York, to Hollywood and Santa Monica Pier in California (where we heard in most detail from our Spotlight Story, Lenny Hoops). Ending with historical reenactments, we encounter a rigorous level of costuming most concerned with accuracy in reproduction. Beware the FARB.

COSTUME CONVERSATION # 10
David Blevins
a.k.a. Khrys'taaal and Remy D.

My Costume, Myself ♦ 175

On their Facebook page, black drag queen Khrys'taaal writes "This is home for my people i affectionately call 'The Movement.' WE are a people not categorized by race, gender, religion, or social class but are a people moving towards common goals; to better not just ourselves as human beings but to help better the lives of our families, friends, and our communities. Our mission is not merely to survive, but to thrive; and to do so with some passion, some compassion, some humor, and some style. Gone are the days where we allow our hearts to be troubled by Basic things & Basic bitches of this world. Gone are the days of us dumbing down and watering down our unconventional lifestyle just to have the world's acceptance. Gone are the days where we allow man to steal our joy, our happiness, our peace of mind, our rewards and our faith. We are not inferior, we are not thugs, we are not statistics, we are not disposable. We smell like smoke because we've been through the flames of bigotry, ignorance, verbal-sexual-physical abuse, poverty, depression, and suicidal thoughts. Nevertheless, we have endured and will continue to do so because we will no longer allow man to discredit or rob us of what we have accomplished & achieved. You are the muthafu*kin sh*t, you are great...... you are magnificent.... you can do whatever you wanna do in this world, put your mind to it, put your grind to it and you can do it ." The October 1, 2018, post concludes with a passage from Revelation 3:11, "Hold on firmly to what you have .... and LET NO MAN TAKE YOUR CROWN."

In a wrestling match hosted by Rocky Mountain Pro at Wimmer Arena in Englewood, CO, flamboyant Remy D., who holds the title of *Charged Champion*, sashays (for lack of a better word) into the ring. His flowing curly hair bounces up and down as he wiggles his hips in a shiny blue outfit (resembling a one-piece Sports Illustrated bathing suit) with matching knee-high boots, as he mocks any one of the "Haterzzzzzzzzz" (with extra z's) who might challenge his right to represent in the ring. When he speaks, his patter is fast-paced, high-pitched, lyrical, and slightly reminiscent of Chris Tucker's extravagant character

Ruby Rhod from *The Fifth Element*. It is pure – and inclusive - entertainment. The crowd loves him.

Both Khrys'taaal and Remy D. are the creations of David Blevins, and he enjoys playing both of them with gusto. Originally born and raised in Detroit, Michigan, he has been a resident of Colorado for approximately a decade. "Graduated college back in the day. Michigan's job market was in the toilet, so I moved out here. Took a leap on faith, and everything has been very prosperous, very progressive, and awesome since I've been out here."

A drag artist for approximately 15 years, David started in college, helping his friend Jeremy, a dance major, with a senior capstone project. This was about the time RuPaul's *Drag Race* premiered on television. "He wanted to show the art of movement with a little drag twist to it." The largest and most muscular of the models, David was ironically assigned the most feminine role. He laughs, the first of many times. "Broke college kids; had to do what we could. We went to the thrift store, and I got this polka dot dress. It was very June Cleaver, very apple pie like the Joneses, and I just looked a hot mess. That was the genesis of me getting into it."

Once he moved to Colorado, he had no intentions of continuing in drag. "It just kind of found me. I had a friend here; we went to a drag show. Never knowing I did drag, he's like 'I bet you can't do that.' So, I kind of hustled him a little bit." Laughs again. "Yeah, I got up there, did my thing, the producer talked to someone, and the rest is history. I had to repolish myself; restart from the fundamentals of this being a business and treating it as such. I wasn't nonchalant about it – 'Oh, I'm just a drag artist' – I had business cards, a website, I made a LLC, things of that nature. You just domino from that." Since then, Khrys'taaal has been featured in multiple articles and magazine publications, has toured the country for presentations and events at colleges (which is how I found him), and even headlined at Red Rocks - Colorado's most prestigious and renowned outdoor amphitheater.

"This character, Khrys'taaal – like the champagne, makes you bubbly, makes you happy - it's just been a blessing." Big smile. He goes on to explain that his version of drag is different than many approaches. "Back when I started it in 2008, you had to have the body, you had to have the pads, you had to have the chest, the big glam wigs, and everything." Instead of following that norm, David turned instead to his interest in cosplay. "I always was a big lover of Comic Con, of cartoons. I've done Carnage, Skeletor, Chung Lee, like all kinds of characters." He then incorporated those styles and inclinations into the drag industry. "It took a while for people to get accustomed to it, but I think that set me apart. It made me more of a novelty, and people want to be a part of my journey, a part of my brand."

The success with Khrys'taaal prepared him for his move into professional wrestling, and the creation of Remy D. Once again, the inspiration came from his love of comics and cosplay. "I'm a big X-Men fan, and Gambit – or Remy LeBeau – he's one of my favorites next to Storm and Phoenix. I always loved that name. And D is for David, Detroit. I always represent my city as best I can. It's always had a bad reputation, all cities do, but we are a very resilient people. We press on in the midst of hard times. I still represent that to this day. And it's also a play on the word 'remedy.' I like to say I'm the remedy to all this *basic* entertainment they have. I'm the cure, the answer, the solution." Laughs.

David sees little to no distinction between the energies, intent, and expressions of the two personae. "I don't think there is any difference. Once again, I already know how to brand myself, who I am as a character. Know the do's and don'ts of social media. In wresting they call it *kayfab*, which is another fancy word for being in character." He explains to me that if I were interviewing Remy D., instead of David, it would be a very different experience. "I would never break the Remy D. character for anything. I would have to stay in that zone the entire time. So, David can't come out. Khrys'taaal can't come out. It's all about Remy. I have to stay in that realm. That's *kayfab*."

I ask him about any overlap that might exist between David and the characters he has created. "I don't feel any different. If anything, I think that Khrys'taaal and Remy D., they're just like me, just amplified times ten. And just a lot of glitter and a lot of rhinestones! Normally I'm - I don't want to say reserved, I'm still very much an extrovert – but I'm more to myself. I think they just give me a reason to get out and have fun." Addressing the issue of costumes and *work*, he adds, "I'm always thinking of new things to add to each character. All those things are my work badges. I wouldn't say there's a distinction between all three; it just depends on what work badge I put on that day."

Whichever badge he is wearing, David feels obligated to give it his all. And the costumes he creates are a direct extension of that commitment. "Especially if it's something I've created from scratch, and I put like a ton of man-hours in. When it's finally done and I put it on, and I'm like, 'I did that. This is crazy.' Because people said I couldn't do this, way back in the day. But now I'm doing it. Now I feel like a superhero. Especially when I'm wearing it, and it's not wearing me – too baggy, or too tight, or something like that. It's a liberating feeling. It's like my work uniform. I feel like I'm going to work. I feel like I have a job to do. Entertain the people. Give them their money's worth."

Obviously, David's work ethic and work badges have been successful. "It has been bananas," he says of his newfound career. "I debuted in our big pay-per-view Shocktober last October. And the crowd's reaction – they had never seen anyone like me – you know, the style, or the way I talk, or present myself – they were like 'Who the hell is this guy?' It's not even drag. Remy's more of an androgynous character. Kind of makes Boy George look like Jim Carrey's The Riddler. He's a representation across the board. Not just race, not just gender, not just sexuality – just across the board. And people can see a piece of them; whether it's the athleticism, or the way I speak, or style, or anything. I just talked my smack. I was a 'heel' at the time, a bad guy, and I got what's called 'heat,' that's when you get like a bad reaction from the crowd, you get heat from the crowd. They hated me – *and I loved it*." Laughter and smile again. "When you're 'over' with the crowd, when you get a reaction from them, you're good! You don't want crickets, otherwise we'll have to write you out of this particular script."

He became so popular with the crowd, the promoters needed to covert him away from being a villain. "I am not a bad guy anymore. It was kind of hard. As much as I would talk smack and heckle the audience, they would start cheering me. It was the weirdest thing. So, the powers that be were saying, 'Yeah, Remy, we gotta take the plunge. We gotta turn you. You're more of a novelty. You're more of an attraction as a 'baby face' - a good guy. I'm a good guy now."

Given Remy D's glitzy and purposefully androgynous characteristics, David is pleased that the crowds have responded so well. "I was cautiously optimistic going in, but I'm at a point in my life where I feel very liberated. I'm not apologetic. I've gotten to the point where I was sick of watering down my talents and myself to make others feel better, because it makes them uncomfortable or they considered it – quote, unquote – 'an abomination' – or all those terms that they use nowadays.

But I'm entertaining people. Kids are excited to cheer on someone that they can relate to."

And kids are the main reason he does this. That is the biggest takeaway from David, from Khrys'taaal, from Remy D. They are all an inspiration to the next generation. "They come here with their parents. The narrative is not being pushed. Their parents are there, they're laughing, they're having a good time. They don't see anything except an outrageous, eclectic, flashy, rhinestone-sparkly character. 'I like him.' And that's all they need to know, that's all they need to care about. And that's why they come each and every week."

In all situations, David's goal is to provide that inspiration. As Khrys'taaal, when touring college campuses, he loves connecting with the students. "I have a real good meeting of the minds with younger people, especially college kids. I don't want any younger person to go through the hardship to the extent that I did growing up, without having the resources. Or having someone to simply say, 'Hey, you can make it. Hey, you look good today.' Just a little positive reinforcement. Being able to have those conversations when we have meet-and-greets, that means the world to me. You make those connections to keep them going." As Remy D., following an injury that laid him up for a while, he continued to hang around the ring and remain active with the junior athletes. "This is like my pastime; being able to motivate the younger wrestlers. They're encouraged to keep pressing on."

Whether it's promoting merchandise or an upcoming event, or bringing him in for motivational work, David loves the opportunity to engage with others. "I love being inspiring and motivating people – because I never had that as a younger kid living in Detroit," he tells me. Taking on the most serious tone since the start of our interview, David concludes, "I try to make myself duty bound to do that; my due diligence to do that." I believe him.

Get up, get out, get motivated, get inspired & get to your destiny.
Khrys'taaal, FB post, 10/18/21

COSTUME CONVERSATION # 11
John C. Luzader
a.k.a. Patrick Gass (Lewis & Clark Expedition, retired)

"To me, the authenticity is paramount. We're a historic resource, a teaching resource. This is like having that character coming back in time for a moment to say something. The research is there. Better than ever before. To me, there's no excuse. If you want to be authentic, if you want to give the best representation to the public, who paid to be there either monetarily or by their time and effort, to be at whatever site you're at, whatever program you have, we have an obligation to them." These are the words of author, trainer, and history expert John C. Luzader, regarding the roles and responsibilities of those who perform historical reenactments.

Looking back, John says there are two main reasons he got involved in living history events. The first is where he was raised. "I grew up around battlefields all my life. I lived in Sharpsburg, Maryland, which is where the battle of Antietam took place – one of the most critical battles in the American Civil War. All the farms around were owned still by the families who had been there during the Civil War. I went to school with their descendants, so we all were Civil War nuts as children. I started out as a drummer boy."

The second reason he got involved was his father. Now, in interviews like this, it is not surprising to hear someone say they got interested with one thing or another because their mother or father encouraged them in the activity. John's case is a little different. He got involved in historical reenactments because his father, who was a professional historian for the United States National Park Service, *loathed* it. "The uniforms were terrible. You could order them through Sears & Roebuck or Wards. They were nylon, and they were considered good enough to go on the battlefields with. My father hated it! He is a historian of great renown of the American Revolution and thought that this was nothing more than play-acting. I thought, 'This is great. Dad won't be hanging around, and he'll have to pay for it all, so what the heck!' That was my beginning."

"From that point on," John continues, "I have done a Civil War activity of some sort every year until the 145th anniversary." Over the course of 40 years, John has participated in numerous other living history events, portraying a variety of historical figures. It was during this time that John's father and two colleagues wrote a thesis for the National Parks Service about how *terrible* living history reenactments were. "So now there's another good reason to protest," John says, leaning forward with a conspiratorial grin. "It would annoy him, because we both have the same name. He, John *Franklin* Luzader, is being quoted by the Park Service as saying 'this is ridiculous.' And yet John *Charles* Luzader is out there teaching this at historical sites and national park sites." John sits back with a satisfied expression, lifting his hands palms up as if giving me a gift. "So, there you have it."

Of the many personae John portrayed over the years, he has three favorite characters. "One is a generic representation that I did; the *factor* of Bent's Fort." The historic site, located on the mountainous edge of the Santa Fe Trail, was home to peaceful fur trading between settlers and the local Cheyenne and Arapahoe tribes. "Fur trade forts were run by a factor, or a manager. Factor is also used as a manager's name in slave areas as well. I luck into becoming the factor at Bent's Fort for about 32 years." He adds that a true reenactment needs to present the individual as they most likely were, even if that means being rude or unpopular. A factor, for example, was not necessarily a friendly person. They were slave catchers. "Do not expect me to sit there and give you a wonderful dissertation about the wonderful aspects of every African American contribution to American history. I'm here to catch slaves." As he spoke with the public, he looked for those whose eyes lit up and said, "we want to know more." He would recruit those individuals to join in as volunteers. "About 80% of them came into the program and were trained, and continued for at least 10-15 years. That's probably my most famous and also my most enjoyable."

He continues. "The second is my great-grandfather, John *Michael* Luzader, who was captured at the Battle of Gettysburg. I had the honor of wearing the clothes he wore at Gettysburg at the 135th, as a prisoner. He was an educated person before the war, a cousin to Stonewall Jackson, and after the war refused to admit that the south had lost, and that there *was* a *West* Virginia, and would not take mail addressed to him in West Virginia, and refused to pay West Virginia taxes. He would send them to Virginia. I thought, *that* kind of cantankerous old man is the type of person I want to be."

The third of his favorites is the person he is dressed as today; a man named Patrick Gass. Gass was a member of the Lewis and Clark expedition, an 1804-1806 military trek mapping the Louisiana Purchase and the Pacific Northwest. "Gass is the first man who actually published a book on the Lewis and Clark expedition, pretty much against orders," John explains. "The men were supposed to turn in all their diaries, all their materials, and make no money from these activities. In 1809, years before Lewis publishes anything on the expedition, Patrick Gass publishes a book about the Corps of Discovery. Much of it might have been ghost-written, and we know much of it was probably exaggerated, but here you have a common soldier – who was renowned by William Clark as being 'better suited for taverns and the dock areas of towns.' You're looking at someone who's not a gentleman. Someone who enjoyed himself. I got intrigued by him. Here's a great character to look into."

In researching his character, John contacted seven descendants of Gass himself. He tells me, "With each family member, we knocked out some things they didn't want to hear, and then they knocked in some things that I had never heard. The more I got involved, the more I enjoyed it." He portrayed Gass the explorer until he eventually "aged out" of the character. At that point, he presented himself as the older Gass who could now look back on his days with the expedition. "At the age of 60, he married a young lady of about 15. He was living in her father's Inn, tavern, and they fell in love, went across the river, got married in Pennsylvania, and came back. I chose that year because he just gets married; I introduce it that way. 'I'm Patrick Gass. It's 25 years since we returned. I appreciate you coming to talk to me about the expedition. I have turned 60 this year, and I just got married! To a 15-year-old young lady.' And of course, everybody's like, they're cheering, or like 'oh my gosh, a pedophile story!'"

Despite the fact that the young Gass was no gentlemen, John informs me he treated his young wife with amazing respect. "And he outlives her. And he outlives every other member of the Lewis and Clark expedition. And just short of his 99th birthday, he dies." John clearly relishes these facts, and you can see his enthusiasm for the character. "There's so much fun with him. You have this rotund-ish gentleman in front of the audience, sitting in front of the tavern talking about the Lewis and Clark expedition – of course *improving* the stories in a way that it sounds it should be the *Gass* expedition! Then, at the conclusion, invites them into his father-in-law's tavern for a drink, which he'll pay for. That's one of my better characters."

Now that we have met John's favorite characters, we return to the question of *accuracy* in historical costumes. Ironically, accuracy was not insisted upon by many of the organizations which hosted the events. It was the pressure from professional historians, like John's father, that lead to the authenticity movement. On this point they agree. "This was, for a majority of people, something that the audience was taking as verbatim, as the truth." John is extremely critical of those actors who have lax attitudes, especially those who add things for humorous effect, or avoid difficult scenarios, or bypass authenticity because it is too expensive. John is committed to authenticity to the point that he has stopped portraying some of his favorite roles. "One of the reasons for leaving Bent's Fort is I aged out. I stopped doing Civil War activities because I was too old to have participated."

He contrasts this with the result of a lawsuit held in the 1980s. A young woman wanted to participate in a Civil War reenactment as a female soldier; something that did not exist at the time. John laments, "She didn't win her federal court case because she was a woman. She won because the Park Service was not *enforcing* an authenticity aspect, which was their defense. 'There were no women in the battles.' Well, there were no pot-bellied Confederate soldiers who have beards down to their knees, or age 70 and 80 years old, either." Because physical accuracy was not enforced with the male participants, it was settled that anyone could portray the characters. This opens the door for the dreaded FARBs to enter.

"FARBs, farbisms, whether self-induced or whether accidental, are the biggest bane on historic sites. I think we're cheating a public who is already being cheated in many classrooms across the nation. We're cheating them." John points out the challenge that exists because history limits you to the truth, whereas FARBs can go in more entertaining directions. "Sometimes the inauthentic is the most vibrant and entertaining, and will get the cameras rolling, and the public will take it; 'Oh, I saw they all had gunfights in the middle of the street at noon. It's in the movie. It's got to be true!' In consequence, when I teach, or go into a training session, I have to sit there and go, 'It never happened. That's not how it occurred.' You're talking about taking a historical activity and bastardizing it to create an entertainment moment instead of a historical interpretation. And I was always taught that bad interpretation is always worse than none."

He provides an example of one such "bad interpretation." "I once went to a gathering of Lincolns – people who did Abraham Lincoln. 156 of them. There were short ones, there were fat ones, there were African American ones, there was a Chinese one, there were female Abraham

Lincolns. So, you've got this, this, this, this, and this, for the public to see, and which one is the real Lincoln? The public has to decide on their own which has the better reference and is the better resource. A gaggle of Lincolns is a confusing situation."

I asked him then, what are the opportunities for women or people of color who want to participate in living history? He understands the delicate situation, but stands fast on his push for authenticity. "In today's society, whatever political stance you take, we're being pushed to not teach authenticity. But everyone in the program should be authentic. If I have an African American working next to me, there better be a reason. 'Why is that person here?' In today's society, we get squeaky on that. And being pressured to become 'authentic' in their mindsets, which is not usually authentic to the feelings, the emotions, the culture, and the backgrounds of the people being represented, is very difficult. Working with that, we lose that, and it bothers me." He insists, however, that embracing diversity is still possible without having to change what really happened. "We want inclusiveness, so they're making up aspects when they don't have to. It's already there. So, instead of being Lee, I'm Lee's guard. Instead of being Abraham Lincoln, why not bring in his barber from Springfield, Illinois, who was an African American? Which nobody knows. Why don't we talk about one of his secretaries, who have their own opinion, probably very venerating. Why don't we talk about the men who worked with Gass, or the family of Gass, as well? And then we don't create the conflict."

To clarify his point, John looks to my wife Maki, who is Japanese. "I can't be of your heritage, no matter how hard I try. I'm not of your heritage, and never should I try to emulate your heritage under any circumstance. And neither should you emulate my heritage. You'd be a terrible Sephardic Jew. Male. It involves a whole different lifestyle." He emphasizes this by adding, "If you want to do entertainment, go to Comic Con. That's fantastic. That's what they're for." Jumping on that observation, I ask John about the difference between living history and cosplay as found at typical Cons. "The difference between cosplay is, it's fiction to start with. To me, that's one of the best beauties of it.

Growing up in my timeframe, I've watched Superman become various images, depending on the person drawing and editing. That's part of the story. Do *Star Wars*. It's a fiction. You can play with that to your heart's desire. But we don't have Abraham Lincoln as a black African-American, because he's sympathetic to their needs, yet there's a black vision out there being done of Abraham Lincoln, which sometimes overshadows the true Lincoln as we know him. I would say, it *can* be done, it should *not* be done, in historical interpretation."

Continuing with the distinction, he believes that costumes are the main point of focus in cosplay. Not so with living history. "The costume is not the story." Pointing to himself, he says, *"This* is the interpretation; this is the story. This is the storyteller." He adds to this, emphasizing again we are now the richest time period for historical portrayals. "Every week something new is learned. Through an archeological dig, through the finding of another diary or set of letters." With that in mind, he concludes, "I'm but a teacher. I'm but an instructor who learns every day something I've done wrong, and I try to improve the program. In fact, when I do my biography, and put my first slide up on the wall, it shows everything I've done in my life in living history, and I end it after I turn off the slide by saying, 'And none of it matters unless I do a better job today than I did yesterday. Period.'"

COSTUME CONVERSATION # 12
Andy Mosher
a.k.a. Con Stapleton, City Marshal, Deadwood, SD

On August 2, 1876, famed Old West gunslinger James Butler Hickok is shot and killed while playing cards in a Deadwood, South Dakota saloon. Better known as "Wild Bill" Hickock, the folk legend was known for his times as a soldier and scout, as a figure who operated on both sides of the law (cattle rustler and lawman), as a gunslinger and gambler, and as an actor and performer in his friend "Buffalo Bill" Cody's *Wild West Show*. Hickock's assassin, Jack McCall, was eventually found guilty of murder and hung.

For almost three decades now, a group of actors – known collectively as *Deadwood Alive* – reenact those events, along with other shootouts and stories, in the streets of Deadwood every day during the summer months. In the evening, they reenact the trial of shooter Jack McCall. Additionally, the troupe hosts multiple activities from Spring until Fall, ranging from storytelling hours to walking tours of the famed city. The director of these events, who among other characters portrays Con Stapleton, the real-life Marshal during Wild Bill's days, is Andy Mosher.

Andy grew up in Concordia, Kansas. He became a firefighter and ended up being Deputy Chief. It was there he discovered that politics was not for him. In 2004 he came to South Dakota to attend the annual motorcycle rally in Sturgis. After the rally, he quit his job and moved to the Black Hills. "This is my 13th season with *Deadwood Alive*. I started out as a newbie like all these other guys, and now this is my 6th season as Director."

(Author's Note: Interestingly, while Andy shared a bit about the essence of *Deadwood Alive*, I got my most detailed description from the previous interviewee, John C. Luzader. He was quite familiar with their reenactments and, while speaking highly of the troupe, doesn't view what they do as "living history." "*Deadwood Alive* is really this wonderful place that has entertainment as a primary, on a site that is primarily entertainment anyway. It is, as one of my colleagues once stated, the largest whorehouse in the West. What a great character play. You've got the death of a Western hero. You've got all those dramatic moments that are real, so Deadwood has this stage that's ready. Is it historically accurate living history? You don't want it to be. Would I call it authentic? No. It's a theater, which is great.")

Returning to Andy, I learn – not surprisingly – that Halloween was his favorite holiday growing up. "When I was a little kid, my mom used to make all of our costumes. I would win prizes in school for the Best Monster that mom made from scratch. It was awesome! I started out making my own costumes for Halloween as a teenager. My first big one that I made was a Grim Reaper costume that I sewed myself. This was in the early '80s probably, and LEDs weren't a big thing yet, but I got ahold of some and put these glowing red eyes behind the screen of the mask. I made a robot-looking skeleton hand, and they'd move with my fingers. I've always built crazy costumes for Halloween. Before I moved to Deadwood, I'd never been in a costume contest I didn't win. Once I moved here, I haven't won once! There's some high-quality stuff here." The next costume he has planned is that of a zombie *victim*. "My zombie is going to be a puppet with sound, of course – I've already recorded the sounds – so he can growl and attack me and everything. I'll have my fake arm, the whole works. I think that's what I'm doing this year."

Despite his love for costumes, he's never tried cosplay – though he admits he finds the idea of steampunk appealing. "There had to be something mechanical or electronic in it for me to make it interesting. It was not just an outfit, but everything under the outfit, and everything involved. It is, to me, just the mechanical parts of it." For example, one year he decided to be Barf, John Candy's Chewbacca knock-off from the movie *Spaceballs*. "I even found robotic ears I ordered from Japan that worked off of brain waves so, if I was excited, I could actually make the ears perk up. It was weird." To exemplify his love for creating things, he points to the various set pieces surrounding us. "I built that wagon, I built that sign, I built that stage, most of everything that we use here."

Given Andy's love for costumes and for construction, it makes sense that he ended up volunteering for *Deadwood Alive*. "I was a poker dealer at the Slim 10 for a long time. I liked to wear a derby hat and the arm bands when I could. One of my buddies was doing the street shows and asked if I would be interested, because they had an opening. So, I showed up to their improv class/meeting/rehearsal and they figured if I was willing to be an idiot and roll around on the floor and do whatever they told me, that I could probably do it. That's how I got into it. I'd never done any acting before that, or anything along those lines, but I liked to dress up and play cowboy."

After roughly seven years of participation, Andy moved up to become the troupe's director. "Part of it is being an *acting* director, like you would imagine in a play," he explains. "What we do is a lot of acting. A majority of my time, other than getting people up to speed for their parts, is just being a manager. A lot of time spent on budgeting, and manpower, and planning for the next season. Each year we try to add new things; new performances, new shows, all kinds of new stuff." Currently, there are 15 people in the troupe. The audition process is rather informal. "Each spring, depending on how many people we need, we start out early in the year – January, February – getting the word out to people that we want to fill a couple positions. And we get guys that'll come in, and will come to our rehearsals, and kind of see what we're doing, and we'll audition them. We'll do a bit of an acting audition, a little bit of an improv audition, and do an interview with them. If it acts like it's going to work out, we go from there."

In addition to the daily shootouts and evening trial of Jack McCall, they provide an information Chuckwagon and stagecoach rides. Weather permitting. The day we were talking was drizzly and chilly. It had been raining that morning, so the stagecoach rides were cancelled early. "Yesterday was the first time in my 13 seasons that it rained all day," Andy tells me. "It really threw a wrench in the works. Normally, even if it is a rainy day, we can sneak in between storms. Yesterday was a big exception." More challenging than the rain can be the summer heat. There are regularly sweltering, humid, summer days in the Black Hills. "I'm constantly saying to my guys, 'Go drink something. Get in the shade. Relax.' And of course, we're all not real smart, and we wear dark colored hats. It is miserable out there in that heat." He emphasizes his point by showing off his gray vest, explaining that it used to be black, but has now faded from constant exposure to the sun.

That's a perfect lead-in to ask about the costumes themselves. Where do they come from? Andy informs me that they are a non-profit organization, so they don't have much of a budget for outfits. "A lot of the guys buy their own stuff, or it's hand-me-down stuff." Unlike the living history events overseen by John C. Luzader, *Deadwood Alive* is less stringent about authenticity. "We try to make it look as close as we can to accurate, but we can't be 100%. A lot of the contests you'll go to, those guys, everything's perfect. We just can't go that far. We can't afford to do it with our budget." Andy does prefer that clothing items be used and a little worn out, rather than brand new. He shows me his hat, telling me it's finally broken in after 15 years. His costume policy? "We go by the ten-foot rule. If your costume looks good from ten feet, then it's alright."

If there is flexibility with costumes, is there also flexibility regarding the actors? "We have a lot of wiggle room. It's difficult to find people that look right," Andy explains, and then adds, "First of all, it's difficult to find people that will do this; that will walk around in the heat all summer long and do this six days a week. So, we're lucky to get enough people to do it. A lot of times what we'll do is find a Deadwood character that looks like *them*. I don't know what Con Stapleton looked like. We don't really have any pictures of him, so I'm okay with that character. We each play several roles during the day, several different roles, so we can't look like all the characters." Given that, I ask him what is allowed for women actors and/or people of color? "We have a couple of female characters. We looked back and found Doc Flora was a doctor here in town, so we use that as one of the character names for those ladies. If you are a female and you want to play a guy role, I don't have a problem with that. As far as race goes, most of what we have done and the actual characters that we have, generally looked like us. But I don't have a problem with hiring somebody that doesn't look like us. There's no reason why I wouldn't."

Wrapping up, I ask Andy to share with me his views on work costumes and identity. "I learned a long time ago when I was doing Halloween, and that's why I enjoy this so much, is that you put on a costume, you can be whatever you want to be. It's really liberating. And in this job as well, I get to do something different than boring old me. I'm the guy that mows the yard and works in my wood shop. I'm not a guy out there that's slinging a gun and arresting people. It's a lot of fun to put on a different identity." I ask him, even though it's a different identity, do his character choices reflect any aspects of his inner self? "That's a good point. It does make sense. Mostly what I do is things that I'm interested in. I was a firefighter and a fire investigator. I had arrest powers. I was a lawman when I did that, more or less. And then I end up here as the town Marshal. I guess that is a part of my personality, a part of my personality that I haven't explored."

However, Andy adds one final stipulation. "I just like to have fun."

CHAPTER 5
Fashion and Lifestyle Costumes

A positive relationship exists between one's inclination toward fashion in dress and the desire to make an impression through communication. Henry Higgins knew that Eliza Dolittle must both look like and talk like a lady.
Gorden, Infante, and Braun, 1985, p. 162

From "Bride" and "Groom" t-shirts and underwear to Ugly Christmas Sweater contests, from Toys for Tots Poker Runs to Black-Tie Affairs, our lives are filled with opportunities to dress up outside the norm. Some reserve it for holidays, like wearing green on St. Patrick's Day even though you're not Irish (see Costume Conversation #13), while others make it part of their daily preparations (see Costume Conversation #14). Sometimes the effect is subtle, like wearing non-prescription Warby Parker eyeglasses to look more intelligent. Other times, it is more obvious. For example, across the country it is becoming common for cosplayers to step outside the world of Cons and create social meet-and-greets in public spaces, restaurants, and bars (see Image 5.1). Whenever and wherever worn, per our working definition of "costume," these choices are *a conscious decision about clothing, recognizable as outside the everyday norm, that an individual wears in specific or public locales, in order to make a statement or send a message.*

Shukla (2015) reminds us that "daily dress reflects personal identity...what we wear is affected by our body, age, gender, socioeconomic class, personality, our taste and style." She concludes by stating, "Dress is who we are" (p. 3). It is part of our lifestyle. This chapter is going to look at a handful of situations, outside of cosplay, Cons, and work obligations, where people put on some level of identifiable costume-wear. This is not going to be a how-to guide providing color scheme suggestions for major holidays. Wearing red, white, & blue on the 4th of July, red on Valentine's Day, and your favorite team's jersey during the Super Bowl, are pretty straightforward recommendations. Instead, we're going to step back and look broadly at some events, groups, and communities that have lifestyle-specific attire. Before we dig deeper into these lifestyle communities, we're going to take a quick look at *style* itself. How and why do clothes make a difference?

Image 5.1 *Haunted house "Foreman" Josh Randall and Star Fleet officer Sam Baca enjoy a beer at a monthly cosplay gathering, Outworld Brewing, Longmont, CO*

Fashion and Identity
One of the most visible and universal ways that people express themselves is through their clothes. Safdar, Goh, and Choubak, 2020, p. 36

Granted, many of us do not put a lot of thought into what we wear. Whatever matches. Whatever is clean. But none of us can deny that certain clothes, like something brand new, make you feel different. Better. Barnard (1996) explains that "the purchasing and wearing of new clothes is an increasingly well-documented way in which some people attempt to alter their mood…it seems that more and more people are becoming 'addicted' to the feelings they get when they do wear something new" (p. 57). Well, new or not, clothing impacts the way we present ourselves and the way we feel, as noted in this detailed observation by Lewis and Lewis:

> The game of dressing up teaches us the importance of apparel upon our own moods, the message we wish to convey to others, the suitability of clothing to our varying activities. In everyday life people dress to fulfill their subconscious vision of themselves. The effect of clothes upon one's psychological outlook is unlimited: the stance and manner of an athlete can be assumed by wearing a pair of jogging shoes and a sweatsuit; a well-tailored suit reinforces a businessman or woman; a handsomely cut tuxedo establishes an air of sophistication; a flowing chiffon gown allows a woman to feel ethereal and elegant. In our personal lives we play many roles, and dress to benefit the occasion. (1990, p. 7)

The word "fashion" itself comes from the word *facere*, a variant of the Latin *factio*, meaning making or doing (Barnard, 1996). Interestingly, it is the same root from which we get the words *fetish* and *fetishism*. As Sellnow explains, a fetish occurs when a person "gets pleasure from openly looking at an object" (2018, p. 245), that is, the object itself is visually satisfying. Most often the terms are applied to sexualized attractions, such as an obsession over lingerie or décolletage. However, it can apply to anything upon which we can gaze and desire, such as art, cars, or collectibles. But the link between *fashion* and *fetish* is undeniable. Clothing and accessories (e.g., high heels, lipstick, power ties) are often fetishized commodities.

In addition to fostering wanted or unwanted visual desire, clothing can produce a variety of communicative outcomes. In their research on personality and clothing, Burgoon, Buller, and Woodall (1996) identified four orientations: clothing consciousness, exhibitionism, practicality, and designer image. An individual with *clothing consciousness*, a heavy awareness of and focus on clothing choices, tended to be inhibited, anxious, compliant before authority, kind, sympathetic, and loyal to friends. Someone who enjoys showing off their fashion, thus high in *exhibitionism*, was found to be aggressive, confident, outgoing, unsympathetic, unaffectionate, moody, and impulsive. *Practicality* in clothing choices, such as emphasizing comfort over trends, correlated with being clever, enthusiastic, confident, outgoing, and guarded about self-revelation. Finally, those with *designer image*, who fancied themselves or aspired to be a fashion designer, also tended to be cooperative, sympathetic, warm, helpful, impulsive, irritable, demanding, and conforming. What do you think? Do these sound like anybody you know?

Looking at it from a different angle, Forsythe, Drake, and Hogan (1985), use the ancient Chinese terms Yin and Yang to help guide and interpret clothing choices. Arguing that clothing "is an important medium through which personal characteristics may be communicated" (p. 269), they explain that Yin is associated with traditionally feminine characteristics like gentleness and warmth, while Yang is correlated with traditionally masculine traits like strength and forcefulness. Thus, when making clothing choices, one might lean toward Yin for a family celebration but Yang for a job interview.

The authors provide design components for each (see Figure 5.1 for summary). Yin (feminine) fashions are characterized by "short broken lines; curved lines; rounded silhouette; gathered fullness; horizontal and upward movement of line; small scale; soft, dull, delicate textures; medium to light colors; soft intensities; and cool hues." In contrast, Yang (masculine) is manifest in "long, unbroken lines; straight, angular, and continuous lines; vertical and downward movement of lines; straight or modified straight silhouette; large scale; heavy, stiff, and coarse texture, few details; dark, bold colors; strong contrast in values, and warm hues." (p. 269). Putting that into practice, a Yin outfit might include acid-washed blue jeans and a light-colored or lightly pattered cotton shirt. A typical pin-striped wool suit would be a classic example of Yang. One can only assume that these principles apply to cosplay and costume creations as well.

Yin (feminine)	Yang (masculine)
Traits: warmth, gentleness	Traits: strength, forcefulness
Style: short broken lines, curved lines, rounded silhouette, gathered fullness, horizontal/upward lines, small scale, soft/dull/delicate textures, medium/light colors, cool hues, soft intensities	Style: long unbroken lines, straight/angular/continuous lines, vertical/downward lines, straight silhouette, large scale, heavy/stiff/coarse textures, few details, dark/bold colors, strong contrast in colors, warm hues

Figure 5.1: Yin-Yang and Clothing, based off research by Forsythe, Drake, and Hogan, 1985. Image Source: Wikimedia Commons.

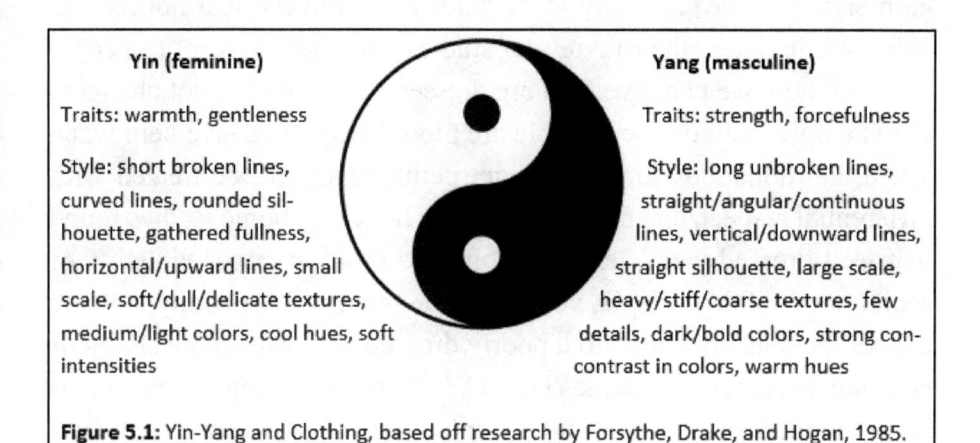

Figure 5.1 *Yin and Yang fashion characteristics*

Gender

While the Yin-Yang distinction was meant for all genders, one cannot help but notice the typical binary differentiation between the sexes. Barnard (1996) acknowledges that gender and power differences exist, but labels them as mere "historical accidents." However, he adds, "fashion and clothing have the function of making them appear to be legitimate, right and almost the work of nature rather than people" (p. 40). In other words, gender differences are natural, but clothing and costume distinctions are purposeful acts dedicated to making a statement about power. Research to that effect has been straightforward and, to the modern reader, perhaps a bit sexist.

In a study of "the female clotheshorse," Solomon and Douglas (1985) began by describing the use of clothing by women to "project a role image and to communicate location or status in society." Her clothing, they argued, revealed her self-identity and aesthetic taste. "A woman elegantly dressed in the latest fashion was viewed as part of the fashion elite, while a dowdy housewife suggested the personality and life-style of the hausfrau. Similarly, the woman dressed in Bohemian garb signaled her proclivity to deviate from conventional norms" (p. 389). While dated, their review of studies find that we react to people based on how we perceive they are dressed. That fact has not changed. For example, well dressed people are more likely to receive help when asked, get donations for charity, get petitions signed, be treated with differential respect, and treated with more honestly. Some studies found that well-dressed people are also followed more in minor violation of social norms. For example, you would be more likely to copy a nicely dressed person, compared to a poorly dressed one, when jaywalking or crossing the street despite the "Don't Walk" signal. Solomon and Douglas point out that clothing is not the only cue used by others when forming impressions. Factors like perceived self-confidence also come into play. However, they note, clothing "can also be an important internal cue affecting an individual's self-concept, and in particular, his or her self-confidence" (p. 389). The argument, then, becomes circular. If you dress well, you feel self-confident. If you feel self-confident, people will intuit that and, coupled with the fact that you are dressed well, treat you better.

Similar views are expressed in Buetow's (2020) more recent research on body image and men who are underweight. Initially, the work seems body-shaming, but you cannot deny his observation that "thin men often feel demasculinized by societal expectations" (p. 430). He suggests that these men wear fashionably masculine clothing, such as the Yang power suit described above, "in order to extend the male body, literally and metaphorically" (p. 430). Using a play on words, he explains the individual can "man-age" concerns about their body image in healthy ways. He adds that clothing therapy has been studied as a way of dealing with cancer and mental illness, to which he adds this perspective on body image anxiety. It is there that Buetow's study takes shape.

Rather than just limiting our focus to thin males, we can expand his viewpoint to all, applying his notion of "performativity of clothing" which helps an individual become a "transparent and authentic being within social transactions" (p. 433). He calls this socially determined and reinforced self-image "enclothed cognition," and suggests that health providers and clinicians engage in clothing therapy and give fashion advice to those with body image issues. Clothing therapy? Not a bad idea.

In some respects, we have come full circle. We started this book by looking at cosplay, and the enormous social and psychological benefits found by those who participate. Now, in this non-cosplay half of the book, while looking at simple fashion research, we find the same kind of conclusions. Whether it is a costume or not, whether it is at a Con or not, the clothing choices we make can improve our lot in life. In fact, let's take a quick look at a of a couple whose love of clothing and costumes turned into both a personal and business relationship.

> **Spotlight Story – Rob Sims and Kyla Swanberg**
> Though both have day jobs, artists and cosplayers Rob and Kyla, of Orlando, FL, wanted to take their hobby to the next level. Kyla, who goes by the username "MisStiched," is a seamstress. Rob specializes in photography, lighting, and tech. Together they created *CosFX Studios* (i.e., she does the 'Cos'tumes and he runs the special "FX"). They describe their business as creating "interactive photo opportunities for guests and cosplayers alike to jump into their favorite movies." (Though a quasi-paid gig, it's being included here under lifestyle because it is only part-time, an occasional offering, and people can participate for free.)
>
> Carnival employees have long been known as *carnies* (sometimes spelled *carneys*). In a few pages, we'll learn that workers at Renaissance Festivals are referred to as *rennies*. Well, since Rob and Kyla like to attend comic *con*ventions, they call themselves *connies*. They attend whatever shows they are able, offering a photo booth

with backdrop, with them in matching costumes, where people can enter worlds such as *Beetlejuice*, *Ghostbusters*, *Addams Family*, and *Back to the Future*. So far, they've attended Fan Expos in Orlando, Denver, Boston, and Dallas – with hopes to eventually take their business around the world. When I met them, they were dressed as Riff-Raff and Magenta from *The Rocky Horror Picture Show* (see Image 5.2).

Image 5.2 *Your author (center) with Rob/Riff-Raff (left) and Kayla/Magenta (right).*
PHOTO CREDIT: CosFX Studios

In the booth, attendees get to hold props, interact with the characters, and take pictures on their cell phones – with the opportunity to purchase professional photos which they provide. "It brings us joy as artists to do what we do when we see how much fun people have," states Kayla, adding, "We create a safe space for all humans to enjoy and leave their troubles outside."

The couple met while working as characters at a theme park. Rob wanted to do a *Beetlejuice* wedding booth at an Orlando horror show, and asked Kyla if she would dress as the Lydia Deetz (Winona Ryder) character. As fate would have it, Kyla had crafted Lydia's red wedding dress earlier that year. They now admit that first effort was barebones compared to their later creations, but both their business and their relationship blossomed from there.

In addition to the *Beetlejuice* wedding scene (Lydia in red dress, Beetlejuice in purple tux), Rob also wears the famous black and white striped outfit, and they've even created a Hawaiian Honeymoon version of the characters, turning their booth into a gothic luau. When they do *Ghostbusters*, Kyla plays Gozer the Gozerian while Rob portrays Dr. Janosz Poha (from *G II*), holding a brush to the Vigo the Carpathian painting. In *Back to the Future* Rob is Marty McFly to Kyla's Jennifer Parker (Marty's girlfriend). Their *Addams Family* setup includes a larger cast with friends, joining Rob as Uncle Fester and Kyla as Wednesday. Out of all these sets of characters they don't really have a *least* favorite. Their favorite *and* most requested is Beetlejuice and Lydia.

Kyla tells me that the costumes really impact the way they feel and the way they work together. "When we are in these characters, we become them. The two of us interact as those characters. We can turn it off as needed like a light switch but we have much more fun when we are in character. If we are visible in our booth we are switched on because anyone can see you at any time and it gives a better quality of show overall." During the weekend of a show, she adds, "we practically live at the booth."

Overall, their Con experiences have been rewarding. They are well received, and they love hanging out with the vendors, artists, and cosplayers. Rob shares a story of a sweet Gothic couple they met at a Halloween convention. "The lady's two small kids were with her, they played, got their photo and left. But then the boyfriend came back by himself. We thought at first that he left something at the

> booth. He asked if he could bring his lady back here to propose to her since Beetlejuice was her favorite film. He brought her and the kiddos back. He was shaking and so affectionate with her, said some sweet words, and got down on one knee. She cupped her hand to her mouth with tears in her eyes and then replied 'Yes!' She turned to her kids and said, 'did you know about this?' and they giggled 'yeah' and jumped for joy as one family."
>
> Noting that the couple above was dressed in Goth style, I asked if attendee attire (e.g., street clothes, cosplay light, full costume) seemed to make any difference. Both were quick to point out they treat everyone as a guest, no matter if they are in costume or not. For them, Kyla tells me, "A cosplayer can be anything- no matter what shape, size, color, gender, or even how much they look like that character. We just love to play and celebrate what we love with other people in fandom." That said, they really enjoy seeing people who take specific characters to "the next level." They love talking shop with fans about costume construction and props. At their first show, there was a guest who was "full on" Dracula from *Hotel Transylvania*. As he hit them with taglines like "I do not say the blah blah blah," they countered back and forth while staying in true *Beetlejuice* form.
>
> "Conventions are such a great way to meet like-minded people and celebrate fandom," Rob concludes. Kyla agrees, adding, "That is what we love most about cosplay. It is the putting on of costumes and playing as that character. Then you meet another person who is from a different comic, movie, or game and they interact with you playing their character. It is a crossover of all crossovers."

At this point we'll turn to some of those settings and communities promised at the start of the chapter. Let's begin with the grandaddy of them all – Renaissance Fairs and Festivals (hereafter referred to as Ren Fairs). As noted in the last chapter, this is a venue that has both official *workers* in costume and a number of lifestyle attendees similarly dressed. And, as noted throughout the book, Ren Fairs were the *starting* point for many to enter the world of costumes.

Ren Fairs

For those who've never been, a Ren Fair is essentially an outdoor gathering on summer weekends, modeled in a simulacra version of the Renaissance, in which Lords, Ladies, Knights, and the like gather to eat, shop, play games, and entertain/be entertained. These fairs can be found throughout the country – Arizona, California, Colorado, Maryland, Michigan, Minnesota, New York, North Carolina, Ohio, Oklahoma, Pennsylvania, and Wisconsin – with the largest of them all in Texas. With attendance levels in the hundreds of thousands (the one outside Houston, TX, has an average draw over half a million), these are perhaps the largest costumed events in existence. Of course, not everyone has to be in costume, but a number of guests enjoy the opportunity to put on a festival gown, a knight's crest, or a jester's mask as they enjoy the day. It is an opportunity to yell "Huzzah!" – an archaic holler of delight dating back to the early 1500s.

American mythology has the notion that people regularly would "run-away" to join the circus; that the circus was the home for many a misfit, outlaw, or outcast. Current sources indicate that Ren Fairs may be the new safe haven for individuals who feel more comfortable on the road than they did in their previous town, church, or job. To get a better understanding of the facts versus fiction, I conducted an interview with West Roberts (2022), who has worked as a vendor and entertainer at multiple Ren Fairs. His description was colorful:

> The Renaissance Festival incorporates a lot of different cultures. While the name implies that the fairs are Renaissance themed, the reality is that they function more as *fantasy* festivals. At the fair you can find members of a royal court, jesters, knights, maidens, pirates, Vikings, and mermaids. You can eat food like the iconic turkey legs and sausage on a stick. You can listen to professional musicians play original and covered tracks with the hurdy gurdy, guitar, harp, drums, bagpipes, and more. You can play games like throwing axes, shooting bows and arrows, and climbing "Jacob's ladder." But arguably the biggest draw of the fair is the environment itself in which these

things combine to allow people from varied walks of life to congregate with friends, family, and strangers and experience the embodiment of so many other peoples' imaginations.

Roberts differentiated for me a few of the cultural subgroups found at a typical Ren Fair.

First are the *Road Rennies*; those who work at the fair for life and treat it like a regular job. Some work for the same company at several fairs around the country, and others work for multiple different shops based upon where in the country they want to travel. He describes the lifestyle as "liberated" and "relatively nomadic." Rennies range from those who treat their job like a relatively normal occupation (e.g., some level of career trajectory), that simply involves a unique brand of uniform, to those who embrace the nomadic lifestyle, such as working only weekends and doing whatever they please during the rest of the week.

A second category is *Weekenders*. These are locals who work only at a festival happening in their area. Roberts feels this group is most into the "huzzah" culture. It is less of a job and more a chance to enjoy the magic of escaping from the "real world" for a few weekends. He explains, "Weekenders can range from cast members of the royal court and stage performers to people who work consistently at a single shop when their local fair is active, to people in food service, to people who will just work part of a day in exchange for entry into the fair to enjoy the rest of the time inside the gates."

Finally, we have the *Patrons*, the attendees, who seem to break down into several subcultures of their own. A majority Roberts defines as *General Patrons*; those who attend simply to experience something new, shop through the products, or see what the hype is all about. These individuals are more passive; they like to see the shows, play the games, and just people watch, more so than actively engage themselves. Roberts notes, "A lot of people have also been going to the fair long enough that it is a staple event they look forward to all year long and/or want to share with their friends and children."

Next in terms of engagement are the *Cosplayers* who attend. They show up in their non-Renaissance characters, ranging from *Star Wars* storm troopers to *The Witcher*'s Geralt of Rivia. A costume is a costume, right? Nobody said it has to match the theme. It is also a chance, Roberts adds, for people to dress as "characters that they have developed in their own minds or have described in self-authored novels." Thus, not much different than a Con; just outdoors, with different food. Finally, we have the *Playtrons*. "These people are often the ones with the most impressive or handmade costumes," Roberts explains, "that are better looking than the paid performers or royal court." Many of the playtrons are regulars, who treat their local Ren Fair as "a lifestyle and a staple of the year."

Finding a strong parallel with earlier observations about cosplay, Roberts speaks to the progression of costume proficiency that occurs as attendees advance from one subculture to the next:

> They may begin as a new visitor who isn't sure why, but they purchase a pair of bracers because it's something small, relatively affordable, and looks kind of cool. They may not know what to do with them outside of the fair, but they enjoy wearing them and feel better about themselves for it. They begin asking themselves questions about what else they might enjoy wearing, slowly build a costume, and with it, a character. Before they know it, they have gradually created a whole new persona for themselves. They make or buy items for their costume based on what will develop their character further. They see themselves differently while wearing garb and discover that that person looking back in the mirror has a backstory, and motivations that are their own.

Before you know, he adds, there is a new batch of wizards, archangels, satyrs, dragons, warriors, time traveling steam punks, princesses, fairies, Vikings, pirates, and a host of other characters wandering the Ren grounds, "interacting with one another and appreciating each other's creativity."

Role Play, Living History, and More

In the last chapter we talked about living history events like historical reenactments, pointing out that, like a Ren Fair, it was "work" for some and a "lifestyle" volunteer event for others. Just as there is overlap between work/play in those two venues, there is also overlap in a multitude of other role-playing, live-action activities. It would be a jumbled mess to try and analyze each format as a discrete and separate entity. For example, some at a Ren Fair participate in physical combat events. There may be swordplay, jousting, and the like. The same may be true of a living history event focusing on medieval times. Likewise, a really interactive game of Dungeons and Dragons could involve some swordplay, as would a Boffer War (done with foam weapons) or a rousing gathering of *Star Wars* Jedi (though the weapon of choice would be light saber). To get a better picture, let's spend a little time on the two more prominent types of events.

Society for Creative Anachronism

According to their website, the Society for Creative Anachronism (SCA) is an "inclusive community pursuing research and re-creation of pre-seventeenth century skills, arts, combat and culture. The lives of participants are enriched as we gain knowledge of history through activities, demonstrations, and events" (www.sca.org). Described as "the Current Middle Ages," the SCA's "Known World" is divided into twenty kingdoms worldwide. Each kingdom is comprised of hundreds of Cantons, Shires, and Baronies to which an individual can belong. The re-creation of medieval times is accomplished through the practice of martial activities (e.g., combat, archery), equestrian skills, the practice of heraldry, and the understanding of arts and sciences for the time.

From her research, Shukla (2015) maintains the "SCA provides an outlet for creativity, aesthetic delight, and psychological release, achieved partly through the mandatory donning of historic garb" (p. 131). While newcomers are welcomed, even before they've had a chance to develop their medieval name/character or build a costume, they are asked for at least a basic attempt at period attire, "such as a plain-colored skirt and peasant type blouse, or plain trousers and an untucked tunic-style shirt."

In May of 2022, I had the opportunity to attend the annual baronial investiture of the Barony of Unser Hafen in the Kingdom of the Outlands. After thanking the outgoing court, King Barekr inducted His Excellency Freana and Her Excellency Richenda as the new Baron and Baroness (see Image 5.3). The members of their court include a head of household, court heralds, baronial guards, and ladies in waiting. As one might expect, the ceremony was geared to be as realistic as possible, from the costuming to the use of Olde English phrasing and terminology. Not being properly attired, I stayed to the shadows and used a telephoto lens (though I was permitted on grounds after the ceremony for a group shot; see color section).

Image 5.3 *SCA Baronial Investiture ceremony*

The SCA is not free from criticism. Some chapters have been accused of inappropriate actions, but those are more the result of transgressive individuals than any institutional practices. Of more general concern is that, when you are trying to re-create the history of a time and place that was patriarchal, colonialist, and even genocidal, those traits might carry over. Unlike the steampunk communities, who can cherry pick which parts of the Victorian era they wish to emulate, SCA members must stick to history. That very orientation, some have claimed, make it an attractive setting for misogynistic white men. On that, I have no comment, other than to say it was not my experience at all. Everyone was welcoming, egalitarian, and appeared to be having a fantastic time.

Live Action Role Play (LARP)
If you want the energy of a Ren Fair and the organizational structure of SCA, then *Live Action Role Play* (LARP) might be for you. While often based in medieval time periods, like SCA, there is greater flexibility in character portrayals, like a Ren Fair. So, while you might have a King, Queen, and Royal Court, you might also have fairies, elves, trolls, and other figures of fantasy. Wikipedia offers the following description: "The players pursue goals within a fictional setting represented by real-world environments while interacting with each other in character. The outcome of player actions may be mediated by game rules or determined by consensus among players. Event arrangers called gamemasters decide the setting and rules to be used and facilitate play."

Unlike SCA, which has a single, international governing body, LARPs are put on by a variety of independent groups and organizations worldwide. On occasion, the events might be labeled as Live Role Playing (LRP), free-form role playing, or interactive literature. Unfortunately, we did not encounter any LARPers in our travels. For many, me included, the only exposure to the activity comes from the 2008 movie *Role Models*. In it, two men (Paul Rudd, Seann William Scott) are sentenced to 150 hours in a Big Brother program, and end up mentoring a LARP participant, Augie, who belongs to LAIRE (Live Action Interactive Role-playing Explorers; an actual tri-state organization in NY, NJ, and PA). What begins as your typical R-rated gross-out comedy actually culminates in a very supportive and touching portrayal of live action role play. Well, like they say, any publicity is good publicity.

Tattoo Culture

One thing that SCA and LARP groups might not tell you is that tattoos were fairly common during the medieval period. The Crusaders, in particular, were most likely adorned with religious symbols (Endres, 2007). Granted, tattoos are not costumes, per se – but they definitely hold a place in modern-day comic and fantasy fandom. Jones (2015) explains that "the fan tattoo is an expression of the fannish self that exists at a deeper level than simply clothes or accessories can demonstrate" [1.2]. Tattoos are imbued with symbolic richness and meaning. We have already seen this demonstrated in our Costume Conversations, with Eric's (#1) KISS signatures and Casey's (#3) Batman ink. Jones compares this as similar to Emile Durkheim's concept of the totem and sacred identity. For example, fans of the Dr. Who television series describe themselves as part of a community ("Whovians"), and they identify the time-traveling police phone box – the TARDIS – as their totem. Getting a TARDIS tattoo would be an affective demonstration of that fandom.

Jones goes on to use the word *sacred* to describe tattoos - not as Holoka did earlier in this book, by equating it with religion - but as that "which is socially transcendent and gives a sense of fundamental identity based on likeness (kinship) constructed and sustained by difference or opposition over and against" the alien [3.3]. In other words, our everyday world and routine is mundane. To inscribe our meanings in ink upon our skin takes our commitment level up a notch or two. And, as Endres (2013) notes, "tattoos have lost much of the negative social stigma once associated with them, and have become for many an accepted practice for proclaiming one's identity" (p. 37).

For example, in a show-and-tell assignment in my popular culture class, student Nathan Stromberg (2023) shared with his classmates his connection to DC's character *The Flash*, especially the Barry Allen storyline. Nathan explains that Allen's character has endured everything from watching his parents die to seeing literal worlds end, but somehow he would never "give up or go dark." He especially likes this quote from Allen, "Sometimes the only way to move forward is to revisit the things in your past that were holding you back. You have to deal with them head on, no matter how scary they may be. Because once we do, you will see that you can go further than you ever imagined." For Nathan, the narrative provides a strong life lesson. "That's an example I try to follow every day, and so far, it's worked wonders. Despite any struggles I've faced, I've remained hopeful that my life will get better. I'm happy with my life, and a few years ago, I never would've imagined being where I am now. I credit a lot of that to the example The Flash set for me." As a reminder, he has the Flash's signature lightning bolt tattooed on his arm. It is his daily reminder to maintain hope.

In similar form, communication professional and scholar Curtis Sullivan has the iconic "Death of Superman" image – Superman's tattered cape blowing forlornly in the wind - tattooed on his arm (Image 5.4). Brownie and Graydon (2016) note that this image, which was selected by fictional photographer and Superman's pal Jimmy Olsen as the one to print in the *Daily Planet*, as the visual "that most effectively symbolizes Superman's sacrifice" (p. 23).

When Curtis was 22 years old, his father passed away from stage four cancer. This left the young man with a complicated mix of trauma, ego, loneliness, and entitlement which he gracefully describes as follows: "The hypocrisy of my then-mantra of goodness and excellence was a stark contrast to the toxic perception of my own reality that I was a flawed and problematic man who would inevitably and foolishly leave a path of great destruction in his wake while attempting to positively impact my world" (2023).

His solution at the time was to get the tattoo. A long-time comic book fan, he read *Superman* titles more than any other. In 1992-93, the *Death of Superman* series traced the battle between the hero from Krypton and an almost indestructible monster named Doomsday. Their battle destroys much of Metropolis and, though Superman defeats the behemoth, he does so at the expense of his own life. "Obviously, I related to the champion of champions laying down his life to protect the world. Obviously, I understood the emotional complexity of leaving brutal destruction in the wake of good intentions. This narrative was so meaningful to me during a formative time in my life, that I simply *knew* that this MUST be my next tattoo." The tattoo meant everything to him; he believed in the message.

Image 5.4 *Death of Superman tattoo.*
PHOTO CREDIT: Curtis Sullivan

Now, years later, he doesn't embrace the tattoo like he once did, but he still thinks the message is important. "I believe many people have good intentions; many of us want to 'save' things – to protect them, and in doing so we sometimes miss the mark and cause damage. Now, the fading image is more of a reminder than anything: a reminder that people grow and they change – that ideals were once bold and prominent but change and even fade over time; it is a reminder that while we *can* cause damage to others unintentionally, we definitely *do* cause damage to ourselves with gusto."

This is a book about costume. But, as you've learned, I also research and write about tattoos. The full story Curtis shared was too long for these pages, but I'm certain to find a place for it in other venues. For now, I'll just state the obvious. Unlike costumes, which can be removed, tattoos are more-or-less permanent. They can be covered or lasered off, but some aspect will always remain. If you get inked, be thoughtful about it. That way, like Curtis, you will have peace with the decision, "I am grateful for my youth, though riddled with coulda-woulda-shoulda and regret, but it made me who I am."

Drag and Burlesque

In our Costume Conversations thus far, we've met both a Drag Queen (male who entertains as a female) and a Drag King (female who entertains as a male), and learned about other varieties of drag performance, such as hyperqueens (females who perform as females) and the ever-growing categories brought about by non-binary and trans performers. Digging deeper into the history and standards of drag performance falls outside the scope of this book. For those wishing more information, in addition to watching things like RuPaul's *Drag Race* (now in its 15th season), I recommend academic works such as the Mountfort et al. 2019 book *Planet Cosplay*. They provide interesting discussion into the similarities and differences between *doing* drag and *being* transgender, noting "this is where the agnostic but never separable relationship between homage and parody comes in" (p. 240). They also offer the term "dragsplay" which, though self-explanatory, entails a level of description again outside the boundaries of this study.

A similar, often gender-based, lifestyle performance is found in the practice of *burlesque*. Though defined by Merriam-Webster as primarily a literary or dramatic work that seeks to ridicule by means of "grotesque exaggeration," "comic imitation," or "caricature," it seems most commonly understood as forms of entertainment that are "broadly humorous," "often earthy," and which may include "striptease acts." Those needing visual examples can turn to the Kit Kat Club's skits and dances performed by Sally Bowles (Liza Minnelli) and company in the 1972 film *Cabaret* (or, more recently, by Cher and Christina Aguilera in the aptly named 2010 film *Burlesque*).

Though it might seem a fine line, there is a distinction between a striptease act that might occur in a theater or cabaret, and a strip act that takes place in a gentleman's club. Actually, it's less a line that can be crossed, and more of a continuum. Just as there is cosplay, and artistic yet erotic cosplay, and solely erotic cosplay, and cosporn, there are similar gradations in things like pin-up modeling and burlesque performance. As explained in the Preface, the focus in this book is on the more family-friendly end of the continuum. The other levels have all the media exposure they need. I leave it to the reader to make their own decisions about what belongs in each category. Each of us has the right to decide, as did Supreme Court Justice Potter Stewart in the famous 1964 obscenity trial *Jacobellis v. Ohio*, who admitted he couldn't define what was pornographic, "but I know it when I see it."

In performance burlesque, the costume is an important part of the script and character. As explained by performer Minnie D'Moocha (cited in Cline, 2017), "We always say in burlesque that it's not about the nudity, it's the story we tell along the way." She practices a unique form of the art labeled *nerdlesque*, which blends burlesque performance with pop culture themes, such as dressing as comic characters. Ironically, while she feels safe in fetish or goth communities, she observes that the nerd communities tend to be the cruelest. "We are all becoming aware of how we shouldn't shame those that are overweight, or of a different race than their character, or who purchase their costumes," she states, but adds, "I have noticed an awful lot of hate being directed for the cosplayers that also do burlesque. Or that do adult modeling, or artistic cosplay nudes. 'They're not real cosplayers' 'They only do it for the attention' 'They're sluts.'" Minnie points out that she is has won multiple awards in craftsmanship in cosplay. On top of that skill set, she says, "I am a burlesque dancer. I pose for artistic cosplay nude sites. I am not a slut…I do not do it for attention. I do it for my art."

Nudism

When I finished interviewing Angel Cardon, whom you'll meet in this chapter's Costume Conversations, I was reflecting on just how critical the choices of clothing were to her sense of self. Simultaneously, I was reading some of the researcher's comments I'll share next. Suddenly I thought, if what you put *on* can make such a difference to your identity, can the same be said of what you take *off*? Given my definition of *conscious choices* about clothing, *outside the norm,* in *select settings*, I wondered if *nudism* could be a form of costume? Keep in mind, I am not talking about the sexualized form of nudity that takes place in men's clubs or adult websites. Ironically, if your job *requires* you to be nude, your bare skin is just another kind of uniform. The focus here is more about lifestyle choices.

Back (1985) argued that clothing "occupies a special place, as the manner of communication which is closest, metaphorically and literally, to the self. It covers what it to be private and shows the world the presentation a person wants to make" (p. 6). What if, in making that decision, we choose to uncover what most would keep private? As Barnard noted, "the nude or naked body is deeply, and sometimes shockingly, meaningful" (1996, p. 19). Can it be meaningful in the same way that cosplay and costume can be? Even RuPaul's famous and oft-repeated quote "Everyone is born naked. The rest is drag" (cited in Mongan, 2015) gives pause for thought. Drag is clearly a costume which reveals aspects of the performer's personality. Is there something equally revealing (pun not intended) about nudity?

To find out, I traveled to Mountain Air Ranch, a family nudist resort located southwest of Denver, CO. The management was welcoming but cautious. I promised my intent was to celebrate people's stories and that everything would be handled with respect. The rules of etiquette were clearly explained; foremost among them being to *look at people in the eyes*. Also, only first names and last initials are to be used. Obviously, I was not allowed to take photographs that included any people, though I was able to take shots of the entrance sign and a metal family sculpture (see Image 5.5). While we will meet two members in more detail in Costume Conversation #15, I'll briefly introduce you to a few people here.

Image 5.5 *Mountain Air Ranch family sculpture*

The first thing you notice is how comfortable everyone seems to be. While some people are relaxing outside their motor homes as you head to the clubhouse, most people are gathered around the pool or hot tub. It does not take long to experience the truth of an observation by Lewis and Lewis (1990) about constant nudity: it "has a tendency to lose its shock value and does an about-face by becoming boring" (p. 136). Once that occurs, it was easy to look people in the eye and ask them their story. The biggest theme you hear is that nudity is a great equalizer. That seems odd to hear after interviewing so many cosplayers concerned about body-shaming. While clothing (and last names) might create status differences on the outside, they do not exist on the resort property.

Ellen R. made her first visit to the ranch, by herself, on her 30th wedding anniversary. Her husband, a pilot, was overseas despite the importance of the day, and he'd never been interested in checking the place out. Ellen returned home from her visit and filed for divorce, telling me that Mountain Air helped her get through and provided her with "a new community, a new life." She explained, somewhat embarrassed, that she'd been raised with racist views, particularly against Mexicans and Blacks. Now, she tells me, "You forget race, because it doesn't matter." She recalls a time she saw family photos of a friend from the ranch and noticed that his children looked Hispanic. It was only then she realized that the friend himself was Hispanic. For Ellen, when clothing disappears, so does race.

John Y. has been a member since 2002. He tells me that, pre-internet, he was in a bookstore looking for information about hot spring locations in Colorado. "There was a section for nude hot springs, and places to go that were nude. I needed something out of the box, and I wanted to experience the feeling -an awakening, an awakening of the senses - of being in the freedom of the sun and the water." He came to Mountain Air and found what he was looking for. "I really did get hooked."

He is sitting by the pool with his girlfriend, Jen N. This is her first day at the ranch. I discovered that the term for this is "nudeginity" day (a play on the word "virginity"). After they'd dated a while, John told her he enjoyed spending time at Mountain Air Ranch. She thought, "Horseback riding?" He explained that, no, it was nude resort, and asked her if she wanted to go. "I kind of avoided it for a bit, then said alright, okay," she says. And her first impression? "I thought everybody was going to be more 'checking each other out.' Like a runway model. You know, kind of shaming. I was wrong. It's a very liberated free people."

"It levels the playing field," says Kelli S., as she sits in the hot tub with a half dozen others. Her friend Mark S. agrees, telling me that you can enjoy hanging out with 15-20 others, laughing and drinking, yet, "You don't know if you're talking to a ditch digger or if you're talking to the CEO of a multinational bank, because you're all on the same playing field and there is zero judgment." He elaborates, "It doesn't matter freckles, it doesn't matter fat, fur…" A voice behind me agrees. I turn and meet Jesus G. (whom you'll meet soon in #15) saying "Everybody's beautiful…that's it."

Summary
Shukla states, "We are always acting for some part for which we must dress. Every morning, in our most common creative activity, we get dressed, and in getting dressed we answer the question of who we plan to be for that day; we choose an identity" (2015, p. 3). The identity, or identities, we choose reflects our fashion sensibilities and our lifestyle choices. We can examine those choices by looking at personalities (e.g., clothing consciousness, exhibitionism, practicality, designer leanings) or via the feminine-masculine distinctions of the Yin-Yang as it relates to traits and textures. In our Spotlight Story, we meet Rob and Kyla, who manifest their love for costumes in a special effects laden photo booth recreating scenes from popular films. From there we visit the most popular of all lifestyle hangouts, the Renaissance festival, and discuss the various levels of participation. Participation is also the key factor in related activities such as the Society for Creative Anachronism (SAC) and Live Action Role Playing (LARP). The lifestyle focus concludes with stories from tattoo, drag, burlesque, and nudism communities, showing the variety of ways people use clothing, or the lack thereof, to express themselves.

COSTUME CONVERSATION # 13
Michael Schluter
a.k.a. St. Patrick's Day leprechaun

Thomas G. Endres, PhD ♦ 222

At the St. Patrick's Day street celebration, called Blarney on the Block, I stopped Michael because he was the most ornately dressed of all the green-adorned partiers. Initially, I just wanted a picture, but after I explained my book project to him, he let me know he had very clear ideas on the importance of costume and identity. He was not kidding! In some interviews, you have to push, pull, bribe, and cajole people into talking. With Michael I was able to turn on the tape recorder and lean back.

Originally from Lincoln, NE, Michael spent his youth between Nebraska with his father and stepmother, and Colorado with his mother. His dad, trained in finance, and stepmom, in service, owned a restaurant in Scottsbluff, NE – among the top ten in the state - which Michael worked at and occasionally managed. From them he learned the importance of hospitality; it helped shape his life as a professional. "I love hospitality because it engages people," Michael begins. "It adds value." Value, we will learn, is the standard for which he strives. From his mother, he learned to dance, bake, and celebrate life on the stage that was her kitchen. This helped shape his appreciation of holidays and costumes. "I like celebrating holidays. I like going all out on things. Obviously, St. Patrick's Day has kind of been my favorite. But I love Christmas. I dressed up as Santa Claus for my sisters when they were little, and brought gifts. I've done that now with my nieces and nephews. There's a joy of giving."

Of course, it is not just holidays that inspire Michael's attire. It has been an important part of his identity his entire life. "I've always liked to dress up. I'd wear ties to school, and I always liked to look sharp. I always had an interest in theater and music, from a very early age. I loved it. I loved entertainment as a whole. Loved watching old shows on *Nick at Nite* with my grandmother, and variety shows like old *Johnny Carson* episodes. Loved Sammy Davis, Jr. and people that could dance. All these people had unique flair." That love of flair and entertainment led him to an early life-lesson about costume. One of the holidays he enjoyed was Valentine's Day. In high school he sang with a quartet that did singing Valentines. One year, he decided to go solo. He purchased some roses, put on a tuxedo, and tells me, "I made about $600 that day. I made more money in that single day than I ever made before or since."

Opportunities to explore continued to pop up in Michael's life. He was a mascot at both his high school (Enoch the Eagle) and junior college (Carl the Cougar). "I really loved being a mascot. It's fun because it elicits a response, positive or negative. And you get both," he muses, concluding that the worst part about his mascot days was passing out inside the costume because it was so hot. "And I got a scholarship for it; that was kind of cool!"

When not in mascot costume, he could often be found on the theatrical stage. "There's a great community college in Scottsbluff that has a pretty decent theater and music program. I got a scholarship to go out there, and wound up doing some repertoire theater. It was a great place for me to progress and define direction, both in terms of my interest in theater, but also in terms of hospitality, which is what I've spent most of my life doing." He went on to graduate in musical theater from the University of Northern Colorado, "One of the top four 4-year degree programs globally," and then attended the Broadway Theater Project summer training in Tampa, FL, where he spent time with multi-Tony winners like Patrick Wilson and Terrance Mann.

He is currently giving back that experience to the next generation, directing a high school version of Studs Terkel's play *Working: The Musical* – a series of vignettes about blue-collar workers and their jobs. "It's personal. A lot of people take a ton of pride in what they do. They go through lots of hardships. I love the way it impacts people." He informed his students what he expected them to accomplish when they walked in front of the audience: "Within the first two seconds, to know exactly what that person does. Before they say a word, I want them to know their occupation by their costume, by the scenery, by the circumstance – but mostly the costume!"

The big picture lesson he hopes to impart to them is that *what you wear* matters. "When somebody sees you, it's the first thing they know about you. Right? First impression, right? You don't get a chance to go back on it. When you're developing a character on stage or in film, it really can draw into light who you want your character to be. And I believe your 'character' in life is what matters. Your *character*. When you're developing that, whether it's through clothing, or background information, all those things tell a story." Granted, he admits going through phases in his life where he dressed in order to be accepted by the crowd: t-shirts with cartoon logos in high school, rock band t-shirts with leather jackets in junior college, and designer labels and professional styles when hanging around with "musical theater, Broadway wanna-be's." Michael tells his students what they wear will impact people's perceptions of them. "And perception does matter. Everybody says, 'I don't care what other people think.' I argue that you should. If you don't care what other people think," he asks, "how are you going to impact them?"

"We build ourselves the same way we would outfit a building," he continues. "The exterior is the first thing you see. You judge a book by its cover. You do whether you want to or not. Which isn't necessarily such a bad thing." Given that, what style does he follow, or what style does he recommend to his students? "The way you dress should be inviting. It should be not so contrary; maybe a little edgy to define yourself, but not so it alienates other people. There's just such a delicate balance to find in whatever you wear. If it's celebratory, flamboyant – does it engage or alienate? Does it add *value*? Does it not?"

These are good questions, I agree. But where in all this, I wonder, does the leprechaun outfit belong? With a grin, Michael explains, "Life's too short not to celebrate everything you can! Every holiday is worth celebrating, no matter what culture it is, because it's a time to look back and cherish and have fun. There's so much *business* to do the rest of the time, that I think making something special, dressing in a different way, doing anything you can to celebrate those special moments, are fun." He explains to me that, despite being "only a fraction of Celtic descent," he has loved Irish culture since childhood. "Clear back then, I was really interested in gnomes, leprechauns, and Celtic mythology. I had this little family of leprechauns that lived on the refrigerator, and they went on adventures, and I told stories with them –

moving them around on the refrigerator." From that, he and his mother did a "reverse trick-or-treat" each St. Patrick's Day. "My mom and I would make sugar cookies in Irish shapes – a little pipe, a little horseshoe, a little leprechaun hat - and decorate them. We'd go around the neighborhood to people we knew and take them a little plate of cookies. I was dressed as a leprechaun - I got one of those little plastic, junky derbies - and it was fun. We did the same thing with May baskets on May Day. My mom was very much about celebrating. I got a lot of that from her; the creative end came a lot from her."

During high school, the "plastic, junky" derby gave way to a nicer green hat. He replaced the buckle and ribbon because the version from the store didn't look authentic. As with so many costumes we've seen throughout this book, the quality of his outfit improved with time. So did his appreciation of all-things Irish. "Just the mysteriousness of it;

it's such a celebratory culture, and so unique, too. And I love Irish music; just haunting, beautiful sounds in that." In fact, during college, he started working for an Irish pub – one that required its male employees to wear a kilt. "They actually bought it for you!" He now owns several kilts, but the one in our photograph is his favorite; it's the greenest. As time passed, he added the sporran and the high socks "It's just been a real evolution of what that looks like. Kind of a combination of my original leprechaun and also more authentic kilts and shoes and those kinds of things, over the years." For Michael, it helps him do a thing he loves most: "Telling cultural stories."

He has been able to share his story in several venues. In his hometown, he has been photographed a half-dozen times over the years sporting his signature look. In 2022 he even wore the costume to the St. Patrick's Day parade in Boston. Despite being in a "sea of green," he was one of very few in an authentic kilt. "I was actually – optically – the most flamboyant in terms of what I was wearing. Everybody we walked by, 'Nice 'fit.' *(Author's note: slang for "outfit")*. It's fun to get those kind of responses." He was even photographed to be featured in promotional material for Guinness beer!

Of course, one of the most enjoyable elements of wearing a costume is having other people pay attention to it. "I've been *acknowledged*; that's one of my things. Everybody kind of knows that I love it. My wife always says, 'Are you getting the attention you need today? Is this going to last you for a while?'" He pauses here, because he wants to make a serious point. "It *is* fun. I'm not going to say I don't enjoy that. But, at the same time, people *want* to come and take pictures with you. Little kids *want* to come up and say hi. I love that. It's more about what it does for other people than even what it does for me."

That, ultimately, is Michael's lesson. To his students. To those he serves in restaurants. To those he entertains as a leprechaun, or as Santa Claus, or whoever befits the holiday that comes around. Lifting people up. Adding value. "I love bringing people into my circle. My wife says I'm Bacchus *(Author's note: the Roman god of wine, festivities, pleasure)*. I like celebrating; I like bringing people together to do that. These events, whether it's entertainment or community events, parades, all those kind of things are an opportunity to bring people together."

"It's interesting in this post-COVID situation, we lost a lot of those together times, and I think people are really thirsty for it now," he observes. He feels an obligation, given the lessons from his parents and from his professors, to keep the celebrations going. "I love hospitality and theater because it's all about the way you think and the way you portray yourself. Psychology is so intertwined with what we wear and how we present ourselves. There are *definitive* reasons why people wear what they wear. I think, by and large, it gives them purpose and excitement." That purpose, that excitement, is Michael's gift to the world. "I feel there's enough sad things in life," he concludes, having made a clear case for his costumed characters. "Yes, it's celebratory. Yes, it's an attention-getter, but does it add value? I think it does."

COSTUME CONVERSATION # 14
Angel Cardon
a.k.a. Dottie Lucille

In a tone both gracious and no-nonsense, Angel informs me, "I'm a pin-up model. I've been doing that for about eight years now. I love doing that. I call it using my powers for good." And her stage name? Dottie Lucille? "Dottie and Lucille were both my grannies, and I felt very strongly about honoring them by using their names. My pin-up persona is very 50s housewife, girl-next-door, wholesome. I don't do lingerie, I don't do nudity, I don't do bikinis – and so I felt good using their names in my modeling because of that."

Today we are doing a patriotic photo shoot. Memorial Day is fast approaching. Angel's entire ensemble, including purse, gloves, and pearls, are in keeping with the red, white, and blue theme. After learning the basics about her pin-up modeling, she provides more details about her background and employment. "I went to school to become a teacher, and came back after I graduated to start teaching in the school district that I grew up in. I started teaching because I wanted to influence young minds to love learning, when they're most influenceable. I like influencing people in positive directions." After a few years teaching, she moved into the public sector. "For my day job I'm a business consultant. I help small, especially minority owned, businesses to gain government contracts to grow their business."

Outside of work, Angel has found her calling working with a nationwide charity known as the Battlin' Betties, who dress in 40s and 50s garb to honor first responders and veterans. Her first event with the Betties was a 100th birthday party for a veteran. "Both the birthday boy and his partner, they just talked about how wonderful it was to see the outfits and the hairstyles of yesteryear and spend time with people who cared about those things." Beyond just the clothing, Betties are trained to communicate effectively with people who have PTSD and have been in combat situations. "That has been special as far as going out into the community, because we're not just pretty faces. We have invested time in being able to be effective and do good in the community with what we have."

"I participated in Honor Flight for the first time," she says, describing a recent event. "It was the first one they were able to have in two years. It was such a blessing to me. I met a World War II veteran. I was wearing a blue Navy type of suit and he took my hand and asked 'Are you in the Navy? I was in the Navy.' I got to hear his stories, and the stories of all the others that were on the Honor Flight for this session." For Angel, the most heartbreaking and most rewarding part of the event was the opportunity to acknowledge Vietnam veterans "who didn't come home to cheers and celebration – we got to do that for them. They stood up and said, 'This is the first time we came home to someone celebrating the service that we provided.'"

Obviously, the main reason I wanted to talk to Angel was because of the 40s and 50s pin-up garb, but I didn't contact her simply because she is a Battlin' Bettie. There are many Betties available to interview. I wanted to speak with Angel because she doesn't just dress in this attire at veterans or first responder events – it is because she dresses like this *daily*, with or without an event. This is her lifestyle choice. "For me personally, I dress like I'm dressed today pretty much every day. I've always, since I was an adult and could buy my own things, worn pearls and heels and dresses." There are, of course, some minor differences between daily and event appearance. "I usually don't wear a full face of makeup, just eyelashes and a lighter lipstick. I don't wear true vintage in my daily life because I have three little boys, and I really like to preserve my nice true vintage outfits and jewelry. But I do wear replicas pretty much every day. Heels, pearls, dresses, nails, hair."

Some people get it, and some people don't. "A lot of people will say 'What are you so dressed up for?' or 'Are you dressed up for this, that, or the other?' or 'Oh, I like your costume.' For me, it's *not* a costume. These are my real clothes that I wear every day. I actually sleep in pearls, I shower in pearls, I do everything in pearls. I wear heels when I'm cooking dinner or breakfast for my kids. I take them to school dressed like this. I wear yoga pants if I'm going to yoga, but in my daily life this is how I dress. And people will say 'Why do you look like that? Where are you going to?' and I say, 'I just dress like this.'" Recently, she was invited to a birthday party where they planned to go dancing. She was told everyone would be wearing "jeans and glittery shirts," to which Angel had to reply, "I might own a pair of jeans, but they're for yard work!"

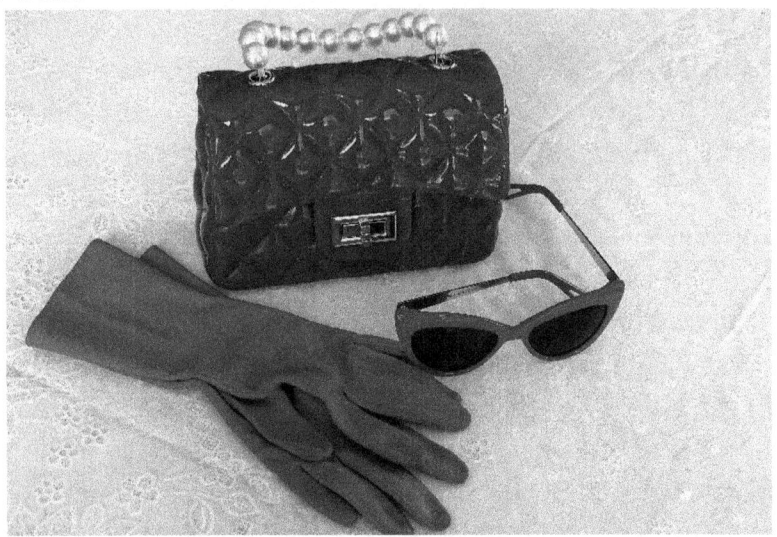

Not only does it frustrate her when people describe her daily wear as a costume, it frustrates her that she has to compete with costume-wearers to find vintage clothes. "At Halloween time, I go to the thrift store to buy my actual clothes, because that's when they put out more of them. But people are there to buy them to just dress up and play. A lot of true vintage has been damaged or destroyed by people ripping it up for dead-bride or dead-Prom Queen or different types of costumes. It really makes me sad, because those are things we can't ever replace. They are not things that were mass produced. Some of them were handmade, and now they're gone forever."

At this point, the obvious question about Angel's attire is…why? What is it that she finds most appealing? "I really like how the community was when they had sewing circles and cocktail parties and potlucks. We shared recipes. We went to bowling night with our partners. On the men's side of things, they had smoking clubs or bowling leagues. I feel that community was more close knit. I miss Mayberry, where everybody was sitting on the porch drinking cherry Coke and just talking and really connecting." Obviously, she realized there were also shortcomings to the time period. "The era I'm representing was very limiting, actually, in being able to represent yourself in clothing. Limitations, first of all, because of the war and access to materials. Second of all, because modestly was a much bigger thing then. We have a lot more freedom now, and it's great that people are able to use that to express themselves. There are so many factors, but it's great that we have the freedom to make that choice, consequences be what they may be."

Even if others chose not to join her, she finds a lot of support in the community. "I get a lot of women who say, 'I used to have a hat just like that. My mother had a hat just like that.' A lot of people give me things that were their mother's, grandmother's, or spouse's, because they want it to go to someone who will cherish it and wear it, or will cherish it and preserve it. I try to always honor whatever that is. I have a collection of things that are precious and vintage that will never be worn, that I just keep safe. And I have a collection of items that are vintage and wonderful, and I get to wear out in public." Speaking of spouses, Angel tells me that her husband fully supports her lifestyle choice, even though he rarely dresses in similar fashion. "He has a bowler shirt with the 8-ball logo, and I purchased for him loafers, but it's not his thing. He does it to try and match me when we go out. Mostly his support is taking care of our three boys so I have the time to invest in doing this. To have an hour-and-forty-five minutes of uninterrupted time to get ready like this, it takes a second person to wrangle three little wild boys."

An hour-and-forty-five minutes? Every day? Yes, Angel confirms, but explains that it is worth it, based on how it makes her feel. "I feel very put together and collected. In the morning, when I'm getting ready, I put on a dress and heels and pearls. It's very light lashes, light brows, and pink lips. Resetting my wig. Lining my eyebrows. Lining my eyes. Getting my lashes just right. Putting on foundation, powder, setting spray, everything. The time and care I put into this look, it makes me feel collected, it makes me feel I invested time in myself and the way I'm presenting myself. That is part of the 1950s woman as well. You were supposed to fix your lipstick, fix your hair, put on a clean apron, and be presentable when anyone came over."

Given the work she puts in daily, coupled with her view that what she wears is *not* a costume, I'm worried my focus might offend. I tell her my definition of costume (e.g., *conscious choice, outside of the norm, special or public settings*), and ask if she is okay being included in a book that has *costume* in the title. She is. "I don't take offense to that at all," she assures me. She acknowledges that her choices *are* outside the norm, but she uses that to create a *new* norm. "For me, I use it to draw my norm to myself, and become part of a community where I felt I belonged and wanted to participate in. I chose my people." On top of that, Angel has a lot of experience with the cosplay and costume worlds, and she understands the importance of costume play in the creation of identity. She worked for a company that did princess parties, so has dressed as "Sleeping Beauty, Elsa, Snow White, most of the princesses. Due to the pandemic, I primarily do that virtually for my friends' daughter's birthday parties. Also, my little boys love superheroes, so I have a bevy of superhero costumes that I'll wear if we're playing around the house."

Knowing that, I ask her about a prominent theme here in the book – culture and appropriation. Would she, for example, dress as ethnic-specific princesses like Jasmine or Mulan? "I personally wouldn't," she answers, "because I have read the Instagram posts and the Facebook posts of women of color who either have been discriminated against by 'house of mouse'-type places, where they are letting Caucasian women portray women of color. Knowing how they feel personally about it, I choose not to do that." Beyond that, however, she is all for people using costumes to explore identity issues. "I personally don't feel there should be a boundary. You know, little boys in princess dresses, little girls in princess dresses, little girls in Jack Sparrow costumes. However you want to dress up and represent yourself, especially if you're doing it as a costume, I think that's fine."

My final question is again one of identity. Is there a difference between Angel Cardon and Dottie Lucille? "Yes. Moreso now than ever," she answers quietly. "Dottie Lucille is really this Marilyn Monroe-esque, blonde, curly, short hair, ruby red lips. Two years ago, I had some pregnancy complications and multiple surgeries, alopecia, staph infection – so now I don't have my own hair; I wear a wig all the time. In my daily life I typically wear a long brunette wig. Initially I had my own blonde Marilyn Monroe hair that I could curl and style. Now, where I do have hair, Angel has salt-and-pepper, gray and white. These are not my eyelashes. I draw in my eyebrows. The type of alopecia and hormone issues I have now, I have decreased coloration in my skin. I wear lipstick." Adding to her story, she informs me she was recently diagnosed with skin cancer. "I'm going to be having surgery on my face, so this interview and photo shoot is very special to me because it will be the last time that I'm photographed and captured in the way that I see myself now, and the way I experience my identity now. I feel like a universe-thing brought us together at time, to capture that before I have a major shift in my identity again."

Author's Note: I contacted Angel after her surgery. All went well and, with makeup, she can conceal any after-effects. Her hair has begun to grow back slowly. I'm confident she will move forward with a positive self-image, complete with her ever-present sense of taste and tact. "If you lay out ham and cheese you have lunch," she told me during the interview. "But if you pay attention to presentation, you have charcuterie."

COSTUME CONVERSATION # 15
Erin B. and Jesus G.
a.k.a. Their Natural Selves

"**I**'ve been nude my whole life," says Erin. "I'm an only child, so I didn't have to compete with anyone; you know, 'who's got the clothes?' And plus, I was in dance, so I was used to changing clothes in a group of people constantly. My modesty is very low."

In contrast, my modesty level is higher. I've been doing ethnographic research for over four decades, and this is the first time I've ever conducted an interview wrapped only in a towel. I'm speaking with Erin B. and Jesus G. at the Mountain Air Ranch (MAR) nudist resort discussed earlier in Chapter 5. While going over the regulations with the front office staff (such as first names and last initials *only*), it was made clear to me that members would be less willing to speak with me if I were fully clothed. Well, when in Rome.

You've already encountered a number of smaller quotes and stories from MAR members, but I wanted to have a more comprehensive interview for a Costume Conversation. Erin and Jesus happily agreed. The couple has been together four years. Both have children. Each is divorced and, due to both having "very bad former partners," they have promised to stay true to one another, but never live together or get married. They have, however, created an LLC together. Jesus assures me, "An LLC means more than a ring!"

Continuing with her "nude my whole life" quality, Erin explains, "I might walk around my house naked. I might walk around my backyard naked. But to be able to go and get food, to get ice cream, to go and say hi to people with no judgment – that's the part that I didn't have." As for Jesus, he did not have the same kind of upbringing. Originally from Puerto Rico, where public nudity is illegal, he didn't really think about it until he attended college. "Miami, when I went to university, was the first time that I explored my community nudity. But I had never been on a ranch, or with a larger group of people, until here."

Given Erin's comfort level and Jesus's curiosity, exploring nudism seemed a natural thing to do. For a while, they tried going to Air B&B's and being exclusively naked there, but that still had its limitations and kept them indoors. Then they hit a spell, a couple of months, where Erin was feeling very down. Jesus knew he had to find something more permanent and reliable. He states, "I said, you know what? I'm going to do what we always wanted to do; I'm going to find a place, and I found MAR and *(snaps fingers)* instant liberation."

They now spend every weekend at MAR, and have even started helping out with the staff. Jesus serves as an ambassador, doing meet-and-greets with newcomers, and Erin has started working in the kitchen. She tells me, "We love it that much, that we want to keep this thing living and thriving." In fact, just that day, they put their names on the waiting list to get a spot for their camper. Given that there are second and third generation families that still belong to MAR, the typical wait time for a spot is around five years.

One thing they appreciate about the resort is the security and protection for its members. A review board meets regularly and evaluates the behavior of all who enter the gates. Jesus explains, "You got to keep in mind, this is a family resort – there's kids. When something goes a little bit off color and families are present, any minor transgressions, any minor trespass, it's dealt with immediately." I asked if they've seen any such behavior, and get a tag-teamed response:

Erin: "We've not seen it…"

Jesus: "…but we've heard rumblings. We've heard… *(pauses, doesn't provide any detail)*

Erin: "…but they get squashed."

Jesus: "Immediately."

Erin: "Right away."

Once again, they assure me, "This is one of the safest places," though Jesus adds the small disclaimer "Whatever happens after hours is after hours."

They reaffirm for me what we heard from the other members in Chapter 5. Nudity is the great equalizer. Jesus reveals, "This is probably the most, in my life, that I have experienced such a large group of people that have absolutely zero judgment. No one knows who I am. No one knows what I do. Some people, we have become friends *(points to a guy in the hot tub),* but I don't know what he does. He could run Microsoft for all I know. I could dig a trench for all he knows. But here, everybody is the same because we are the way we were born." Erin nods, adding that it is the anonymity that is most rewarding. "It's anonymous," Jesus enthusiastically agrees, "There is zero, zero judgment here. None. Everybody here is equal. This is utopic. Nobody is looking at what brand of jeans I'm wearing. Or if I'm wearing a Pink Floyd t-shirt, like, oh, 'Why Pink Floyd? Why not Grateful Dead?' There's no conflicts. Everybody here is in their own skin."

And with that equality comes a sense of comfort, belonging, and freedom. "I think the one beautiful thing, us coming up here," Erin says, "I'm free. I don't have to worry about what I'm wearing. Am I comfortable? Yes, I'm comfortable. *(Pointing to those around the pool),* They're comfortable. And that to me is what this place offers – is comfort. There is something about being in your skin, of being in the mountain air, of being in this climate with other people who aren't judging, aren't making side looks. We really feel at home here." Connecting nudism and costume, she even compares the experience to a cosplay Con by giving the example of a shy youth who puts on a costume and becomes more sociable. "There's something about being 'in your skin,' like the anime people call their costumes their skin; there is something that these conventions do provide, that produce and promote people to be who they really are."

Speaking of Cons, they share a story of taking Erin's boys, ages 10 and 12, to an anime convention. Erin made Jesus stick with the boys to "put the guardrails on" if need be. In fact, they were surprised that a vendor was selling hentai (adult and often pornographic anime and manga). In their eyes, MAR is far safer than a Con. Of course, that doesn't mean their kids are interested. Erin would bring her kids, but they "are of the mindset that this is not for them. I'm trying to convince them they need to come. This would be perfect for them." Similarly, Jesus would like to bring his daughter, "But I'm waiting for the right time." Because MAR is so family oriented, and because the rules about behavior are so clear, they feel it's a great environment for young men and women to learn social skills.

Throughout this book, we've seen the important role that costume – what you choose to wear - plays not only in the development of social skills, but also in one's sense of personal well-being. It's now becoming clear that the conscious choice to not wear something can produce similar benefits. As Jesus already noted, it was because Erin was feeling blue that he sought out MAR. Her view now? "I have never felt more myself than I am here," she says, adding "This place is empowering. I love this place. It's a breath of fresh air. People are a breath of fresh air." Jesus follows up, reminding her of a previous conversation, "The thing that you told me that was so impactful was, that people make you feel so comfortable, it's the first time in your life that you actually felt..." Erin smiles lightly and finishes the sentence for him "...popular."

But, for the couple, it goes beyond that feeling of belonging. Erin tells me that, before coming to MAR, she was struggling with clinical issues and an eating disorder. "I came here, and it was all forgotten. All of it. Why? No one else cares, why should I care?" Jesus, too, wrestled with past trauma. "I went through a hard therapy for two years for things that happened in my childhood. And my therapist exorcised a lot of things. The first time we came in here, I said, if I would have discovered MAR two years ago, I would have never had to go to therapy; would have never!" Erin understands, adding, "If I had come here at eighteen, as a child, never would have needed all the therapy that I've had." For Erin and Jesus, MAR and the choice of nudism is all the therapy they need.

That led me to ask, if they feel so at home here, how do they feel when they have to return to the clothed world? Erin's reply is quick. "Depressed. I'm depressed. Absolutely, I am fucking depressed. 100%. I have to wear clothes?" Jesus agrees, "For me, also, I get bummed out. I go, oh my god, I've got to go back to work Monday, and I'm going to have to put on something to be on a Zoom, and it brings me down. Monday through Friday I have to cater to everybody else. Everybody else wants me dressed, everybody else wants me to work and be a certain way and play a different role. This is the only time, on the weekends, that I can actually say to myself, I am Jesus, I am who I am."

Hoping I will understand the analogy, Jesus says, "This is what Haight-Ashbury didn't get right. This is the refinement of what Haight-Ashbury wanted to do. This is executed right." Having just taught a unit on the 1960s, I know just what he is saying. So many attempts were made in the 60s to legitimize the drug culture. Peter Fonda tried it in *Easy Rider*. Ken Kesey (author of *One Flew Over the Cuckoo's Nest*) drove around the country in a day-glow painted bus with the Merry Pranksters, trying to launch LSD events called "acid tests." Drug guru Timothy Leary encouraged us to "Turn on, tune in, drop out." And much of this counter-culture activity was centered around the Haight-Ashbury neighborhood in San Francisco *("Be sure to wear some flowers in your hair")*. And they all failed. Drugs did not provide the peace and love that the movement promised. Jesus believes that nudism is the answer they were looking for.

Jesus concludes with a series of statements that prove why he is the right choice as newcomer ambassador to MAR. "It's the people. It's the community. Everybody cares for each other. It is a support system." He has proven his point. By this time, I've forgotten I'm wearing only a towel. "If you've ever a conflict with self-esteem," he continues, "if you ever felt judged, if you had to resort to a vice to escape how you felt about yourself, spend a weekend at a nudist ranch, because all that stuff will be forgotten. This is like frickin' heaven."

CHAPTER 6

Research, Rules, and Wrapping Up
*All humans play a number of different roles in their lifetime,
and the transition from one role to another is marked by costume.*
Brownie and Graydon, 2016, p. 34

The quote above originates from Brownie and Graydon's 2016 book on superhero costumes. It is not a book on cosplay; it is an academic analysis of the actual outfits worn by superheroes as depicted in comics and movies. They compare their ideas to earlier studies on "power dressing," where regular humans make choices about clothing to "make the wearer appear dominant, and therefore more successful" (p. 31). The authors equate the superhero who shifts back and forth between alter ego and hero persona with the normal person who takes off their work clothes when they get home and put on something more comfortable. "The two roles that this individual plays, marking home life apart from professional role, are distinct, and the clothes that signify each role can never be exchanged without unwanted connotations" (pp. 34-35).

Along that line, this book also has a dual identity. I'm not sure which part is the "alter ego" and which part is the "secret identity," but I am trying to manage two distinct "personalities." On the one hand, because much of this book is funded university research, there are a few elements I need to include in order to uphold academic principles found in a journal article or a textbook. On the other hand, I also want this project to be user-friendly, as the hoped-for audience extends beyond the academy. Rather than jumping back and forth into a phone booth to change costumes, I have attempted to juggle the academic and the public consumption sides throughout. Hopefully that hasn't created the "unwanted connotations" warned above, but rather a balanced narrative that has both educated and entertained. As we near the end of our journey, I offer closing arguments structured around the headings from the chapter title: Research, Rules, and Wrapping Up.

Research

One of the earmarks of a good research project is a discussion of the study's strengths and limitations. I think the aforementioned decision to combine both the rigor of academic study with the informality and conversational tone of public access was a good one. It might seem lopsided in spots, but I think the overall interplay is successful. For example, a lot of published research has a section titled Literature Review, where the author compiles and summarizes all of their outside resources. Given the 100+ books and journals quoted here, not to mention the dozens of interviews conducted, it seemed best to spread those resources throughout the chapters, rather than clump them all together.

I think another strength comes from the fact that I'm studying what I love. At first you might think, "Oh, yeah, we saw some of his costumes. He loves cosplay." Well, though that's true, what I really love to research is *stories*. My entire career has been about examining *rhetorical communities*; that is, communities of people who are bonded not because of a geographic locale, but rather a *symbolic* one. People who share the same storylines, the same heroes and villains, the same plots and places, and the same reasons for doing what they do. Over the decades, that has led to me examine the cultures of diverse collectives, ranging from single mother self-depictions, to father-daughter relationships, to fraternal organization PR campaigns, to the involvement of laity in religious activities.

Some of those studies required me to take pictures. As I explain in my Preface, I am an amateur photographer at best. But some of the communities, like the biker and tattoo examples provided throughout, needed to have pictures. And here, the costume and cosplay community stories make the best sense when you can *see* the people who are speaking. I think photos help bring the stories to life. Beyond that, yes, I do like costumes and cosplay. Like those pictured in Image 6.1, I grew up loving Halloween and still celebrate it with gusto. I also did theater in high school, so continued my love of costume in plays like *Finian's Rainbow*, *The Odd Couple*, *Guys and Dolls*, and *Once Upon a Mattress*.

Image 6.1 *University faculty and staff annual Halloween celebration, 2022*

Other seeds got planted as well. When I was an undergraduate student, years before Takahashi and colleagues coined the term *cosplay*, I remember studying clothing impact in a course titled Nonverbal Communication. The textbook, by Henley (1977), looked at sexism in fashion. For example, she claimed the tendency to make women's clothing out of fragile materials like lace and chiffon created an associated feeling that women were likewise fragile. In fact, fashion actually reinforced related behaviors: "The frailty of the material, its fineness and therefore difficulty of cleaning (compelling one to avoid getting it dirty), and the design of the clothing have combined to restrict women's movements in many ways. Skirts, for example, have kept many girls and women from engaging in certain physical activities and sitting in certain positions" (p. 90). Fashionable shoes, restrictive undergarments, and contour-hugging designs, making pockets rare and requiring women to carry purses, further limit physical activity.

In contrast, looking at choices for men, she discussed decisions made when dressing the defendants - Haldeman, Ehrlichman, and Mitchell - in the Watergate trial accusing then-President Nixon's confederates of breaking into a Washington DC hotel to steal documents from the opposing party. To relate to the predominantly black jury, the men moved away from their normal pinstripe suits, which might offend, to light colored suits with sporty, non-authoritarian neckties. As history proves, they all received light sentences. Henley titled this section "Clothes Make the Man Not Responsible" (p. 87). So, yes, I got hooked early on.

Years later I was teaching my own course in Nonverbal Communication. My textbook at the time, Leathers (1997), took a similar look at the impact of attire. Recall his suggestion that "dressing to appear credible or dominant" may negatively impact likability and interpersonal attractiveness. As the Watergate study demonstrated, we might respect your power suit, but that doesn't mean we'll like or be attracted to the person inside it. With lessons like that, in retrospect, I was destined to write a book like this.

As for limitations, this study has a few. Story-focused research like this is called ethnography (basically, the study of people and cultures), and the practice itself has built-in potholes. "A researcher has or imposes no control over what he or she sees or hears. The only choice he or she has is where/which location and who to study" (Kawamura, 2011, p. 45). In other words, I might not like what someone has to say, or the way a subgroup acts, but I need to report it anyway. Even more limiting is Kawamura's follow-up observation that ethnographic studies of clothing and style tend to be devalued by academics: "fashion as a research topic is still considered very marginal, on the periphery of any intellectual discussions" (p. 121). She adds that, because fashion is constantly evolving, the modern-day researcher is always chasing the ever-changing images. The same is true of costumes and cosplay. How many new anime and manga characters have been launched since I started writing? Where will the Marvel and DC universes be by the time this hits print? It is almost impossible to keep up.

Brown (2012) points out that formal ethnographic research, such as anthropological studies of culture, require day-in, day-out living with the culture in question. He says that *most* ethnographic research of subcultures like goths, punks, bikers, and the like, merely employ "qualitative ethnographic methods," but do not follow the method in the strictest sense of the rule (p. 283). He is correct, and that is a potential limitation here. A related limitation, which was also addressed in the Preface, is that there is no way to capture all the stories out there. The best you can do is the best you can do, and you hope you cast a broad enough net to capture a representative cross-section. Most important, of those you do catch, you hope to do their story justice. I've been interviewed many times over the years, and often when I read the finished product, I feel like "I didn't say that" or "That's not what I meant." All one can hope is that a voice was given to someone who previously had not been heard.

The final limitation of research I'll discuss is that of missed opportunities. I had an interview and photo shoot set up with Samantha Oester, who goes by the social media moniker *elemental.cosplay*, during a train layover in Chicago. I was truly looking forward to connecting with Samantha, as her powerful story of struggle and triumph exemplified what I was trying to capture in this book; the power of costume to transform a life. Unfortunately, she was under the weather at our meeting time, and I had a train to catch. But sometimes you luck out, and the limitation can be salvaged. It is unfortunate we were unable to meet but, via email, Samantha shared her story and photography links with me and gave me permission to share them with you.

> **Spotlight Story - Samantha Oester (in her own words)**
> I was first diagnosed with cancer near the beginning of 2013 and went through many different treatments through finally receiving the stamp of "full remission" at the very beginning of 2022. I'm a conservation

biologist who also started my PhD program the spring semester of 2013. The first several years (especially the first few) of being in and out of cancer treatments and going through constant surgeries, I maintained my overachieving personality. I achieved partial remission multiple times, but even during those times, the effects of cancer and cancer treatments were taking their toll. But I was mostly private about my health issues and did not want that part of my life to impact my career. I wanted to deny this, but I noticed cracks starting to appear in my walls after needing a full hysterectomy in late 2016. Then my husband and I moved from the DC area to Chicagoland in 2017.

At this time, I was also hungry for a creative outlet. Some of mine had gone by the wayside while in graduate school, and I could tell that I desperately needed a new one, the emotional and psychological impacts of cancer seeping into my everyday life. I was previously an invited speaker at Dragon Con in Atlanta; in addition to pop culture icons, celebrities, and artists, they invite scientists to come and do multiple panels each year. I loved it and was blown over by the cosplay. It was amazing!! I had been sewing for decades but hadn't done so in a while. I also had a lifelong love of volunteer work and was looking for opportunities I could do with my growing health limitations. Chicago has many comic and pop culture conventions every year, so I made a conscious decision in 2018 (I think?) to make more time for my mental well-being and give cosplaying, causeplaying, and convention-going a go. I immediately fell in love, in a big way.

I started sharing my craft and parts of myself on Instagram, becoming just a little more forthcoming with my private life with each passing year. I was doing volunteer costuming almost every weekend. I was always working on multiple cosplays at the same time. I was going to more and more conventions, photoshoots, and cosplay meetups. I was becoming more outgoing. And I was becoming more comfortable in my own skin. I had a lifetime of body image issues, but through cosplay and constant photos, I started seeing myself differently. These aspects of cosplay are what carried me through my most recent battle in the war cancer waged in me.

My doctors determined near the end of 2020 I needed a full bilateral mastectomy. I thought it should not have been a big deal to me, considering all I had been through. But by this time, I had been struggling with cancer for more than seven years, encompassing chemo, multiple rounds of radiation, more than 30 surgeries, and a wealth of medication to combat cancer and the lasting health issues that went along with it. Every year became more difficult, but the rate at which these difficulties occurred increased around the time we moved to Chicago. So when I received this news, I was already battered. Beaten. Covered in scars, inside and out. And exhausted beyond belief. I was having trouble coming to terms with the fact that I was not and would never be the person I once was. This became my most strenuous time with cancer. As you can see in the captions to my social media posts, I panicked over losing more of myself. I was already in pieces. I needed all those pieces I had left. The thought of losing more became nearly unbearable.

But when I couldn't sleep one night, I got the idea to do something emotionally daring. I decided I wanted some kind of photos before I lost yet more. Not photos as a character, but as myself. I became friends with many local photographers through my cosplay "career" whom I felt I could trust with these precious fragments of me. Thus, it turned into three sets of photos -- before mastectomy, after mastectomy, post-reconstruction -- so I could use the photography as a means to speak openly and publicly about cancer. Then my creative side took over, and it eventually turned into eight sets of photos at different stages, representing various aspects of dealing with cancer that I was going through. When I started posting them, a lot of people said it made them feel seen, seeing these (at times) raw images and putting my story into words they had been struggling to find for themselves.

> Going through this time with cancer while being so isolated due to the pandemic was difficult, especially since this battle gave me the most anxiety. My husband couldn't be with me as much as we wanted him to in the hospital, and that was very hard. But these photos and the vulnerability I was now sharing with thousands provided me with a community who knew what I was going through. I had never been this raw and honest, even with friends, but the many friends I made through cosplay got to know me on a deeper level. I was trusting so many people with my struggle, allowing them to hold these snapshots of my journey. My turmoil. My thoughts. I had never been this exposed. And my ability to do such a thing all boiled down to cosplay.
>
> I truly believe if it wasn't for cosplay, this may have broken me. Being more comfortable in my own skin was exceptionally helpful in dealing with the changes to my body. Being more open helped me finally share my story. Being used to being photographed allowed me to have these images taken, having evidence of my triumph that I could look upon and turning my strife into beautiful works of art. I had never made so many friends before as I have through cosplay, feeling for the first time that I truly had a real community that I learned to lean on.
>
> I am now in full remission, after nine years. I am now an award-winning cosplayer who has been published many times, speaks on panels at conventions, and guests at conventions.
>
> There are eight sets of photos, each containing three photos -- Vulnerability, Strength, Change, Grief, Support, Resilience, Conquest, Triumph. The captions get longer and more open as they go. I have made a LinkTree for you, to keep them organized: https://linktr.ee/elemental.cosplay.breastcancer

Rules

In both ethnographic research works and in popular press regarding cosplay, it makes sense to lay down some ground rules. In this case, many of the rules happen to overlap. Let's look at this section through the cosplay lens, and I'll weave in those comments most relevant to the researcher. We'll begin with one of the most important topics of them all. Taking pictures.

Photography Rules

Whether you are writing a research article or people watching at a Con, if you don't have permission to take someone's picture, DON'T DO IT! Just as I had to get written permission from everyone whose photo shows up in this book, you should also get verbal or written permission from any cosplayer you want to photograph (see Endnote regarding specific requirements for sanctioned research of this nature).

This may seem a bit counter intuitive. As Han (2020) points out, "A long-standing inside joke in the cosplay community is that all cosplayers are hopeless attention-seekers. After all, we don't go through all the trouble of making costumes and dressing up just to prance around in our living rooms. We expect to be stopped for photos whenever we go out in costume. We want people to take photos of us" (p. 93). Similarly, Mountfort et al. (2019) argue that cosplay "lends itself most willingly to the medium of the photo essay" and that cosplayers "can snap into or out of character in an instant, especially when cameras appear" (p. 10). In fact, those authors coin a few new words with this sentence: *Cosphotography* "transcends its immediate settings, and feeds into a larger economy of desire: to be seen and acknowledged within the *cosphere* that is constituted by a vast assemblage and physical and virtual spaces" (p. 57, *emphasis added*).

While all this might be true, it still is common courtesy to ask permission. Granted, if this is a red carpet walk, or a fan group meet-up posing for shots, you do not have to ask permission from all those in the group who are obviously posing for a picture. I'm talking about the individual in the hallway, the one who doesn't see you, the one you are trying to capture clandestinely without their knowing it. That's just creepy. As Zarin (2017) explains, "Cosplayers face an almost constant stream of harassment. Audiences – convention goers, photographers, judges, and industry heads – take photos for adult use without permission, and often fetishize, fat-shame, and slut-shame cosplayers." Noting that many cosplayers come from historically underprivileged groups (gender, age, ethnic minorities), he adds, "It is unsurprising they have concerns about their safety." Mountfort and colleagues are there once again with the correct term, labeling the "pervert" photographers who snap pictures for their own "private fetishes" as "hentai-lech" (2019, p. 132). Even an apparently "candid" shot, like this couple eating in a restaurant (Image 6.2), took place only after permission was granted.

Image 6.2 *Scarlett Witch (Eleanor Dobbles) and Luke Skywalker (Michael Gomer) take a Con break and enjoy lunch at New York's Tick Tock Diner*

As for those larger group shots, snap away. Mountfort et al. go on to say that photography is the *sine qua non* (an essential condition) of cosplay and related media. "Where cosplay groups are concerned," they suggest, "when a camera is raised the whole 'troupe' may spontaneously shift into mode, posing in forms that can resemble posters promoting a Marvel movie or anime show" (p. 61). While visually rich, photos are "superflat" in terms of narrative structure; however, they can be "consumed at leisure" (p. 69). Finally, the scholars comment that such poses evoke memories of the 19th century practice of *tableau vivant*, in which actors would stand still to re-create a pre-existing scene or piece of artwork in detail. Today, cosplayers similarly re-create scenes and poses of their favorite characters. You may photograph those to your heart's content.

Speaking of you as the photographer, here is the final thought on the topic. Rauch and Bolton (2010) argue that the cosplayer is really only half of the equation. The other half, they claim, "is the cameraman (or woman), and there is a strong sense that the photograph is the privileged end product of the entire enterprise" (p. 179). Basically, they argue, photographers have unique and often contradictory goals for their photos. Some want to reproduce the animated frame or manga page as in the *tableau vivant* examples above. Others want to intrude on the frame or the subject, leading to questions about social contexts and relationships. Still others want to see the person emerge from their costumed persona, and even try to pry them out. As such, they conclude, "It is futile or contradictory to construct a canon of cosplay photography" (p. 177). Okay, no *canon* may be possible. But a socially accepted standard of polite behavior is not too much to ask.

Anti-Harassment Rules

Of course, it is not just when taking pictures that we can expect socially appropriate behavior. We need to eliminate all forms of harassment from the cosplay and costumed communities. For many Cons, this has gone beyond just an informal perspective to an enforced rule. Many cons post signs as reminders and have in place anti-harassment policies and forms for reporting incidences of inappropriate behavior. For example, mega-host FanExpo posts a Zero Tolerance Policy on their website with the following statements:

> Threats, threatening language, or any other acts of aggressions, violence or sexual harassment made toward or by any attendee/exhibitor/staff will NOT be tolerated. For purposes of this policy, a threat includes but is not limited to any verbal or

physical harassment or abuse, attempts at intimidating or instilling fear in others, menacing gestures, flashing of weapons, stalking, or any other hostile, aggressive, injurious and/or destructive actions undertaken for the purpose of domination or intimidation. Fan Expo HQ expressly prohibits any acts or threats of violence or sexual harassment by any attendee, exhibitor or staff against another in or around the convention facilities or elsewhere at any time. All reports of violence or sexual harassment will promptly be investigated by show security. If an investigation confirms that a threat of a violent act, or violence/sexual harassment itself has occurred, Fan Expo HQ will take swift appropriate corrective action with regard to the offending person, up to and including immediate discharge from the show and the facility.

Whether officially posted or not, the credo "Cosplay Is Not Consent" is the one that needs to be most ingrained in our psyches. Just because someone is in a costume does not give anybody the right to accost them. Even the "sexy" versions of any character are not an invitation to touch. As the cosplayer named Stage, whom we'll meet shortly, correctly observed, "If someone is upset with you for setting boundaries, it's because they benefit from you not having them." And as Gracie articulated so clearly in Costume Conversation #7, "Cosplay is for everyone. Cosplay is not consent. Don't be a troll about it. Don't be a jerk." Even more forceful was a sign Winge encountered at a Con reading "Have Fun! Don't be a Dick!" (2019, p. 91). Don't do it. If you see it and you're able, step in and stop it. Otherwise, report it immediately.

Rules for Cosplayers

In addition to rules for photographers and fans, there also need to be rules which cosplayers, and those in costumes at other venues, must follow in order to be on *their* best behavior. Here are a couple quick examples.

In 2022, I attended a Con panel titled "Do's and Don'ts on In-Character Cosplay." I'll admit, I read the title too quickly. I thought it was about do's and don'ts of how to treat people dressed *in* cosplay character. Rather, it was how people dressed *in-character* cosplay need to treat their audience! Most of the session was spearheaded by a professional cosplayer known as Stage (@stage-props-cosplay). She began with her warning from experience; there are a lot of toxic cosplayers out there who tend to ruin it for everybody. This is particularly true of those characters who are, in the source material, unpleasant. Just because you are dressed as the villain, does that allow you to be villainous? "Even if your character is rude," Stage teaches, "please don't make comments in-character about a person's race, size, weight, or gender." She points out that comments made in-character are not free of consequences once out-of-character. Her other advice is equally helpful, including the following thoughts and recommendations: You don't need to be perfect. You don't need to be in-character all the time. Take breaks. Read the room. And know when to deescalate; sometimes you just need to step away.

In his book on armor construction, prop master Thorsson (2016) also provides advice to those in costume. Immediately in his preface, he gives a warning about interacting with children: "To some of the kids you encounter, you're not just some person in a homemade costume. To them, you *are* the character you're dressed as. Remember that when they see you and start getting excited. It's one thing if they kick you or abuse you, but otherwise, be the hero they think you are" (p. x). He follows with common-sense advice like obeying the police and having situational awareness (e.g., don't wear a mask into a bank), and concludes with two suggestions, started purposefully in all caps to make his point:

DON'T FRIGHTEN THE NORMAL. Simply wearing a costume in public shouldn't be a problem, but it may make a lot of people wary of you. Acting outrageously and being obnoxious is a bad idea. Don't do this.

DON'T HIDE BEHIND THE COSTUME. Dressing up as a villain doesn't make it okay to mistreat people. Playing with your friends is fine. Harassing random strangers is not! (p. xi).

Perhaps the best rule for everyone is less a rule and more a way of thinking. Burlesque artist Minnie D'Moocha (cited in Cline, 2017) sums it up as follows: "Cosplay is about acceptance. Acceptance of all. Then we must love all. We must accept all. We must support all, challenge all, and only this way do we become greater." The best rule is love.

Wrapping Up

Here is the part in a research project where scholars are asked to pull things together. The biggest question we have to answer is "So what?" Now that we know all this great information and have met all these great people, what are we supposed to do with it? How does it apply to us? A second question, which I'll address at the very end, is where should this project go from here?

Let's start with "So what?" Officially, as a communication scholar, I have viewed all the content encountered – all the books, articles, photos, and interviews – as *text*. You might see the word "text" and think only of the written word, like a book or even a text message. But, as Sellnow explains, a popular culture text "is any set of interrelated written, oral, or visual signs and artifacts" which focus on objects, actions, and events in our lives (2018, p. 6). These texts are important, because they shape the world and suggest to us what we ought to believe or how we ought to act. Sellnow explains that the scholar's job is to evaluate the meaning and significance of the messages. "You do so by considering the various audiences who might view it and how it might influence them to believe and behave as a result. What impact might it have on individuals and groups?" (2018, p. 15).

I think my "various audiences" are quite diverse. I obviously assume a few of you reading this are cosplayers. And some of you are academics. Maybe both? There might also be a smattering of people interested in costumes in general, either within or outside of cosplay realms, who want some insights on where to begin and where they belong. Some of you are devotees. Some are just passing by. That's okay. The conclusions that follow are for all of you.

Parents

I have a special message here for parents of cosplayers and beyond, who might be worried about this activity and wondering what their kids are getting into. Take heart. As a parent myself, I am overjoyed to see the diversity, openness, and acceptance within the community. Costumes are a great outlet for creativity and, as seen throughout these pages, a great resource for building confidence, increasing social skills, and exploring otherwise muted aspects of one's personality. Definitely a character builder (no pun intended).

Remember that classic movie *The Breakfast Club*? The one thing those kids had in common – a brain, an athlete, a basket case, a princess, and a criminal – is that they all had terrible relationships with their parents. Presumably, the parents did horrible things, ranging from physical abuse to pigeon-holing them into slots to ignoring their very existence. My goal has always been to *not be a Breakfast Club parent*. Costumes/cosplay is something everyone can get behind. Support them financially, if possible, but first and foremost support them emotionally and spiritualty. Heck, maybe even dress up with them, like these pirate parents do with their daughter (see Image 6.3). The family that cosplays together, stays together!

Anybody Can Be Anything….

Well, it took a couple hundred pages to get here, but *this* is the main takeaway message from the book. I want to strongly proclaim that – as long as you are not hurting anyone (see next block on cultural appropriation) – *you are free to dress as whoever you want*. Outside of historical reenactments that demand accuracy, it does not matter what gender you are or identify with, what size you are, what color your skin/hair/eyes are, what your level of ability/disability is, where you come from, how rich or poor you might be, what (if any) religion you follow, who you choose to love in your personal life, or how accurate your costume is, I'll say it again - *you are free to dress as whoever you want*. Anybody can be anything.

Image 6.3 *The Jiron family at Pirate Fest
(l to r: Shawn [father], Samira [daughter], Lynette [mother])*

Remember Mia Rios, the black cosplayer from Chapter 3 who was shunned and even banned from TikTok for posing as a Japanese anime character? Fortunately for Rios, a number of Japanese artists and cosplayers came to her defense, explaining that she was practicing the art of "kawaii" (translates to "cute"), a portrayal of women harkening back to the 1960s. Emphasizing an "aesthetic of adorableness," women are imagined as hyperfeminine, shy, and charming. "I want to ask my Japanese friends, did she really do something wrong?" said Haruka Kurebayashi, a kawaii artist, influencer, and model who argues that kawaii culture is for everyone. "It doesn't matter if you are a beginner. Nor does your nationality, gender, age, or skin color matter" (Montgomery, 2021). The same holds true for all such portrayals.

Remember Rule 63? It states that, for every fictional character that exists, there is a gender-reversed version of them somewhere out there. You want to be a female Vision or Flash? No problem. A male Nebula or Mera? Go for it. Brown explains the wonder and value of Rule 63 by observing that the "various forms of superhero gender reconfiguring undertaken by fans demonstrate what is often described as fandom's 'transformative' function – transformative not just in the surface representation of the character but in how audiences understand the character or the entire genre" (p. 145). Not only do you get to celebrate a favorite character however you want, but you also get other people thinking and opening up their minds as well. Win-win.

And honestly, this is nothing new. Brown continues, stating that comic books have long used the concept of *multiverses* – "different realities that the primary heroes can visit and where stories can explore what-if scenarios outside the scope of central continuity" – to gender swap iconic male heroes. "For example," he shares, "DC Comics has designated Earth-11 as a parallel reality where all of the characters' genders have been reversed" (p. 145). On Earth-11, the multiverse is only being used to swap gender. Why not swap anything and everything?

This is just what occurred in the 2022 smash hit *Everything Everywhere All at Once* (2023 Best Picture) starring Academy-award winners Michelle Yeoh and Ke Hay (a.k.a. "Short Round," "Data") Quan. In this fantastic story, beleaguered housewife and laundromat owner, Evelyn Wang, finds she is a key link to a multiverse war between good and evil. Able to tap into the skills and traits of her counterparts in other dimensions, she experiences everything from being a skilled marital artist, to having impossibly long "hot dog" fingers, to becoming a sentient rock with googly eyes. In the process, by embodying all these different personae, she finds inner strength, survives an IRS audit, and, of most importance, learns to accept her daughter Joy's non-Asian girlfriend. What a fantastic metaphor for the potentiality of costume.

Similarly, superhero movie franchises have finally started integrating the multiverse storylines from their comic books. In addition to the multiverse portrayals in the TV series *Loki*, the Marvel Cinematic Universe (MCU) got a running start with 2021's *Spider-Man: No Way Home*. In it, Peter Parker (Tom Holland) asks Dr. Strange (Benedict Cumberbatch) to reverse the conclusion of 2019's *Spider-Man: Far*

From Home, when Mysterio (Jake Gyllenhaal) reveals to the world that Peter is Spider-Man. In a botched spell caused by Peter's ongoing list of requests, Strange opens a portal to other universes, through which previous Spider-Men (Toby Maguire, Andrew Garfield) and their various enemies enter.

That storyline then exploded in 2022's *Dr. Strange in the Multiverse of Madness*. Strange encounters universe-jumper America Chavez (Xochitl Gomez) as she runs from Wanda Maximoff, The Scarlett Witch (Elizabeth Olsen). Wanda wants Chavez's ability to traverse dimensions, as she wants to live in the universe in which she has children. Turns out we, the viewers, have always been privy to the storylines from universe 616. Strange and Chavez eventually end up in universe 838. There, the leading band of superheroes is not the Avengers headed up by Captain America; it is the Illuminati under the direction of Reed "Mr. Fantastic" Richards of the Fantastic Four. His troop includes Carol (616's Captain Marvel) Danver's friend, Monica Rambeau (played by Lashana Lynch), as a black Captain Marvel. Also, in this world, the Marvel "What if..." scenario has occurred, in which Steve Rogers does not receive the super serum. Rather, Agent Peggy Carter (Hayley Atwell) does, thereby becoming Captain Carter. The multiple universe scenario then travels to the subatomic level in 2023's *Ant-Man and the Wasp: Quantumania*. By the end, we are shown an arena full of dimensional variants of the evil conqueror Kang, ranging from lizard-skinned to an Egyptian pharaoh lookalike.

Not to be outdone, the DC multiverse is found mostly throughout their comics, cartoons, and television shows. McFarlane toys offer an increasing number of DC Multiverse action figures such as Red Robin, Solar Suit Superman, and Endless Winter Aquaman. 2023's film release *The Flash* centers on a storyline where the hero's superspeed causes a collision of worlds, bringing together classic friends and foes such as the once-dead General Zod (Michael Shannon) and multiple Batmen (Ben Affleck, Michael Keaton). Outside of DC and the MCU, you might remember that Family Guy did this as early as 2009. In the season 8 episode, "Road to the Multiverse," Stewie [the occasionally evil baby genius] and Brian [the always pompous family dog] travel to multiple dimensions, such as one where they appear to be drawn by Disney animators. In 2012, it was even released as an interactive video game.

What is the point here? Just this. Since all of these storylines tell us that – in the multiverse - we can be anything from hot-dog fingered to made of paint, then we can create and dress as any character we desire. In Chapter 3, I asked if there was any problem having a black Batman. The answer is "no problem at all." Same with a Native American Superman, an Asian Captain Jack Sparrow, a female Thanos, a One Punch Man in a wheelchair, and an endless list that goes on and on. In their self-published book on getting started, Cosplaymom and her daughter Kiogenic (2012) provide a similar argument: "Cosplay is for Everyone: The Only Rule is to Cosplay What You Love. So if you are a woman, you can cosplay a male character? Yes. If you are human can you cosplay a robot? Yes. If you are full-figured, can you cosplay someone slim? Yes. If you are 70 years old can you cosplay Elsa from *Frozen*? Yes. If you are skinny, can you cosplay a muscular character? Yes. Cosplay is for everyone, of every gender, shape, ethnicity and religion" (p. 6). On these points, we all seem to agree.

Of course, the biggest reason we need to be flexible is, drumroll please, these are all *fictional* characters! Luke Skywalker is only a white male because somebody wrote him that way. *He himself is not real.* And because these characters are not real and never will be, you can edit those writings in any fashion you want and present a new text to the world.

...HOWEVER, Be Prepared...
When you pick something that is outside of the norm, pushes the envelope, or challenges comic canon for diehard purist fans, you can expect some pushback. As many of the interviewees have pointed out, the biggest enemy to a cosplayer is a fellow cosplayer, and canon purists can be the worst. Have you seen the 1980 *Superman II* with Christopher Reeve? There's a scene where he pulls the "S" symbol off his chest and throws it at the bad guys. The shield grows and becomes a big piece of

flypaper to which they get stuck. That ability is not part of Superman's catalog of powers. I'm still reading angry fan reviews for that scene. The movie was released more than 40 years ago! It's time to move on!

What I'm trying to say is, our decisions have consequences. Turning again to Cosplaymom (who, incidentally, is real-life scholar E.G. Nichols, cited throughout) and Kiogenic, they add, "We are not going to promise you that you will never get a negative comment about how you 'don't look enough like the character.' We wish we could, but this can and will happen. The thing is, though, that the vast, overwhelming majority of the cosplay community is open, welcoming and warm" (2012, p. 6). I hope for you that is true, but still recommend that you need a thick skin to go along with your new costume. If you are ready for that, proceed.

...And Ask Yourself, "Appropriate or Appropriation?"

When your costume choice butts up against social, racial, and cultural storylines, traditions, and portrayals, just ask yourself, "Is what I'm doing *appropriate* or *appropriation*?" Even though the characters may be fictional, *history is not*. Make sure you have done enough homework on your character to know if there are any past or systemic inequities that might serve as a warning to your costume decisions. If your intent is honorable and respectful, it is more likely to be appropriate. If your portrayal is more of a cultural kidnapping, taking on characteristics and presenting them in a stereotypical way, it is appropriation. Consider, for example, these Indonesian Muslim women (Image 6.3) who have rented kimonos to wear, along with their hijabs, outside of a Buddhist shrine in Tokyo. Their intent is to celebrate and participate in Japanese culture. No offense is intended, and none is perceived.

Incidentally, I confirmed this perception with my Japanese wife. Since the women were paying homage to Japanese tradition, she was in fact pleased with their portrayal. In contrast, I asked her, what if somebody had rented that same kimono, and hiked to up to their thighs to show off fishnet stockings and stiletto heels. "Sexy" kimono. That, she agreed, would be disrespectful and therefore appropriation. The difference is generally easy to see.

Image 6.4 *Non-Japanese Muslim women celebrate Japanese culture*

This is most true when it comes to skin tone. Consider the following by Yaya Han: "There are no real people with green skin on Earth, so painting yourself green to play an alien, such as Gamora from *Guardians of the Galaxy*, indeed does not hurt anyone. However, there are billions of dark-skinned people living in the world. Emulating a living race through cosplay does have real-world implications, regardless of whether or not the source material is fictional" (p. 2020, p. 149). She goes on to explain that, in our Western culture, light skin is the norm. We must beware the danger of thinking we are *so open minded* that we "don't see colors" (p. 149). That's a great perspective to start with, as long as we remember that, for non-Caucasians, skin tone is *identity*. Han explains this in articulate fashion:

> By darkening your skin tone to emulate another real human race, whether it is African, Native American, or Pacific Islander, you are pointing out to an entire marginalized group

of your peers that for you, skin tone is interchangeable. It highlights the fact that you can choose to wear someone else's skin tone for one day to enjoy your cosplay without having to experience the negativity that marginalized people often have to live with.... A white cosplayer might see dark makeup as no different than putting in colored contacts or using a wig to change their appearance, but it can come across as mockery to people of color. (2020, p. 150)

In the end, Han concludes "cosplay whoever you want, but don't darken your skin. Cosplay Katara, Storm, or Pocahontas to your heart's content. Rock it out in their costumes, but do so in your own skin tone" (p. 156). This is excellent advice.

Pulling together views from our various interviewees, it is safe to say that children are exempt from these rules. If a little white girl wants to be Moana or Mulan, nobody really has a problem with that. Parents might want to consider using it as a teaching moment. For teens and above, one needs to be thoughtful. In our culture, this is especially true for Caucasian cosplayers, as they have universes of source material to pick from. Ultimately, cosplay and costumes are all about respect. Respect for self and the identity you embody. Respect for others and the culture that defines them. Respect for the community where you showcase your creations. Respect for the variety of roles that people play and the level of expertise that they bring to the table. Then we truly have cause to celebrate.

Where Do We Go From Here?
Since no resource is the be-all and end-all of the conversation, good research always needs to end with a look ahead. We've covered a lot in these pages but need to finish with a few ideas about future directions and future trends.

One thing we didn't look at, though it sounds mighty interesting, is the phenomenon of copycat or real-life superheroes. Kirkpatrick (2015) explains that sometimes ordinary citizens are "moved to practice social activism or vigilantism by imitating the costuming practices of fictional superheroes; often emulating their crime-fighting behavior. They lift from the page and take to the streets" [5.4]. That is fascinating, but far outside the scope of this study. For those interested, there is a 2011 HBO documentary titled *Superheroes* you might want to check out. Directed by Michael Barnett, and using the tagline - "What if Superheroes were real?" - the film follows the exploits of actual people who dress up and engage in activities such as patrolling their neighborhood streets at night. While they are in general criticized by the police, and even Stan Lee, for taking the law into their own hands, there is that fanciful seduction of getting to live out your superhero fantasies. While an intriguing area for research, this project neither studies, nor endorses, real-life costumed vigilantes.

Another area worth investigating is the link between cosplay and costume activities and the stories found in fan fiction. Peppard (2021), addresses the genderswap function of fan fiction, noting that it "has historically been dominated by female fans re-writing connotatively masculine genres, such as science fiction and action-adventure" (p. 136). This goes beyond the "affirmational" fandom, which tends to follow the rules of the source's original text, and becomes "transformational" fandom that twist the storylines to the fan's own interests. Is there a layer at which fan fiction and costuming practices intersect? Which comes first, the story or the costume?

Other avenues for investigation look more at the connections between cosplay and evolving technologies. Lamerichs (2015), for example, studied the rise of Cosplay Music Videos, or CMVs. Calling this a "transmedial process" she claims that "CMVs have increasingly become a means to extend and share the cosplay performance" (1.4). That warrants a closer look. Next, Mountfort et al. speak to the increased usage of virtual reality (VR) and augmented reality (AR), noting that the world is increasingly complex and traditional models of understanding are eroding. They offer fandom and cosplay as "emotional and psychological touchstones that fill the gaps that have emerged in the wake of structural changes" (p. 278). Interestingly, they spoke about these structural changes in 2019, a year before the entire world was changed by

COVID. How much more have those changes created a place for cosplay, fandom, and reality-centric technologies? On that note, not one study encountered discussed the interplay between artificial intelligence (AI) and fandom communities. Now that ChatGPT has caught our attention, should we view it as an instrument of assistance or the embodiment of evil as we seek to answer questions of identity, and the ways in which costumes can make them manifest?

Finally, I want to end on an observation made by Winge (2019). "The future of Cosplay," she wrote, "is female." She argues that girls and women have the most influence in cosplay fandom, manifesting itself in the range of being both the creator *and* subject of fandom storylines. She also says it is "present in the fandom's multigenerational composition, which could benefit the future of the fandom" (p. 185). To this she adds the skill set of women, not only in areas like sewing, but also in interpersonal engagements like follow up recognition and empowerment. If this is the case, we need to be careful not to recreate historical costume trends of males co-opting and taking over what was feminine. A classic example, cited by Churchill (2019) is that kilts were originally a fashion piece for women. While the huge Scottish military kilts, which were as much blanket and hood, had been around a few centuries, the shorter pleated versions were worn by Irish women during dances as part of an Irish cultural revival in the late 1890s. "As political adornment, dance costume articulated Irishwomen's self-identification within a broader political collective" (p. 160). Following a Civil War (1922-23), the political powers began to institutionalize "gender difference and the primacy of family" (p. 154). Women got to stay in the home and, in a tradition that has now lasted 100 years, men got to wear the kilts.

Who *does* the future of cosplay belong to? Women? Men? That is a question to be answered by someone else at a later time. Putting in my two cents, I hope that the answer is "the future of cosplay belongs to everyone, regardless of biological sex, psychological gender, or any other attribute on which we may divide ourselves." Hopefully these pages have shown it belongs to all.

Summary

In addition to being a labor of love, this lengthy tome has a two-fold purpose; to serve as an educational resource in academia, and as a source of entertainment for general consumption. For the author, it is the culmination of a decades-long interest in topics like fashion, gender, and power. With all such works, there are strengths and limitations. The truth is, it is impossible to capture all the stories we want. Sometimes we luck out by being able to share powerful stories like Samantha Oester's journey. Moving on to rules, whether one is a photographer, a fan, or a cosplayer, there are expectations of etiquette regarding photography and, in all cases, harassment is not allowed. Cosplay is not consent. Following some quick advice to parents, we wrapped up with the key takeaway from this book: if you're not hurting anyone with your costume, then anybody can be anything and dress however they want. That said, one must be prepared for backlash, and remain constantly vigilant on the question of "appropriate or appropriation?" Looking ahead, there are plenty of opportunities for future study, ranging from real-life superheroes, to ongoing societal and technological changes, to the question of whose hands hold the future of cosplay. With those thoughts in mind, we turn to the final three Costume Conversations, selected here because they seem to most embody the lessons of this final chapter. They get it.

Endnote: Brown (2012) notes that many universities "require ethnographic projects to be approved by a human subjects review board before research can begin in order to ensure the rights and safety of both the researcher and the proposed subjects" (p. 282). An Institutional Review Board (IRB) examines factors like elements of risk, and whether subjects have received and signed an Informed Consent Form indicating they know what the study entails and are willing to participate. Under new guidelines, in-depth interviews like the ones here are exempt from IRB protocol under CFR 45, Part 46. According to 46.102, scholarly activities including oral history, biography, and historical scholarship that "focus directly on the specific individuals about whom the information is collected" are considered journalistic in nature. For example, unlike traditional research, you cannot guarantee confidentiality or anonymity because you are, in fact, taking people's pictures and telling their story. That said, everyone involved in this project read and signed a release form consenting that their image and their words could be used in this publication and related materials. Subjects agreed that author could edit content in a fashion that corrects or clarifies grammar (either spoken or written) and put them in their "best voice." Finally, unlike traditional consent forms, the one used here promised subjects that their information would be treated in a respectful manner. They knew their story was to be celebrated, not exploited.

COSTUME CONVERSATION #16
The Bond Family
a.k.a. High Plains Ghostbusters

In 2016, a *Ghostbusters* reboot was launched, starring women (Melissa McCarthy, Kristen Wiig, Kate McKinnon, and Leslie Jones) as the paranormal protection squad. Ches Bond Jr. (hereafter referred to as Ches) was living in Hawaii at the time and, though it is his least favorite of all the films ("the social politics took all the fun out of it"), he liked it well enough to realize "there was a resurgence of Ghostbusters into the public zeitgeist." Local Halloween stores were selling Ghostbuster gear at reasonable prices, so he purchased a costume and started participating with the Ghostbusters Hawaii Division. That was the beginning of this ghost story.

He later moved back to his home state of Colorado and, wanting to continue the connection, initiated the High Plains Ghostbusters starring friends and family members. When I encountered them at an event called Greeley Monster Day, complete with proton packs and Ectomobile, the crew consisted of Ches, sister Mandy (as Gozer the Gozerian), and their father Ches Bond Sr. (hereafter referred by his childhood nickname, Newman). The event, which in part celebrates the contributions of local monster movie propmakers Distortions Unlimited, also promotes the "Don't be a monster" anti-bullying campaign in the school district. In addition to Monster Day, the High Plains Ghostbusters participate in a number of regional get-togethers, fund raisers, birthday parties, and toy drives, and were even asked to appear at a local movie theater for the premier of 2021's *Ghostbusters: Afterlife*.

Newman tells me that they collectively decide on the directions the group moves. "One of the things that keeps this going," he explains, "is how people, regardless of age, ethnicity, or life story show so much joy when they see the Ghostbusters." His favorite movie is the first, because it establishes the canon. Like his son, he doesn't care so much for the 2016 version. "They tried too hard." Both Mandy and Ches equally agree that the first Ghostbusters (1984) is the best.

I ask the trio to describe some of the events they do, and share with me any favorite stories. Ches begins: "I will do anything we are requested for. I have done charity events, birthdays, parades, car shows, sporting events, and even was featured as part of a Ghostbusters themed booth for JBS' [local factory] trick or treat event." The surprising part is that, for all the effort, nobody gets paid. "It is all volunteer," he continues. "The goal is to make people happy. Occasionally people will give us donations, but I don't seek them. The goal of this group is to generate happiness and joy in people or, in the style of *Ghostbusters 2*, to generate positive psychokinetic energy. I really just want people to smile when they see us."

One of Ches's favorite moments occurred Monster Day 2021. "I met a boy named Gavin who might've been 4 or 5 years old. He had a hand made proton pack and a jumpsuit from a store. He was so excited to see us and hang out at our booth. I decided to give him a toy proton wand that I had painted to be more screen accurate, and he got so excited." This year Gavin, and the upgraded proton wand, returned. "His mom told me he had specifically come to the event to hang out with the Ghostbusters. I like to think he sees himself as a member of the group. Gavin is who I was at his age, and it really makes me happy to make Ghostbusters real for him."

For Newman, it's hard to pick one favorite memory, though he recalls, "We have done Hockey games where we are just as popular as the game to the crowd. We did a porch appearance once, where this kid got so excited, he started to cry." Mandy has a similar struggle to pick a favorite. "It is really hard to choose from one story because there is so much great energy from people." As a female, however, it is especially meaningful to her to see women or young girls get excited about interacting with them. Just that day, she enjoyed sharing time with a young girl who was showing off her new monster claws.

Costume-wise, Mandy is clearly Gozer the Gozerian, a prominent character in both the 1984 and 2021 films (played, respectively, by Slavita Jovan and Shohreh Aghdashloo). Both Ches and Newman are, essentially, themselves as Ghostbusters. Explains Ches, "I think there is this neat part of the greater Ghostbusters community that has established a world beyond the movie. In a way, the community has made it so that a person could join the Ghostbusters in their area and be their very own unique character. We don't necessarily create backstories, but if I was asked, it would relate strongly to my own story." Newman chose to be more of himself, "because I want people to see that the story goes beyond the characters in the movie. Plus, if you put a name of a movie character on your suit, people expect you to be that character. The name on my suit is the name I had as a child. It feels good to use that name."

Good points, all. I personally would not want to try and fill the shoes of the likes of Dan Aykroyd or Bill Murray. Being yourself as a Ghostbuster makes great sense. Mandy empathizes with that view. She also cosplays as Disney princesses and finds "it is very difficult to assume those identities because there are so many technical demands. So many people are familiar with them." While everybody knows Gozer, it's more of a visual character, which she embodies well.

A couple of times now, Ches has referred to the Ghostbusters franchises or communities. To what extent do they work together or compete with one another? "I would never choose to make another Ghostbusters group a foe," he tells me. "Sometimes, just like in any collaboration, it can be hard to come together. In terms of The High Plains Ghostbusters, I am very dedicated to being interactive and as positive as possible. Sometimes, when we partner with other groups, we have to contend that those groups may not be as interested in the openness or the performative nature of our appearances as I would like, but that is never more than an annoyance. I generally get along with anyone I work with, and I want to ensure that that professionalism shows through."

One aspect of that professionalism is the striking believability of their costumes and props. They do all the sewing, constructing, modifications, and 3D printing themselves. For example, Ches explains, "All of the parts have some level of our own touches on them. The packs are generally store-bought. I've added a variety of parts to all of the packs to make them more screen accurate or to repair them." The process, he adds, gives him the chance to learn new skills and techniques. "I've specifically learned some electrical engineering strategies and different paint techniques to get the perfect patina on the packs." Add to that the bonus of getting to spend quality time with his father. Newman chimes in, adding that kids don't care if the props are screen accurate, but "hardcore fans will notice if a screw is out of place." His bigger concern is to make the props "bomb proof, because it sucks when things break." Mandy agrees, noting it's always a good idea to have a repair kit and a sewing kit handy. "Costumes always break."

The biggest prop (aside from a huge inflatable Stay Puft Marshmallow Man, not with them today) is their car, the Ecto. Ches tells me, "I chose a Subaru because it has good contours that are reminiscent of the movie car, but also something economical. Dad and I generally do the work, but since it serves as my daily drive car, I do a majority of the upkeep. The best part of the car is the *Monday morning moment*: frequently, I will pull up next to a person at a red light and see the person glance over at the car, then do a double take with the largest grin on their face. It's the best on Monday mornings when that person may not be excited to be headed to work."

Those smiles are truly important to Ches. After serving five years in the Marine Corps, he was worried that his demeanor had changed, and that people perceived him differently following his service. "One of the things I struggled with after leaving the military was expressing that, despite my military service, I am not defined by it. Dressing up as a Ghostbuster has helped me, and sometimes forced me, to lead with the fun-loving, creative, and positivity that felt atrophied during my service. As ridiculous as some may think driving an Ecto around town is and wearing a proton pack is, it has had a very profound effect on being who I am and who I want to be."

At that point we've reached the message of this book. The importance of costume and how it makes you feel. When Ches straps on the pack, "I feel like a Ghostbuster. It's amazing to see how excited people get when they see us out and about. In their eyes, I AM a Ghostbuster and that feels really cool. That being said, it can be a lot of work. Putting the costume on is a performance. I am very careful to make sure that performance is special to everyone. I essentially have to put away anything that detracts from that, like my own shyness, feelings of tiredness, fears, sadness, etc. I love it all, so the work is definitely a labor of love."

Newman's views are similar, "When I put the suit and pack on, it makes me be more extroverted. I am naturally introverted, but it forces me to be outgoing because that's what makes the experience special for the people that come to see us. If I was standing there being shy, it wouldn't be special to see the Ghostbusters. I feel a responsibility to be a good showman when I have the gear on."

The same holds true for Mandy, who adds, "Anytime you wear a costume, things are heightened. You have a heightened awareness of things and people around you. You are more aware of what people need to make that experience special. I think for me, when I wear a costume that is an actual character, it gives me license to be evil, or to assume the characteristics of a character that I may not share, but it also allows me to be selective with those traits. Maybe I turn the evil down for a kid, so they feel comfortable, or I go full evil for an adult who wants the full experience."

Best of all, they experience this as a family. "I feel like we can rely on one another and feed off of each other's energy," Mandy shares, adding, "Personally, I feel safer having my Dad and Brother nearby in case I have an uncomfortable interaction with a person because, unfortunately, that does happen occasionally." Ches follows up, saying "There is so much value to it. We are the Ghostbusters family, which really is backed up by a huge culture of *okay* in the family. And the level of support that comes with family is valuable beyond measure." And dad, Newman, concludes, "It gives us all a creative outlet. Ches and I have so many neat conversations as we plan and create the gear. That's probably my favorite of all of this." With a smile, he adds, "I like to be the one who first does risky things, so if it goes bad, it can be my fault -- that's the dad in me."

Speaking of risk, Newman shares that he lost a leg in a motorcycle accident. With his jumpsuit's left pantleg hemmed short, you see an artificial limb adorned with a Van Gogh inspired Bat signal. "The leg is actually a big part of what I do because it is part of me. I want to show the prosthetic because I like to incorporate what could be a handicap into what could be a positive. I've turned something that may be tragic into a symbolic thing."

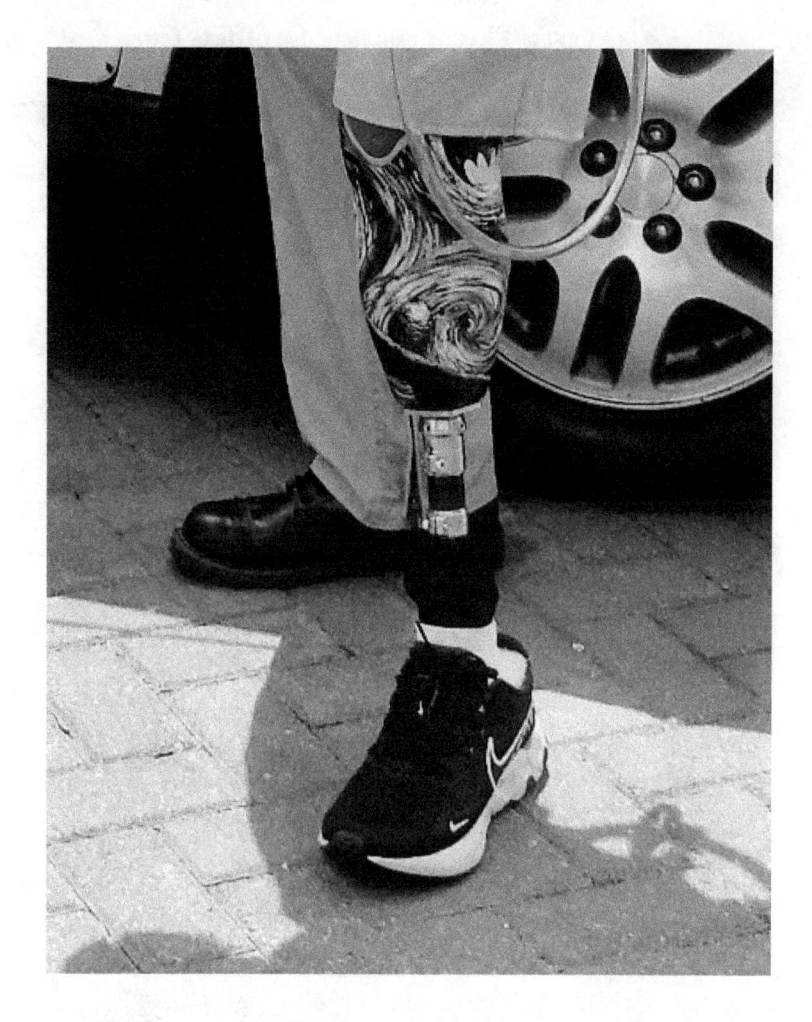

Again, the power of costume and adornment. All of it to serve an empowering purpose. "I think with all the negativity in the world, people need more ways to escape," Ches concludes. "That is something I think we do." And that is why they support costume events. "Cosplay is a safe community where everyone is welcome," says Mandy, to which her father adds, "Cosplay is not much different than when everyone wears the jersey on game day. Everyone should try it."

COSTUME CONVERSATION # 17
Rachel Taulbee
a.k.a. Terra Thesaurus and Countess Cora

"**M**y whole life, I've known that I am a singer. I was in choir all through school. I went to college to be a music educator. I wanted to do theater both in high school and college, but those programs always competed with each other, so I always chose music. That felt like my core." So begins the life story that Rachel so graciously shares. Her speaking voice is actually musical; melodic, lilting, evocative, cadenced. "I started as an elementary music teacher in my hometown. I loved it, but I also had this feeling like 'Oh my gosh, if I stay here, I'm going to stay here my whole life.'" Knowing this, a fellow teacher told her, "Rachel, there are kids everywhere to be loved. Go have an adventure."

And that's just what she did. First, she signed on as a singer for a cruise line. "Did that for four years. Really cut my teeth on singing pop and Top 40. That also taught me that I *cannot* have a 9-to-5, and that I *can* do interesting, creative things with my life." After departing from cruise life, she earned a certificate as a holistic life coach. Knowing it would take time to build clientele, she started a side job entertaining – as Anna from *Frozen* – at children's parties. "I have all the right skill sets. I love fashion, I have worked with kids a lot, I love costumes, and I can sing." Things went well, but it wasn't perfect. "I started to realize I don't like princess culture. It's just kind of gross. I don't want to put kids in boxes, especially gender boxes, teaching them to curtsy and be kind and polite. There's more important things for kids to know."

Instead, she turned her talents to delivering singing telegrams. "And that was FUN, because I got to be in character for adults, and be things like a gorilla, a clown, and all sorts of wacky stuff." From there, she moved to a company that did corporate events, and added characters like Zoltar, Lady Gaga, Madonna, and Marilyn Monroe. Eventually that led to gigs where she could create her own characters. As for the life of a telegram singer, Rachel is enthusiastic. "It's so delightful. It's a custom process. It's wonderful to be able to cater to exactly what would be nice for this individual person. A singing telegram is very intimate. They require being good on your feet. You've got to be flexible." She sings at retirements, birthdays, anniversaries, holidays, and even get-well telegrams for people in the hospital. She strives to learn about the person to whom she will sing, so she can tailor lyrics to their special occasion. "That's when you can really get in there and create a special moment that people will remember forever."

That practice and exposure gave her the confidence to pitch a character to an event called Folks Fest. "I went to Folks Fest and was talking with a friend. I explained to her all the different things I wanted to do. I was like, 'I really want to do this *for* the festival. I see a hole in it.' 'See that guy over there? That's the VP of Planet Bluegrass. Go tell him what you just told me.' And so I did, and he's like, 'Can you remember an email address?' I emailed him and we worked out a deal where I could be the *Fairy of Folks Fest*. I dress in a different costume each day, and that's where I really got to start exploring my fairy characters more." For Rachel, portraying a fairy has distinct advantages over playing a princess. "I can talk with kids about nature, and I can be whimsical and magical, but I can also talk about deep things with them. I can get into the seasons and the cycles of life and death and rebirth. So, great! I can make very inclusive characters for kids." Her favorite experience there was connecting with a little boy with autism. "He loves to watch me dance. I can't go and hug him. I have to be careful how I look at him, because it could turn him away. It's very important to pay attention to how people want to interact with me. Sometimes people don't want to talk, they don't want to go there. That's okay. I cannot be pushy with them."

The original character she is modeling today is named Terra Thesaurus, a kind and enthusiastic dinosaur who loves books. Originally designed for an event called "T-Rex Express," Rachel got to create the program from scratch. "I got to choose the books, the songs, the dances that I would do. This is so fun! I get to choose how I present these things to kids, and what I talk to them about." Terra's key feature is that she attracts people to a place where they can explore feelings. "Because who doesn't love dinosaurs? Beings like Terra live in that gooey place. Terra Thesaurus welcomes people in. Anybody. She appeals to any kind of human. She's like frontline because a lot of times people need softness. They need someone to invite them in to play."

During the creative process of character development, Rachel occasionally runs into difficult feelings and obstacles. She calls this her shadow work. To demonstrate, after the Terra photo shoot, Rachel's mother Cecilia Taulbee helped her get into a costume showcasing the darker end of the spectrum. We meet the Countess Cora. "She takes me into the hard places, and she tells me the truth. She doesn't coddle me, but she's there for me." I'm curious what sort of topics are discussed with and via Cora. "Social conditioning has been a big one for me. Really examining the person that I am embodying; is that really me, or is that who I've been told to be? One of the beautiful things about my character, or any other character, honestly, they give me an opportunity to embody a certain part of myself, and help me be a little bit more brave in that area. I'm authentic in my characters. I find a piece of me that I can explore more, and I just use it as a mechanism to have real conversation and really connect to people with love."

Rachel continues, explaining how the Countess gives her the ability to confront problems within herself, or conflicts experienced with others. "With Cora, she really taught me how to go deeply in myself. How to embrace the places where I am dark, where I'm ugly, where I'm complicated, where I'm rubbing up against parts of me that make me feel uncomfortable. She's like, 'I've got your back, but if you want to know who you really are, you've got to go in there. Let's do this. I'll tear up whatever person comes in here and tries to fight you on it or keep you from being who you are.' Cora is the warrior that stands at the boundary around my heart. She stands around the soft, gooey, precious part of who I am. You will not fuck with her. She is my ultimate protector."

Via that inner reflection and shadow work, Rachel has developed around 40 different characters, including a sexy gorilla with cone boobs, and Wonder Nurse (a mashup of nurse and Wonder Woman, to celebrate front line workers during the pandemic). Her closet is filled with costume items that can be mixed and matched to create new characters. In 2021 she launched an LLC business to cover all the things that she is and offers. "I want to be very choosy about who I work with and how I give my time. Time is currency. I am a visual artist, I am a singer-songwriter, I am a character actress, and I love burlesque, and I need a big umbrella that focuses on all of those, because when I try to choose one, it doesn't work. I'm all of it. And the more I try to do all the things I'm good at, the more magical my life gets. It's been such a wonderful adventure to be able to create as I create. I'm so much bigger than I thought I was, and the more I allow space for my bigness, and focusing on what I really love, it also creates more space for me to now start building community and doing things with more and more people."

Our conversation moves from there to the costumes themselves; what they do and how they make her feel. "Costume is a mechanism to know yourself better," she answers. "And to invite people in to get to know themselves better. To build relationships with others. To invite people to play. To invite people to grieve. To invite people into who they really are and go a layer down. For me, it's been a mechanism for me to learn more about who I am, and be a more authentic human being myself, and how I am in the world." In those interactions with others, she sometimes must enforce boundary lines. When playing Marilyn Monroe, or sexier characters like saloon girls or flappers, she encounters men who do not behave. "Men just come in and say whatever they want. And hit on you. And think they can take pictures, and they put their arms around you, and they touch you in certain ways. It really got to me. I've been more choosy about the kind of jobs I'll take, because I don't want to put myself in that situation. I don't have to. Other people might not be bothered by that, but I am not an object. I am a beautiful human being and I get to set my own boundaries about what I do and how I interact with people. Who I touch. When I touch. When they touch me. With that said, it's also important to honor other people's boundaries, because I might do the same to them. I don't want to do that."

In her exploration of borders and boundaries, she has played around with gender swapping. Her favorite male character is Bartholomew the Bard, a polite and joyful medieval entertainer who combines chivalry and flirtation when he encounters beautiful women. "It's so funny, but through these characters, these male characters that I've embodied, it's really given me an opportunity to explore myself. I don't know, maybe there's something deeper to this? The more I've allowed myself to do the shadow work, that's one of the things that I found in there. I'm really quite queer. And so, I'm giving myself time to explore 'Is there something more to this for you? Let's go check it out.'" Rachel laughs (also melodic) and adds, "So, I'm not even sure; there's a chance that I'm actually *she/they*, so we'll keep you posted!"

While she is comfortable portraying male characters, she is very cautious about crossing cultural boundaries. That was not always the case. "A few years back, I bought an Afro wig for my '70s character. I got rid of it. I had a whole Cleopatra costume. It's problematic. So, I got rid of that. Oh gosh, I had this *Cinco de Mayo situation*. I have this picture of me in a sombrero and I had a big mustache. I'm like, 'You are making a caricature of a culture! You can't do that. Stop.' There are other people who will do it. Great. I'm not going to." Other past memories are equally haunting. "When I was a princess, there were times I would play Jasmine. I was tan, but I also darkened my make up a bit. That no longer feels comfortable. Even back in the cruise ship days, we had a party around Disney characters, and I dressed up as Tiger Lilly. Oh my gosh, what was I doing? That feels really wrong now. I want to say this because I have made mistakes. 'Rachel, you're white. You're white, white, white, white, white, white, white! No, this is not for you!' That's not you! It's not your culture. It's not yours.' It doesn't matter how respectful you're doing it. It's problematic. 'You're white. There's a whole world you get to embody, so don't do any of that.'"

With her more culturally aware standards, Rachel is ready to change her corner of the world. "I had a woman at Folks Fest tell me, 'Just watching you makes me want to be more curious, and explore more about who I am in myself.' Great! That makes me want to cry. What a beautiful thing. I figured out how to do it, and that is one of my many purposes in this world. It is my gift to give, and I'm honored to do it." Most important, she now understands that her characters put on display facets of her inner self. They are characters, but they are also Rachel. "You really are embodying the character, but you're also embodying yourself. You know when someone's playing a character, but you don't actually *feel* them? I'm not that. I deeply connect with people. I can't even tell you how many hugs I get, how many people telling me that they love me, and I'll tell them that right back. That's what we need in our world. I didn't realize how important costume and character work are to building morale and intimacy and friendship in our world. How healing it can be, and what an impact it can make."

"It's important work."

COSTUME CONVERSATION #18
George Gray
a.k.a. Elvis Presley

George is a minor celebrity in the central Midwest, not only for his Elvis shows, but as an early morning disc jockey for a popular station called Pirate Radio. In addition to refreshing local banter, he spins hits from the 1950s-1980s. Surprisingly, he admits "I never was a big Elvis fan. My mom remarried when I was nine, and my stepdad had a lot of albums. I can remember listening to Peter, Paul, & Mary, the Kingston Trio, the Smothers Brothers. I start listening to Elvis albums over and over again. And little did I know, God was putting things in motion. As I got older, I was actually training myself somewhat to having Elvis's reflections and his vibrato." He also admits, "I never was a singer. I never had the opportunity in school to do a lot of extra-curricular activities. I was never in choir, didn't do any of that stuff. I was in band; I was a trumpet player and also a French horn player. So I had an ear for music."

It wasn't until he was in his early 30's that he joined a little theater group, one that would sometimes go to a karaoke bar after rehearsal. His fellow actors would prompt him to get up and sing. He'd refuse until, in his words, "after a couple liquid refreshments, which kind of allowed me to step outside my comfort zone," and he'd go up on stage. Looking through the catalog, he'd recognize Elvis songs from his stepdad's albums and would sing things like *Love Me Tender* or *Teddy Bear*. Sometimes he'd embellish with a lip curl or movement, but it was a rare occasion that he performed.

He eventually started working for a big company that had Christmas parties. One year he was approached by the entertainment committee, who said, "We understand you do this Elvis thing?" His reply was "No. No, I don't do this Elvis thing." But they convinced him, so he bought some teardrop sunglasses at a gas station, borrowed an ill-fitting jumpsuit from the receptionist's fiancé, attached some fake sideburns, and sang *Are You Lonesome Tonight*, modifying the lyrics a bit to include the name of someone in the audience. After his act he thought, "Man, what did I just do? That was embarrassing!"

A few days later he started getting phone calls. "Would you come and sing to my grandmother? Would you come sing at my wedding? Our anniversary? How much do you charge?" He begrudgingly allowed someone from his theater group to make him a better fitting jumpsuit. Still embarrassed, he would do these gigs, with no idea what to call them or what to charge. "I don't know. Twenty-five bucks? Even then I thought that was too much money." Each time he got dressed for a show, he felt the same waves of embarrassment. "I'd stand at the front door of my house, and before I went outside all dressed up, I would look up and down my street and make sure nobody was coming. And then I'd run out to my truck, I'd get in there, and I would take off. And I would freak out if I came to a stop sign or stoplight, because somebody would pull up next to me, and they'd look at me, and they all go 'Hey, it's Elvis! What's shaking, baby?' Beet red! I was just totally embarrassed to do these things."

This went on for a few years. One day, when he was working as Executive Director for a non-profit organization, he was speaking with the director of a local hospital. "She said 'I understand you do this Elvis thing.' In the back of my mind I'm thinking, 'Tell her no. No, I don't do this thing.' I said, 'Yeah. Yeah, I kind of do this thing.'" She asked if he would come by and entertain an elderly woman named Edie, on her third bout with cancer, who was in hospice and had about a week to live. He agreed. When he arrived, he found that Edie's family had hired someone to film the entire thing. The hallway to her room was filled with balloons and "We Love Elvis" signs. The doctors and nurses were all lined up and wanted to take pictures. After about 10 minutes he suggested he'd better go see Edie. Then one of the ladies said, "Oh my gosh, here she comes."

George looked up and saw a frail woman at the end of the hall, hanging onto an orderly's arm on one side, and the hallway handrail on the other. The same lady tells him that Edie got up and put on her favorite dress and best wig for the day. Then, George tells me, "She approaches me, and I walk towards her, and she pushes the orderly away and says, 'He's here for me,' and she falls in my arms."

George explains that, at that time in his life, "Like a lot of us, I had a fear of death. Didn't even want to think about it." They talked for a bit, and he suggested they return to her room so he could sing her a few songs. "I get down there. The room is packed. Everybody is in there. The doorway's packed. Everybody's crying as I'm trying to sing to this lady and, of course, I'm getting a lump in my throat, right? And if I talk too much about it, I'll start crying here. But we had this wonderful, beautiful moment." At the end, Edie said, "Thank you so much. You don't know what this meant to me in my life." Before he left the hospital, he was asked to stop by and sing a song to another patient who was dying of congenital heart failure. He sang *Teddy Bear*.

"And when I went home," George continued, "I didn't get undressed. Normally my MO was I'd get dressed at the last moment, run out to my car, do the thing, and once I got home, I took off the Elvis outfit and hung it up and closed the door, because I didn't want to look at it. I sat down in my rocking chair for *hours*, trying to process what just went on. I couldn't process; I didn't know what was wrong with me. And the more I thought about it, the more I'd think 'I need to go back and talk with her.'"

George went back, as himself, to visit Edie every day. Her family lived a distance away and could not visit as often as they'd like, so Edie appreciated the company. They talked until the wee hours every night, up until the day she passed. "I still think about her a lot. That's kind of the door that opened to me up to 'there's a lot of people out there that are hurting, fighting battles, and sometimes it's the smallest things," he states, because he thinks of what he did as a *small* thing, "that can make a big difference in somebody's life." He concludes the story of Edie with this realization, "That didn't cure me about wanting to do Elvis, but it started the ball rolling."

The next call came from Relay for Life (fund raiser for the American Cancer Society), and he started doing shows for them. "I can remember my first show with them. I finally had a new seamstress and she made me a black Elvis jumpsuit. And this time I thought, 'I'm gonna do it up right.' I spray painted my hair black with the washable hair dye, put on these nicer looking sideburns, and I get out there – 9 or 10 o'clock in the morning - and I'm doing my thing. Sun's coming out, and I start sweating. I started getting these black lines running down my neck. The dye is washing out of my hair because I'm sweating. Sideburns are peeling off. I do this half-hour show and afterwards they said, 'Man, that was amazing. We want you to come back next year and do an hour-and-a-half long show as our main event.' And in the back of my mind I'm going 'When is this going to stop? When is this going to stop?'"

Well, it hasn't stopped yet. George decided to grow out and properly dye his hair. He had another jumpsuit made, one that could be thrown into the wash. He still had no confidence about his performances. "Because *I didn't want to do it*. I felt silly, dressing up as Elvis. But I also told myself I'm not going to get up there and do a caricature of him – curl my lip, (*imitating exaggerated Elvis voice*) 'Thank you, thank you very much.' I didn't want to be that guy. I just wanted to keep the music and spirit alive."

He found a local three-piece band, and they decided to create a little Elvis tribute group. They had some rehearsals, made some calls, and started playing. Within a year they had a 12-piece band with saxophone, trombones, trumpets, two keyboardists, a lead guitar, bass, and backup singers. "I mean, it was just crazy on how big this thing was getting. And then we got our break." George knew the manager at the town's Civic Center and broached the idea of doing an Elvis holiday show. "About a week goes by and he calls me up: 'You know what we'd be willing to do? Let's go ahead and do a holiday show, so to speak. But don't make it all holiday music. Do some of his rock-and-roll stuff.'" Their first holiday show was to a sold-out crowd. Over the years he would bring in different choirs or high school groups to join him. Now in its 13th season, the show continues to sell out year after year. And each year that passed, George's confidence in himself as a performer grew.

He acknowledges that, to a large extent, it's the costume that makes it work. "That's the magic. I'll be out and about dressed just like I am, George, and I have people say, 'Hey, c'mon over and sing a couple of Elvis songs to us,' and I say, 'Elvis only comes out when he's got the jumpsuit on.' Part of the magic of those concerts is me getting dressed up. I'm not Elvis, but that's when I kind of embody who he was. Without the jumpsuit, I'm just a guy singing Elvis songs. With the jumpsuit, now all of a sudden, I become a *mirage* of Elvis. And that's what really draws everybody to the concerts. They say, 'Oh my god, that was crazy. I've never seen Elvis back in these days. You do such a good job. You look just like him. You sing songs just like him.' To a part of me, it's just like a magician. If you can make a coin disappear, for him, it's easy; sleight of hand. That's kind of what I'm doing up on stage as well. However, it's the outfits that turn me into the image of Elvis."

"I've noticed for my own self, it really took the costume for me to really get into what I do," George continues, speaking about the transformational effect of clothing. "I can remember when I got this real expensive black leather jacket. I mean, it's like a biker's jacket. And when I put that thing on, I feel tough. I feel like I could go out there and ride a motorcycle and have a big bar fight. Not that I would," he interjects. "It's just interesting how that can transform people."

His transformation into being Elvis has become increasingly professional – and expensive. "It's interesting as I see my progression. I said, 'I need to look more authentic with this whole Elvis thing.' There's a company back east that makes Elvis jumpsuits for professional tribute artists. I contacted them and I got a replica of his '73 Aloha concert one. It's called the American Eagle. With the cape and the belt and everything, that thing ran me like $4400. I mean, I had to save for a long time, put stuff on credit cards. And now I've got this real outfit. Three years into this thing, I need to get a different outfit. Then I got the fringed one. And the red one. So now I probably have ten thousand dollars' worth of Elvis wearables. That's kind of how it started."

The ball that started rolling when he met Edie has been rolling now over two decades. George continues to visit nursing homes and hospices on a regular basis, and to volunteer at numerous events like Relay for Life, and performing at the annual Christmas show. The color photos shared here are from a pre-Easter Elvis Gospel show he put on in Denver, Colorado. He still gets a little embarrassed, but for different reasons. George was raised to believe that charity should be anonymous, and it is tough to be anonymous at a charitable event when you're Elvis Presley. "A lot of times there's a financial aspect of those shows that go to help someone in our community. I'll leave it at that. I don't need a badge to put on me to say, 'Hey, look, I gave to this organization.'" Though he cannot remain anonymous, George has finally come to realize that's a small price to pay in order the help children, seniors, and others in his community. "You know what?" he asks, rhetorically. "This is pretty cool. What we're doing is a good thing. And what I'm personally doing is good." And these days, the sideburns are real.

REFERENCES

- Adams, Eric. (2022, March 26). Personal communication (in-person interview).
- Alexandratos, Jonathan. (2022, March 25). Personal communication (in-person interview).
- Aljanahi, Mona Humaid, & Alsheikn, Negmeldin. (2021, November/December). 'There is No Such Thing as Copying in Cosplay': Cosplay as a Remixed Literary Practice. *Journal of Adolescent and Adult Literacy*, 65(3), 210-218.
- Ayu, Ratya Ratna, & Suharyono, Kumadji Srikandi. (May 2017) The Influence of Word of Mouth (WOM) on Brand Identity and the Impact to Purchasing Decision: A Study on Cosplay Community. *Russian Journal of Agricultural and Socio-economic Sciences*, 65(5), 148154. DOI: 10.18551/rjoas.2017-05.20
- B. Erin. (2022, July 30). Personal communication (in-person interview).
- Bachard, Tim. (2022, June 16). Personal communication (in-person interview).
- Back, Kurt W. (1985) Modernism and Fashion: A Social Psychological Interpretation. In Michael R. Solomon (Ed.), *The Psychology of Fashion*. Lexington Books.
- Barbieri, Donatella, with a contribution from Trimingham, Melissa. (2017). *Costume in Performance: Materiality, Culture, and the Body*. Bloomsbury Academic.
- Bardmi, Rawan. (2022, July 2). Personal communication (in-person interview).
- Barnard, Malcom. (1996). *Fashion as Communication*. Routledge.
- Barnett, Michael (Director). (2014). *Superheroes* (Film). Theodore James Productions.

- Barrett, Casey. (2022, May 15). Personal communication (in-person interview).
- Barrett, Kenneth. (2022, May 6). Personal communication (in-person interview).
- Bealer, Tracy. (2022, March 25). Personal communication (in-person interview).
- Birkedal, Katarina H.S. (2019). Closing Traps: Emotional Attachment, Intervention and Juxtaposition in Cosplay in International Relations. *Journal of International Political Theory, 15*(2), 188-209. DOI: 10.1177/1755088219830112.
- Blevins, David. (2022, April 26). Personal communication (in-person interview).
- Bolling, Ben, & Smith, Matthew J. (Eds.). (2014). *It Happens at Comic Con: Ethnographic Essays on a Pop Culture Phenomenon*. McFarland & Company, Inc., Publishers.
- Brochu, Jean-Philippe. (Director). (2017). *Cosplay Culture* (Film). UBIQUE/Film.
- Brown, Jeffrey A. (2012). Ethnography: Wearing One's Fandom. In Smith, M. J. & Duncan, R. (Eds), *Critical Approaches to Comics: Theories and Methods*. Routledge.
- Brown, Jeffrey A. (2022). *Love, Sex, Gender, and Superheroes*. Rutgers University Press.
- Brownie, Barbara, & Graydon, Danny. (2016). *The Superhero Costume: Identity and Disguise in Fact and Fiction*. Bloomsbury Academic.
- Buetow, Stephen. (2020, January 28) The Thin Man is His Clothing: Dressing Masculine to be Masculine. *Journal of Medical Humanities, 41,* 429-437. DOI: 10.1007/s10912-019-09605-6
- Burgoon, Judee K., Buller, David B., & Woodall, W. Gill. (1996). *Nonverbal Communication: The Unspoken Dialogue* (2nd ed.). The McGraw-Hill Companies, Inc.
- Burke, Liam. (2022). Cosplay as Vernacular Adaptation: The Argument for Adaptation Scholarship in Media and Cultural Studies. *Continuum, 36*(1), 84-101. DOI-org.unco.idm.oclc.org/10.1080/10304312.2021.1965958
- Bush, Kenneth. (2022, May 8). Personal communication (email).

- Camire, Quianna "Ace" (2022, July 2). Personal communication (in-person interview).
- Cardon, Angel. (2022, May 6). Personal communication (in-person interview).
- Cecil-Barrett, Brianna. (2022, May 6). Personal communication (in-person interview).
- Chen, Jin-Shiow. (2007, January). A Study of Fan Culture: Adolescent Experiences with Anime/Manga Doujinshi and Cosplay in Taiwan. *Visual Arts Research, 33*(1), 14-24. https://www.jstor.org/stable/20715430
- Churchill, Sara. (2019, March). Revolutionary Threads: The Mediation of Gender and Political Identity in the 'New Irish Dance Costume,' 1917-37. *Gender & History, 31*(1), 153-177, DOI: 10.1111/1468-0424.12409.
- Cline, Amanda. (2017). *Coping Through Cosplay*. Irregular Misfit Publications, LLC & Panda Inc.
- Clyde, Deirdre. (2021). Flying on Borrowed Feathers: Identity Formation Among Gender-Variant Anime Fans in the U.S. *Feminist Media Studies, 21*(6), 1050-1053, DOI: 10.1080/14680777.2021.1959371
- Cosplaymom and Kiogenic. (2012). *Cosplay for Beginners: How to Get Started in Cosplay*. ISBN: 1985779811, ISBN-13: 9781985779815
- Couture, Suvi. (2022, July 1). *Inclusivity in Cosplay: Promoting Inclusivity and Combatting Bullying in the Cosplay Community* [Conference session]. FanExpo, Denver, Colorado, United States.
- Crawford, Gary, & Hancock, David. (2019). *Cosplay and the Art of Play: Exploring Sub-Culture Through Art*. Palgrave Macmillan.
- Crome, Andrew. (2019). Cosplay in the Pulpit and Ponies at Prayer: Christian Faith and Lived Religion in Wider Fan Culture. *Culture and Religion, 20*(2), 129-150, DOI: 10.1080/14755610.2019.1624268
- Dachs, Ofer Dekel, & Harman, Brian. (2020). Negotiating Identity and Authenticity in Hijabi Cosplay. *Advances in Consumer Research, 48*, 43-46.
- de Casanova, Erynn Masi, Brenner-Levoy, Jeremy, & Weirich, Cole. (2020). All the World's a Con: Frontstage, Backstage, and the Blurred Boundaries of Cosplay. *Symbolic Interaction, 44*(4), 798-818. DOI: 10.1002/SYMB.533

- Duchense, Scott (2010, January) Stardom/Fandom: Celebrity and Fan Tribute Performance. *Canadian Theater Review, 141*, 21-27, DOI: 10.3138/ctr.141.21
- El Jurdi, Hounaida, Moufahim, Mona, & Dekel, Ofer. (2022). 'They Said we Ruined the Character and Our Religion' Authenticity and Legitimation of Hijab Cosplay. *Qualitative Market Research: An International Journal, 25*(1), 43-59.
- Endres, Thomas G. (2002). *Sturgis Stories: Celebrating the People of the World's Largest Motorcycle Rally*. Kirk House.
- Endres, Thomas G. (2007, November). *The skin as sacred space: Reflections on religion and tattoos* [Multi-media presentation]. 32nd Annual International American Studies conference, Hacettepe University, Ankara, Turkey.
- Endres, Thomas G. (2013). The family that inks together, links together: Tattoos as family identifiers. In Marrow, Sherilyn, & Leoutsakas, Dennis. (Eds.), *More Than Blood: Today's Reality and Tomorrow's Vision of Family*. Kendall Hunt Publishing Company.
- Endres, Thomas G. (2022, October 17-22). *Costume Conversations: Resilience and Representation in Cosplay and Beyond* [Keynote address]. The 13th Asian Conference on Media, Communication, and Film (MediAsia), Kyoto, Japan. https://mediasia.iafor.org/costume-conversations-resilience-and-representation-in-cosplay/
- Erningsih, Anit. (2019, January-June). Cosplay Adolescent Community in Padang City (Case Study: White Raven Community). *Jurnal Ilmu Sosial Mamangan, 8*(1), 30-35.
- Esser, Helena (2018, June) Re-assembling the Victorians: Steampunk, Cyborgs, and the Ethics of Industry. *Cahiers Victoriens & Éduordiens, 87*, 1-18.
- Forsythe, Sandra M., Drake, Mary Frances, & Hogan, Jane H. (1985). Influence of Clothing Attributes on the Perception of Personal Characteristics. In Solomon, Michael R. (Ed.). *The Psychology of Fashion*. Lexington Books.
- Freitas, Anthony, Kaiser, Susan, Chandler, Joan, Hall, Carol, Kim, Jung-Won, &, and Hammidi, Tania. (1997, July). Appearance Management as Border Construction: Least Favorite Clothing, Group Distancing, and

- Identity Not! *Sociological Inquiry, 67*(3), 323-335, DOI: 10.1111/j.1476-682X.1997.tb01099.x
- French, Erin, & Reddy-Best, Kelly L. (2021, June). Women's Czech Folk Costume: Negotiating Ambivalence and White Ethnicity in the Midwest. *Clothing and Textiles Research Journal*, 1-17. DOI: 10.1177/088730X211027500.
- Fudimova, E. (2021, March). The Concepts of Historical Costume Reenactment. *IOP Conference Series: Materials Science and Engineering, 10*(4), 1-5. DOI: 10.1088/1757-899X/1079/4/042087.
- G. Jesus. (2022, July 30). Personal interview (in-person interview).
- Gagné, Isaac (2008, June) Urban Princesses: Performance and 'Women's Language' in Japan's Gothic/Lolita Subculture. *Journal of Linguistic Anthropology, 18*(1), 130-150, https://www.jstor.org/stable/43104179
- Gibson, Daniel. (2022, July 1). *Inclusivity in Cosplay: Promoting Inclusivity and Combatting Bullying in the Cosplay Community* [Conference session]. FanExpo, Denver, Colorado, United States.
- Giddon, Donald B. (1985) Ethical Considerations for the Fashion Industry. In Solomon, Michael R. (Ed.), *The Psychology of Fashion*. Lexington Books.
- Gn, Joel. (2011) Queer Simulation: The Practice, Performance and Pleasure of Cosplay. *Continuum: Journal of Media and Cultural Studies, 25*(4), 583-593, DOI: 10.1080/10304312.2011.582937
- Gnojek, Matt. (2022, May 15). Personal communication (in-person interview).
- Good, Kristie "Karmdaa." (2016). *Epic Cosplay Costumes: A Step-by-Step Guide to Making and Sewing Your Own Costumes Designs*. Fons & Porter.
- Gorden, William I., Infante, Dominic A, & Braun, Audrey A. (1985). Communicator Style and Fashion Innovativeness. In Solomon, Michael R. (Ed.), *The Psychology of Fashion*. Lexington Books.
- Gray, George M. (2022, April 20). Personal communication (in-person interview).
- Gunnels, Jen. (2009, September). Jedi Like My Father Before Me: Social Identity and the New York Comic Con. *Transformative Works and Cultures, 3*. DOI: 10.3983/twc.2009.0161

- Haborak, Fiona Katie. (2020, September). Identity, Curated Branding, and the Star Cosplayer's Pursuit of Instagram Fame. *Transformative Works and Culture, 34*. DOI: 10.3983/twc2020.1949
- Hale, Matthew. (2014, Winter). Cosplay: Intertextuality, Public Texts, and the Body Fantastic. *Western Folklore, 73*(1), 5-37.
- Han, Yaya. (2020). *Yaya Han's World of Cosplay: A Guide to Fandom Costume Culture*. Sterling Publishing.
- Harrington, C. Lee. (2018). Creativity and Ageing in Fandom. *Celebrity Studies, 9*(2), 231-243. DOI: 10.1080/19392397.2018.1265295
- Henley, Nancy M. (1977). *Body Politics: Power, Sex, and Nonverbal Communication*. Prentice-Hall, Inc.
- Hjorth, Larissa. (2009) Game Girl: Re-Imagining Japanese Gender and Gaming via Melbourne Female Cosplayers. *Intersections: Gender and Sexuality in Asia & the Pacific, 20*. http://intersections.anu.edu.au/issue20/Hjorth.htm
- Holoka, Beverly (2014). *Cosplay as Religion*. Self-published.
- Hoops, Lenny. (2022, June 15). Personal communication (in-person interview).
- Ito, Kinko, & Crutcher, Paul A. (2014). Popular Mass Entertainment in Japan: Manga, Pachinko, and Cosplay. *Symposium: Signs, Symbols, and Semiotics, 51*, 44-48. DOI: 10.1007/s12115.013.9737.y
- Jones, Bethan. (March 2015). Fannish Tattooing and Sacred Identity. *Transformative Works and Cultures, 18*. DOI: 10.3983/twc.2015.0626
- Kawamura, Yuniya. (2011). *Doing Research in Fashion and Dress: An Introduction to Qualitative Methods*. Berg.
- Khan, Angèle. (2022, July 2). Personal communication (in-person interview).
- Kirkpatrick, Ellen. (March 2015) Toward New Horizons: Cosplay (Re)imagined Through the Superhero Genre, Authenticity, and Transformation. *Transformative Works and Cultures, 18*. DOI: 10.3983/twc.2015.0613
- Kirkpatrick, Ellen. (2019). On (dis)play: Outlier Resistance and the Matter of Racebending Superhero Cosplay. *Transformative Works and Cultures, 29*. DOI: 10.3983/twc.2019.1483.

- Kotani, Mari, & LaMarre, Thomas. (2007, January) Doll Beauties and Cosplay. *Mechademia, 2*,(1), 49-62. https://www.jstor.org/stable/41503729
- Lamerichs, Nicole. (2011). Stranger than Fiction: Fan Identity in Cosplay. *Transformative Works and Cultures, 7.* DOI: 10.3983/twc.2011.0246
- Lamerichs, Nicolle. (2015). The Remediation of the Fan Convention: Understanding the Emerging Genre of Cosplay Music Videos. *Transformative Works and Cultures, 18.* DOI: 10.3983/twc.2015.0606
- Leathers, Dale G. (1997). *Successful Nonverbal Communication: Principles and Applications* (3rd ed.). Allyn & Bacon.
- Letamendi, Andrea. (2015). To Be Like Others is to be More Like Ourselves. In Chuang, Eljen (Ed.), *Cosplay in America, V2.* Optiknerve.
- Lewis, Jac, & Lewis, Miriam Striezheff. (1990). *Costume: The Performing Partner.* Meriwether Publishing Ltd.
- Liptak, Andrew. (2022). *Cosplay: A History.* Saga Press.
- Little, Aimée, Elliot, Benjamin, Conneller, Chantal, Pomstra, Diederik, Evans, Adrian A., Fitton, Laura C., Holland, Andrew, Davis, Robert, Kershaw, Rachel, O'Connor, Sonia, Sparrow, Thomas, Wilson, Andrew S., Jordan, Peter, Collins, Matthew J., Colonese, Andre-Carlo, Craig, Oliver E., Knight, Rebecca, Lucquin, Alexandre J.A., Taylor, Barry, & Milner, Nicky.(2016, April 13). Technological Analysis of the World's Earliest Shamanic Costume: A Multi-Scalar, Experimental Study of a Red Deer Headdress from the Early Holocene Site of Star Carr, North Yorkshire, UK. *PLoS ONE, 11*(4), e0152136. DOI: 10.137/journal.pone.0152136.
- Luzader, John C. F. (2022, May 9). Personal communication (in-person interview).
- Maddie "Audubondage." (2023, Feb. 14). Personal communication (Messenger interview).
- Madonia, Molly Rose. (2016, January). All's Fair in Copyright and Costumes: Fair Use Defense to Copyright Infringement in Cosplay. *Marquette Intellectual Property Law Review, 20*(1), 177-193.
- Melea, Giannoula, Angelopoulos, N.V, Kotrotsiou, S.A., & Bakouras, S.X. (2019, May 31). Personality & Mental Health of Greek Cosplayers, In Relation to Postgraduate 'Mental Health' Students. *Journal of Human*

- *Behavior in the Social Environment, 29*(6), 779-803. DOI: 10.1080.10911359.2019.1612808
- Mongan, Shelby Fawn. (March 2015). Finding Truth in Playing Pretend: A Reflection on Cosplay. *Transformative Works and Cultures, 18*. DOI: 10.3983/twc.2015.0634
- Montgomery, Hanako. (2021, November 24). A Black TikToker Was Accused of Appropriating a Japanese Character. Then She Was Banned. *VICE World News*. https://www.vice.com/en/article/epxn3j/black-cosplay-japanese-anime-tiktok
- Montgomery, Lee. (2022, April 25). Personal communication (in-person interview).
- Moore, David. (2023, Jan. 15). Personal communication (in-person interview).
- Moore, Kellsie. (2023, Jan. 15). Personal communication (in-person interview).
- Mosher, Andy. (2022, May 31). Personal communication (in-person interview).
- Mountfort, Paul, Peirson-Smith, Anne, & Geczy, Adam. (2019) *Planet Cosplay: Costume Play, Identity and Global Fandom*. Intellect.
- N. Jen. (2022, July 30). Personal communication (in-person interview).
- Nichols, Elizabeth Gackstetter. (2019). Playing with Identity: Gender, Performance and Feminine Agency in Cosplay. *Continuum, 33*(2), 270-282. DOI-org.unco.idm.oclc.org/10.1080/10304312.2019.1569410.
- Nichols, Elizabeth Gackstetter. (2021, Winter). Terrifying Allure: The Beauty of Harley Quinn in U.S. and Mexican Cosplay. *Visual Arts Research, 47*(2), 55-66. https://www.jstor.org/stable/10.5406/visuartsres.47.2.0055.
- Nord, Samantha. (2022, April 28). Personal communication (in-person interview).
- Norris, Craig, & Bainbridge, Jason. (2009). Selling Otaku? Mapping the Relationship Between Industry and Fandom in the Australian Cosplay Scene. *Intersections: Gender and Sexuality in Asia & the Pacific, 20*.
- Ogens, Matthew (Director). (2007). *Confessions of a Superhero* (Film). Hunting Lane Films/Smokeshow Films.
- Ogonoski, Matthew. (June 2014). Cosplaying the Media Mix: Examining Japan's Media Environment, Its Static Forms, and its Influence on

Cosplay. *Transformative Works and Cultures, 16*. DOI: 10.3983/twc.2014.0526
- Ohanesian, Liz. (2015). How Cosplay Can Change Lives. In Chuang, Ejen (Ed.), *Cosplay in America, V2*. Optiknerve.
- Peirson-Smith, Anne. (2013). Fashioning the Fantastical Self: An Examination of the Cosplay Dress-up Phenomenon in Southeast Asia. *Fashion Theory, 17*(1), 77-111. DOI: 10.2752/175174113X13502904240776
- Peppard, Anna F. (2021). Adaptation, Fandom and Gender: What Counts, Who Counts, and Why. In Darowski, John. (Ed), *Adapting Superman: Essays on the Transmedia Man of Steel*. McFarland & Company, Inc., Publishers.
- Plante, Courtney N., Roberts, Sharon E., Snider, Jamie S., Schroy, Catherine, Reysen, Stephen, & Gerbasi, Kathleen. (2015). 'More Than Skin Deep': Biological Essentialism in Response to a Distinctiveness Threat in a Stigmatized Fan Community. *British Journal of Social Psychology, 54*, 359-370.
- Porter, Ryan (2015, August 31) Professional Cosplayers Find Fame and a Bit of Fortune on Convention Circuit. *Toronto Star*. http://www.thestar.com/entertainment/2015/08/31/professional-cosplayers-find-fame-and-a-bit-of-fortune-on-convention-circuit.html
- Pushkareva, Tatiana V. & Agaltsova, Darya V. (2021, October). Cosplay Phenomenon: Archaic Forms and Updated Meanings. *Rupkatha Journal on Interdisciplinary Studies in Humanities, 13*(3), 1-13. DOI: 10.21659/rupkatha.v13n3.26
- R., Ellen. (2022, July 30). Personal communication (in-person interview).
- Rahman, Osmud, Wing-Sun, Liu, & Cheung, Brittany Hei-man. (2012). 'Cosplay': Imaginative Self and Performing Identity, *Fashion Theory, 16*(3), 317-341. DOI: 10.2752/175174112X13340749707204
- Rauch, Eron, & Bolton, Christopher. (2010). A Cosplay Photography Sampler. *Mechadmia: Second Arc, 5*, 176-190. https://www.jstor.org/stable/41510963
- Riley, Brendan (March 2015) Zombie Walks and the Public Sphere. Transformative Works and Cultures, Vol. 18, DOI: 10.3983/twc.2015.0641
- Roberts, West. (2022, May 11). Personal communication (email).

- Rose, Carleen. (2022, May 8). Personal communication (email).
- Rosenberg, Robin S. & Letamendi, Andrea M. (Sept. 2018). Personality, Behavioral, and Social Heterogeneity within the Cosplay Community. *Transformative Works and Cultures, 28*. DOI: 10.3983/twc.2018.1535
- Ruan, Li. (Sept. 2018). Promoting Japan's World Cosplay Summit in China's Anime, Comic, and Games Communities: Authenticities in Intercultural Transaction. *Asian Anthropology, 17*(3), 204-220. DOI: 10.1080/1683478X.2018.1506276.
- Safdar, Saba, Goh, Kimberly, & Choubak, Melisa. (2020, January). Clothing, Identity, and Acculturation: The Significance of Immigrants' Clothing Choices. *Canadian Journal of Behavioural Science, 52*(1), 36-47. DOI: 10.1037/cbs0000160
- Saito, Rio, & Lunning, Frenchy. (2011). Out of the Closet: The Fancy Phenomenon. *Mechademia: Second Arc, 6*, 139-150. https://www.jstor.org/stable/41511576
- Sawyer, Kathleen. (2022, April 25). Personal communication (in-person interview).
- Schluter, Michael. (2022, April 20). Personal communication (in-person interview).
- Scott, Suzanne. (2015, Spring). 'Cosplay is Serious Business': Gendering Material Fan Labor on Heroes of Cosplay. *Cinema Journal, 54*(3), 146-155.
- Sellnow, Deanna D. (2018). *The Rhetorical Power of Popular Culture: Considering Mediated Texts* (3rd ed.). Sage.
- Seregina, Anastasia, & Weijo, Henri A. (2017, June). Play at Any Cost: How Cosplayers Produce and Sustain Their Ludic Communal Consumption Experiences. *The Journal of Consumer Research, 44*(1), 139-159. DOI: 10.1093/jcr/ucw077
- Shakespeare, Johnny. (2022, June 16). Personal communication (in-person interview).
- Shin, Layoung. (Winter 2018). Queer Eye for K-Pop Fandom: Popular Culture, Cross-gender Performance, and Queer Desire in South Korean Cosplay of K-pop Stars. *Korea Journal, 58*(4), 87-113. DOI: 10.25024/kj.2018.58.4.87
- Shukla, Pravina. (2015). *Costume: Performing Identities Through Dress*. Indiana University Press.

- Shumaker, Jenny. (2022, May 12). Personal communication (email).
- Solomon, Michael R., & Douglas, Susan P. (1985). The Female Clotheshorse: From Aesthetics to Tactics. In Solomon, Michael R. (Ed.), *The Psychology of Fashion*. Lexington Books.
- Stage. (2022, July 2).*The Do's and Don'ts of In-Character Cosplay* [Conference session]. FanExpo, Denver, Colorado, United States.
- Stillson, Chase. (2022, May 3). Personal communication (in-person interview).
- Stillson, Voniè. (2022, May 3). Personal communication (in-person interview).
- Stromberg, Nathan. (2023, February 22). Personal communication (Canvas post).
- Taulbee, Rachel. (2022, April 28). Personal communication (in-person interview).
- The Boston Women's Health Book Collective. (1971, 1973). *Our Bodies, Ourselves: A Book By and For Women*. Simon and Schuster.
- Thomas, Cathy. (2021). Black Femme Rising: Cosplay and Playing Mas as New Narratives of Transgression. *American Journal of Play, 13*(2-3), 320-355.
- Thorsson, Shawn. (2016). *Make: Props and Costume Armor*. Maker Media Inc.
- Tompkins, Jessica Ethel (2019, September). Is Gender Just a Costume? An Exploratory Study of Cosplay. *Transformative Works and Culture, 30*. DOI: 10/3983/twc.2019.1459
- Villa, Gracie. (2022, May 30). Personal communication (in-person interview).
- Waterman, Elaine. (2022, June 3). Personal communication (in-person interview).
- Wild, Benjamin Linley. (Dec. 2020). Critical Reflections on Cultural Appropriation, Race and the Role of Fancy Dress Costume. *Critical Studies in Fashion & Beauty, 11*(2), 153-173. DOI: 10.1386/csfb_00014_1
- Winge, Therèsa M. (2019). *Costuming Cosplay: Dressing the Imagination*. Bloomsbury Visual Arts.
- Worsley, Harriet. (2011). *100 Ideas That Changed Fashion*. Laurence King Publishing.

- Y. John. (2022, July 30). Personal communication (in-person interview).
- Yamato, Eriko (2016, July) 'Growing as a Person': Experiences at Anime, Comics, and Games Fan Events in Malaysia. *Journal of Youth Studies, 19*(6), 743-759, DOI: 10.1080/13676261.2015.1098769
- Yamato, Eriko. (2020). Self-identification in Malaysian cosplay. *Transformative Works and Cultures, 34.* https://doi.org/10.3983/twc.2020.1771
- Zarin, Babak. (2017). 'Can I Take Your Picture?' – Privacy in Cosplay. *Transformative Works & Cultures, 25.* DOI: 10.3983/twc.2017.01075.

APPENDIX
Studies from Around the World

Much of this book, obviously, is Western-centric and focused heavily on practices in the United States. When searching literature, I encountered works on cosplay, costume, or clothing, published in different countries. Sometimes those sources presented unique and often contradictory counterparts to the western research. This section is to provide space and voice to those studies, beginning with a few works that crossed international boundaries, and then taking each country in turn via alphabetical order.

Multiple Countries

Rahman, Sun, and Cheung (2012) offer brief conclusions. Cosplay is highly stigmatized throughout Asia. Non-participants criticize cosplay, accusing it of having sexual undertones, in addition to being expensive, silly, meaningless, and unconstructive. In comparing countries, they claim that Japan is more accepting than stricter countries like Hong Kong.

Peirson-Smith (2013) discussed cosplay across Southeast Asia (e.g., China, Indonesia, Singapore, Thailand, and Malaysia) but primarily focused on Hong Kong. Most characters were imported from Japan, but some from Hollywood. "The spectacular nature of the presentation and performance of the costumed self is clearly evident at these Cosplay events. Yet, it is the camaraderie, festival atmosphere, and sense of community that strikes the outside observer both amongst, and between, the players" (p. 84). Asian cosplayers enjoyed being looked at and photographed, but only in groups and not by themselves. Looking specifically at Hong Kong, it is noted the country has "deep-rooted conservatism towards issues of gender, sex, and sexuality, and an adherence to dominant heterosexual ideology" (p. 101). Feminized male characters in manga and anime, known as "beautiful boys," provide outlets for both sexes to explore qualities outside the norm. More females than males participate.

Finally, Mountfort, Peirson-Smith, and Geczy (2019), whom we've encountered throughout these pages, conducted a survey of 100 cosplayers (which they call *cosers*) from the United Kingdom, North America, Canada, Australia, Hong Kong, Macau, Beijing, and Tokyo. A majority (70%) were female, and ages ranged from 17-25. Here is a summary of their findings:

- Many Asian cosers picked from the immense catalog of Japanese anime and manga produced over the last 40 years. Asian cons have distinct and accurate representation of characters; other cultures may do generic representations. The focus is more on the character than the narrative or backstory.
- Asian *cosers* are not selecting Japanese characters simply because they're close at hand. "Rather, they are attracted to cosplay on the basis of its capacity to create alternative identities based on axiomatic, or at least familiar, reference points. Further, this cosplay activity offers active participation in a cultural practice that is fluidly interpretative rather than rigidly fixed. As a result, it is highly appealing to a youth demographic in search of agency and identity, given the multi-leveled pressures of contemporary life from parental, peer and social sources" (p. 151).
- Cons in China encourage selection of Chinese characters like *The Monkey King* or 'odourless' texts like *Final Fantasy*. ("odourless in this case meaning they are not overly contaminated by Japanese cultural traits, from plot elements to the portrayal of characters with large eyes and neutral skin tones" p. 155)

- North America and United Kingdom Cons are more relaxed, inclusive, and less rule-based. New Zealand focused on craftsmanship. Australia emphasized photo shoots and skits. Europe focus was digital engagement. Singapore and Hong Kong emphasis was character fidelity.

Australia

Hjorth (2009) discussed Japanese influence, especially as manifest in video games, e.g., transformation of the otaku into heroes, and rise of the technologically savvy woman – "a new girl subculture." They are non-cute, or cute infused with an ironic twist. "In Australia the consumption of Japanese popular culture provides an alternative avenue for imagining localisation and globalisation, it re-orients Australia away from its colonial past and into its geo-ideological proximity in the region. It re-imagines Australia as part of the 'Asia-Pacific'" [22]. She conducted a study of 15 female gamers and cosplayers in Melbourne. Unlike Asian cultures, cosplayers in Australia are more multicultural. Given Melbourne's demographics, the Japanese characters are reimaged in both culture and gender. "Cultural, ethnic and gendered performativity is celebrated rather than undermined" [23]. Cosplay provided participants a safe place to explore self-expression, overcome shyness, and led to deepening interest in Japanese culture.

Norris and Bainbridge (2009) also spoke about Australia's fascination with Japan. The interest in otaku culture is less about hard-core or elitist fandom, but more a form of fandom that "delights in outsiders' incomprehension of their culture and values." Cosplaying, and becoming otaku, allowed the participant to "exist in opposition to the more casual, inauthentic, local mass culture…" [12]. Most of their arguments focus on gender. They argue that, compared to other fannish forms of dressing-up, cosplay is closest to drag. The purpose, they conclude, is intentional disruption of cultural expectations. "This is the 'play' in 'cosplay,' a play with identity and, more often, a play with gender identity" [9]. Ironically, they note, it is through the wearing of another layer that the true nature of gender is revealed. "But perhaps most importantly, we would argue that cosplay should be viewed as a creative act, a performance that is as much about revealing the nature of the fan as the emulation of the character they enact" [12].

Canada

In a study of Canadian immigrant's decision whether to wear ethnic clothes or Canadian clothes, Safdar, Goh, and Choubak (2020) concluded that those who chose ethnic clothing did so to represent their ethnic culture, to attend cultural events, as the result of parental influence, and/or to be seen as unique. "Many of the participants reported using ethnic attire as a way to express pride in their ethnicity, convey ties to their culture, as well as to promote positive attitudes toward their ethnic group" (p. 44) Reasons to wear Canadian clothing included a desire to be viewed as a Canadian, for everyday practicality, as the result of media influence, and/or to blend in. They found many that liked to mix styles, a fusion of ethnic style and dominant culture.

China

Ruan (2018) argued that "cosplay in China has developed into something strikingly different from both its Japanese origins and its counterparts in other countries and regions." Cosplay communities formed within local and university-based groups or circles. These communities ranged from 30 to 200 members. Often there was a distinct division of labor. If you are photogenic, you are the model. Others perform other duties, like sewing or taking pictures. "They enjoy both the photographic and stage performance elements of cosplay and function at a highly professionalized, commercialized, industrialized, and competitive level." The division of labor, complemented by cooperative attitudes "allow the Chinese cosplay circles to deliver impressive stage performances, which last between 10 and 60 minutes and combine the performance efforts of dozens of cosplayers and hundreds of stage props" (p. 211).

Czech Republic

French and Reddy-Best (2021) briefly addressed cosplay, noting that costumes worn in the United States were much more individualized than the comparable costumes found in countries like Sweden. Following that, most of their focus was on Czech ethnic costumes for females. "We found that Czech folk costumes play a significant role in how these women negotiated and communicated their Czech ethnic identities" and "their folk costumes held considerable meaning to them because of the costumes' connections to their family history and ethnic origins" (p. 6). Festivals also created a sense of community. They feel a sense of pride and joy. "Findings from our study can be useful to society as individuals search for a more positive sense of self – that is, if they are looking to feel more connected, pride, or joy, they can consider engaging in some of these cultural practices" (p. 15).

Greece

Melea, Angelopoulos, Kotrotsiou, and Bakouras (2019) looked at mental health of Greek cosplayers. They found that cosplayers overall had higher scores of aggressiveness. Female cosplayers were more likely to have depression and anxiety. The longer one cosplayed, the more they saw symptoms like paranoid thinking, anxiousness, compulsiveness, and obsession. "Cosplayers' personalities, therefore, have more psychopathic, paranoid, hysteroidal, delusionally or non-delusionally self-critical, melancholic and obsessive elements" (p. 795). However, "most cosplayers do not seem to suffer from anxiety syndrome" (p. 795). Much of this, they admit, could be due to stress regarding the economic crisis in Greece. Regarding the activity at large, they argue, "Cosplay is usually interpreted as a transformative tool. Cosplayers cannot be native speakers, locked within as translators with cosplay always as their second language; a tangible interpretation of a uniquely performed complex process, a form of identity transformation that frequently trades boundaries between reality and fiction by carrying their characters from a literary plane into the material one" (p. 784). On the positive side, individuals can experiment with subjective identity. They are limited, however, by their performance ability and material body characteristics.

Indonesia

Ayu and Suharyono (2017) studied two cosplay communities in Malang, Indonesia. They found that word of mouth had "significant influence toward the brand awareness, quality perceived, brand loyalty, and brand association" (p. 152). Costume purchasing decisions by adolescents with access to the internet was greatly influenced by this Word of Mouth (WOM) process.

Erningsih (2019) specifically interviewed a group known as the White Ravens, a group of cosplay teens who love Japan and its influence. They perform only as a group, not individuals, as "cosplay activities are still considered as clowns in the community and their own friends" (p. 32).

Japan

In 2008, Gagné published an early piece on Japanese Gothic and Lolita subcultures. He described the latter as "a fashion-oriented subculture of young females who wear elaborate, antiquated dresses and aspire toward looking, acting, and speaking like 'princesses.'" (p. 131). Participants revived and recreated a "women's language" style of exaggerated politeness called *joseigo* (from *jogakusei kotoba* – or schoolgirl speech). Differs from *noripīgo* style (infantile, lisp) and *gyaru* style (brash, vulgar, unfeminine). He labels all three as hedonistic forms of play "that expresses dissatisfaction with gender ideals and notions of adulthood and responsibility" (p. 133). The Lolitas, however, puzzle the establishment, who want to criticize the counterculture but find it difficult because they are so polite. They follow the three oaths of the speech: "1. Speak slowly and politely; 2. Do not use elliptical words; 3. Be positive when answering in the positive and indirect when answering in the negative" (p. 137). A problem occurs when men take their photos without asking and post on the internet in sexualized ways. They are often confused with young women from the popular Maid Cafes. Lolitas do not view what they do as cosplay. To those he interviewed, cosplay "means mimicry and dressing up as someone, that is, as a specific character from comic books, movies, video games or animation." In contrast, Lolitas said their style "was personalized and was an expression of their 'true' selves, and that they took pride in choosing their own styles and making their own clothing" (p. 141). Gagne states the distinctions in practice are not always that clear.

Image A.1 *Maid Café signs in Tokyo's Akihabara district*

Ito and Crutcher (2014) claim that "Japan dominates the cosplay phenomenon, from both inspiration and participation standpoints" (p. 47). For example, the first World Cosplay Summit (WCS) was held in 2013 in Nagoya. It received support from the Ministry of Foreign Affairs in 2016. Providing real life examples beyond conventions, they also discuss the Meido Cafes (Maid Café) which emerged in Tokyo in the 2000s, adding that, in some, all waitstaff are men in drag. "Again, this sort of gender fluidity and sexual ambiguity is seen throughout Japanese pop culture" (p. 47). Relates it to longstanding Kabuki theater, back to feudal times, when men portrayed both male and female characters. They also mention the Gothic and Lolita groups, along with a more recent cultural role play, *bihaku*, or the maximization of whiteness and pale qualities.

Ogonoski (2014) provides in-depth analysis of Japanese otaku culture and their connections to anime, video games, computers, science fiction, special-effects films, figurines, and cosplay. "At best, otaku is a term that refers to a broad diversity of consumers." Cosplayers combine fan practices as prosumers (producer-consumers) and approreaders (appropriator-readers) [1.4]. They don't just passively consume media but actively and creatively participate in the cultural signification process. Argues that propagation of the term otaku throughout Japanese culture "indicates that otaku practices have more comprehensive historical significance and cultural cachet than do fan practices in North America" [1.4]. Observes that Japanese cosplayers tend to strike a static pose, saying this best fits with the Japanese photography media environment. There is an etiquette to posing. Should be energetic and emotive, not just the utilitarian poses of facing the camera and turning profile. "The otaku themselves called this new consumer behavior 'chara-moe' – the feeling of moe toward characters and their alluring characteristics without relation to the narrative or message of those works" [2.2]. The affective and emotive elements of moe (see Chapter 1), and its ability to evoke feelings, overshadow the narrative significance of the media form. "A production/image/design is judged not according to originality but by its association and referentiality of the moe database" [2.3].

Finally, Mountfort et al. (2019) provide specific analysis of Japan. They liken precincts in which cosplayers gather (e.g., Tokyo's Harajuku, Akihabara, and Ikebukuro areas) to London's Piccadilly Circus being a home to punk rockers in the 1990s, pointing out that the west does not offer this. Discussion here again of Maid Cafes, "where a largely male otaku crowd can simulate interaction with their idols in the guise of young women dressed in outfits from manga, anime and Japanese pop culture. The encounter is highly ritualized and centres around being poured tea and polite conversation conducted in an archaic idiom full of respect forms for the clientele" (p. 66). Though less prominent, there are also Butler Cafes where women are served by beautiful, youthful boys (*bishonen*) or Miss Dandy bars where women are served by women in costumes.

Malaysia

Yamato (2016) addressed cultural events like Malaysia's Comic Fiesta, noting that, despite its influence, Japan provides little commercial engagement. Cosplay is often disapproved by parents, especially the sexualization of characters in a Muslim country. She conducted a survey and follow-up in-depth interviews with cosplayers. All interviewees' parents disapproved, thinking it was a waste of time and money. Some were able to convince parents it was acceptable; others hid their participation. Many used the Japanese word otaku to describe themselves, as it gave them a sense of relatedness and community. Many did organizing and volunteer work, increasing their competence and skill levels; helping them to "discover one's own capability as a working adult" (p. 754).In some cases, cosplay participation led to forms of professional development like selling art or writing fanzines.

In another article, Yamato (2020) again stressed the conservative nature of the country, pointing out that cosplay existed only in safe spaces like conventions. Unlike the West, where race can be a sticking point for character selection, "ethnicity appears not to be very important while cosplaying" because everyone was Malaysian [9.3]. Concludes by pointing out how interesting it is to study this exercise in "appreciating individuality" in a culture which prizes the collective and common characteristics.

South Korea

Shin (2018) looked at the phenomenon of "fan cosplay" or "fancos," where youth dress up and do K-pop cover dances of groups like BTS. While also found in Thailand and Philippines, claims that fancos hit height of popularity in those countries in the 1990s and 2000s and are now becoming marginalized and invisible. Originally served as a "alternative space for young queer-identified women to meet, freely share desire and identity, and find support" (p. 98). Popularity in Korea diminished when current *iban* (lesbian) women began to disparage fancos by labeling them as otaku.

Russia

Pushkareva and Agaltsova (2021) explain that the first Russian cosplayers appeared in 1999, as Iron Curtain began to collapse. Heavily influenced by Japan and America, but also the figurative system of Soviet animation of the 1960s-1980s which "experienced an unprecedented flourishing, leaving works of world artistic level" (p. 11). A popular example is the hero Cheburashka from 1969 Russian cartoon *Crocodile Gena*.

Taiwan

Chen (2007) states that fandom products, like cosplay costumes, shows that fans and pop culture consumers are not dupes or social misfits. They are able to digest the information and translate it for their own use. Taiwanese cosplayers select from Japanese anime/manga, Japanese rock bands, or characters from traditional Taiwanese puppetry. Provides feelings of recognition and not being alone. The emphasis in costuming is on accuracy. "Many experienced cosplayers suggest that a new player should learn to choose a character that is matched to his or her physique rather than one with whom he or she is merely infatuated" (p. 19). Additionally, "Most fans play characters with a personality similar to their own" (p. 19). Argues that anime/manga fandom provides a temporary means to deal with frustrations and stresses of the real world, but is "more likely a symbolic outlet for self-expression and a sense of well-being through artistic achievement" (p. 20). Points to the irony that, by running away from reality by making doujinshi (self-published fanzines) and doing cosplay, participants find a mechanism for personal adjustment and "a harmless outlet for their impulses to be expressed freely" (p. 21).

Times Square, New York City

Bumblebee from the *Transformers* franchise
Costume worn by Mirelbis Peña

Costume Conversation # 1
Eric Adams a.k.a. Gene Simmons from KISS

Costume Conversation # 2
Lee Montgomery & Kat Sawyer
a.k.a. U.S.S. Tiburon Star Fleet Officers

Costume Conversation # 3
Casey Barrett a.k.a. Hospital Batman

Costume Conversation # 4
Ken Barrett & Brianna Cecil-Barrett a.k.a. LOTR Wedding Theme

Costume Conversation # 5
Voniè & Chase Stillson a.k.a. Lady Vo & Chaos Crossfire

Costume Conversation # 6
Elaine & Ember Waterman
a.k.a. Blackbeard & Jim from *Our Flag Means Death*

Costume Conversation # 7
Gracie Villa a.k.a. Jaskier from *The Witcher*

Costume Conversation # 8
Jonathan Alexandratos a.k.a. Non-binary Star Fleet Officer

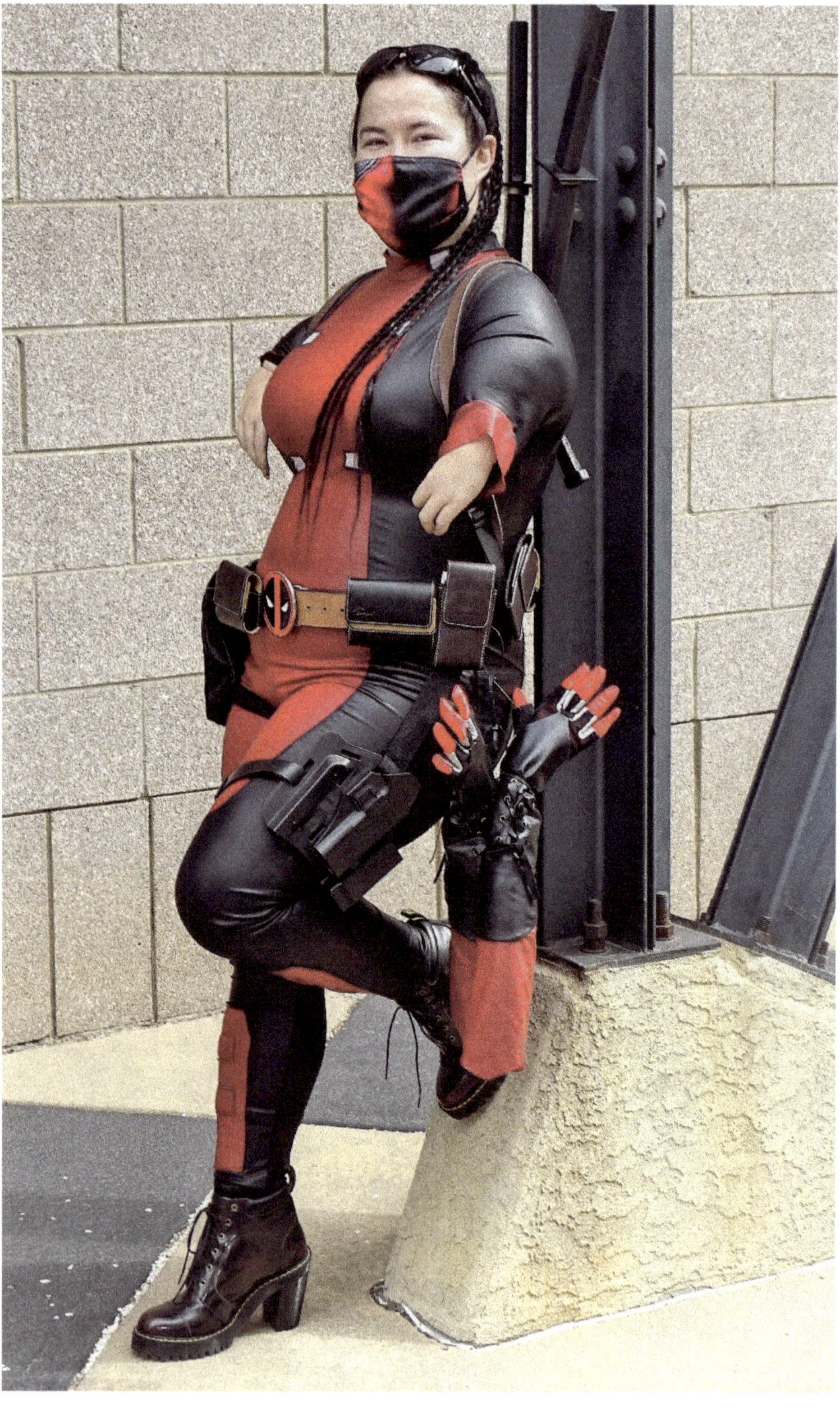

Costume Conversation # 9
Samantha Nord a.k.a. Lady Deadpool (opposite page)
and Lady Loki (above)

Costume Conversation # 10
David Blevins a.k.a. Khrys'taaal a.k.a. Remy D.

Costume Conversation # 11
John C. Luzader a.k.a. Patrick Gass (Lewis & Clark Expedition, retired)

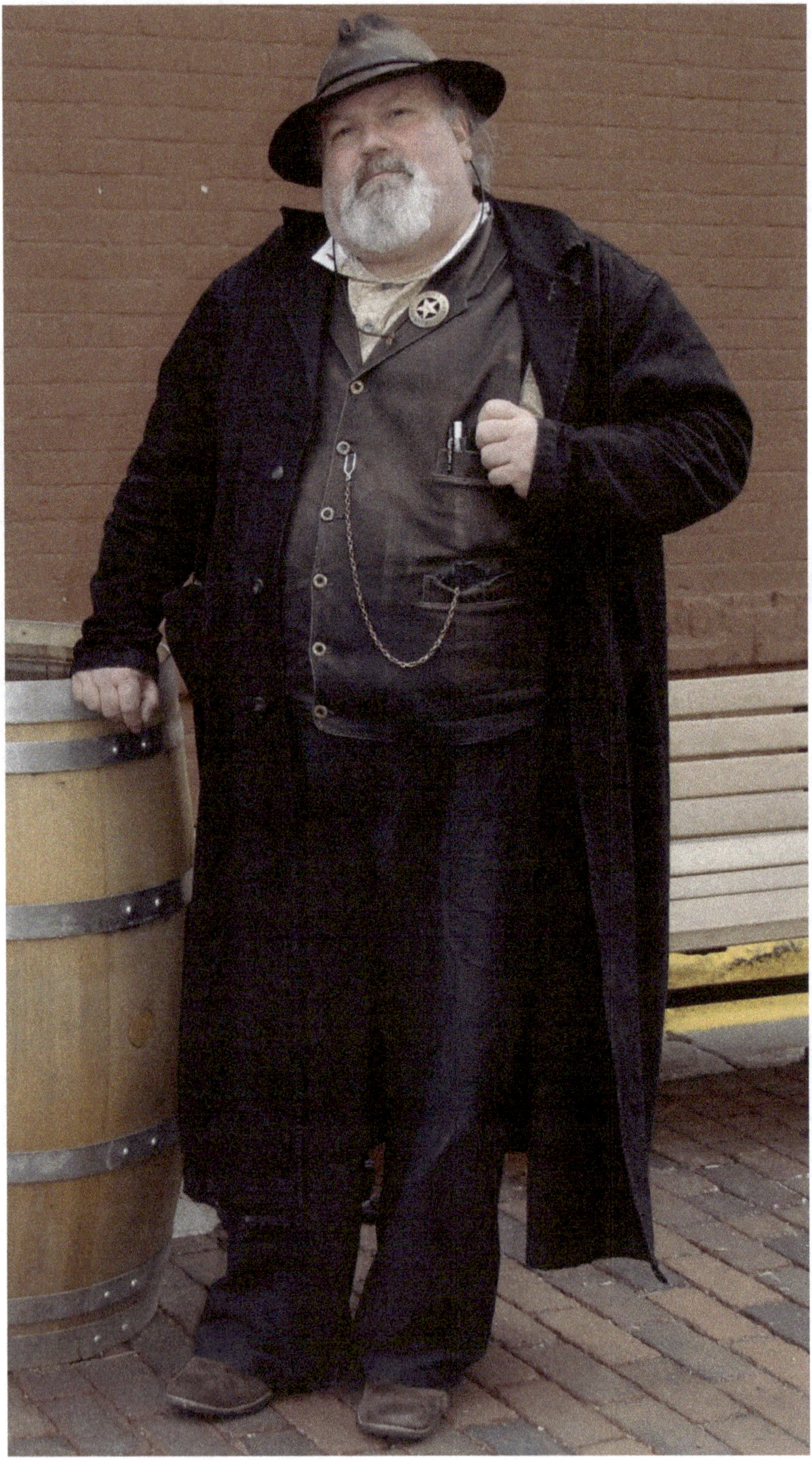

Costume Conversation # 12
Andy Mosher a.k.a. Con Stapleton, City Marshal, Deadwood, SD (opposite page)

Also from *Deadwood Alive* troupe Deadwood, South Dakota

Travis Pearson (above), a.k.a. Wild Bill Hickock

Patrick Harpel (right), a.k.a. Potato Creek Johnny

Costume Conversation # 13
Michael Schluter a.k.a. St. Patrick's Day leprechaun

Costume Conversation # 14
Angel Cardon a.k.a. Dottie Lucille

Costume Conversation # 15
Erin B. & Jesus G. a.k.a. Their Natural Selves
PHOTO CREDIT: Erin B.

Costume Conversation # 16 *(turn page horizontally)*
The Bond Family a.k.a. High Plains Ghostbusters
Left to Right: Ches Jr., Mandy, Ches "Newman" Sr.

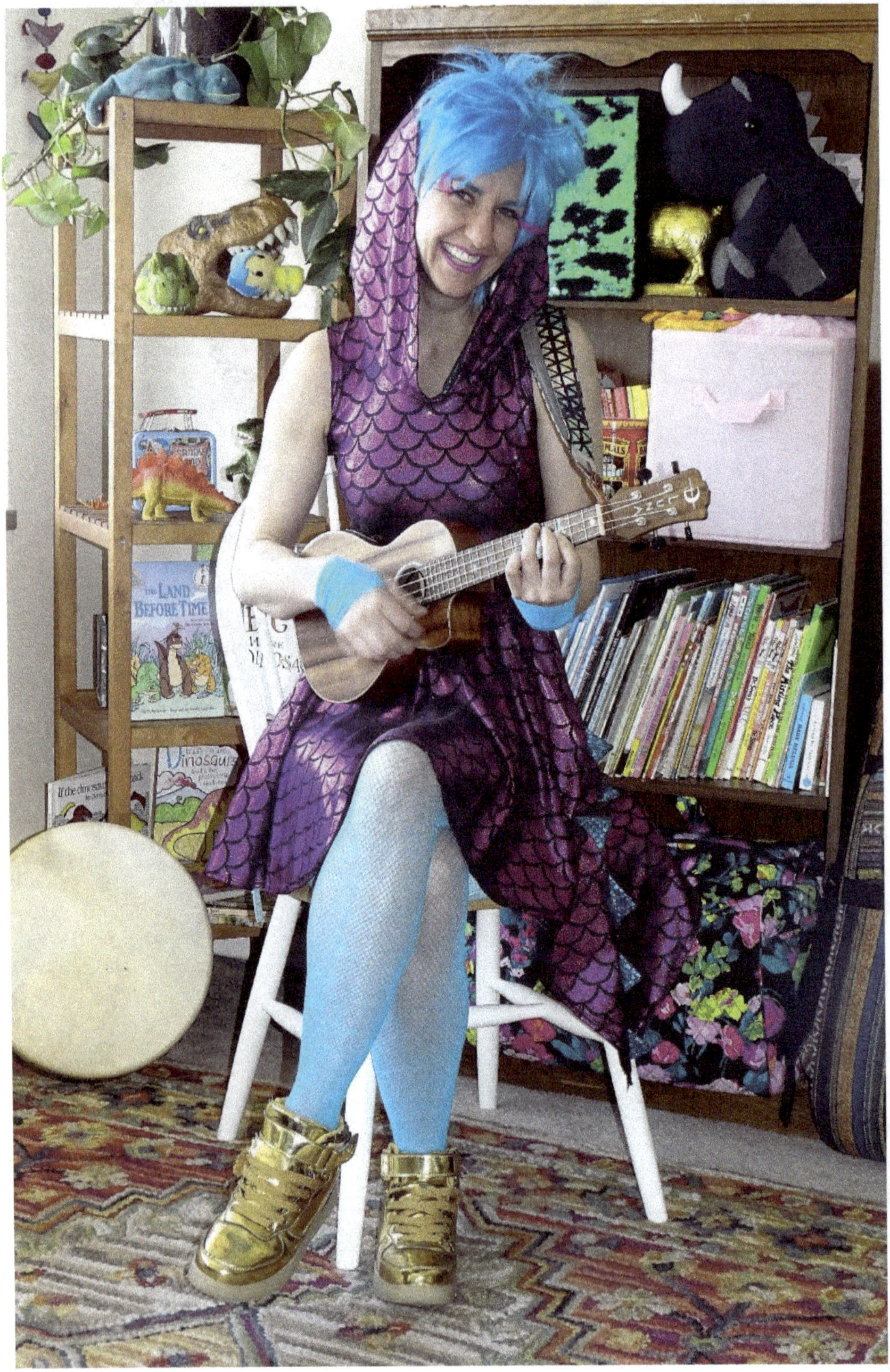
LAND
BEFORE TIME

Costume Conversation # 17
Rachel Taulbee
a.k.a. Terra Thesaurus (opposite page)
a.k.a. Countess Cora (above)

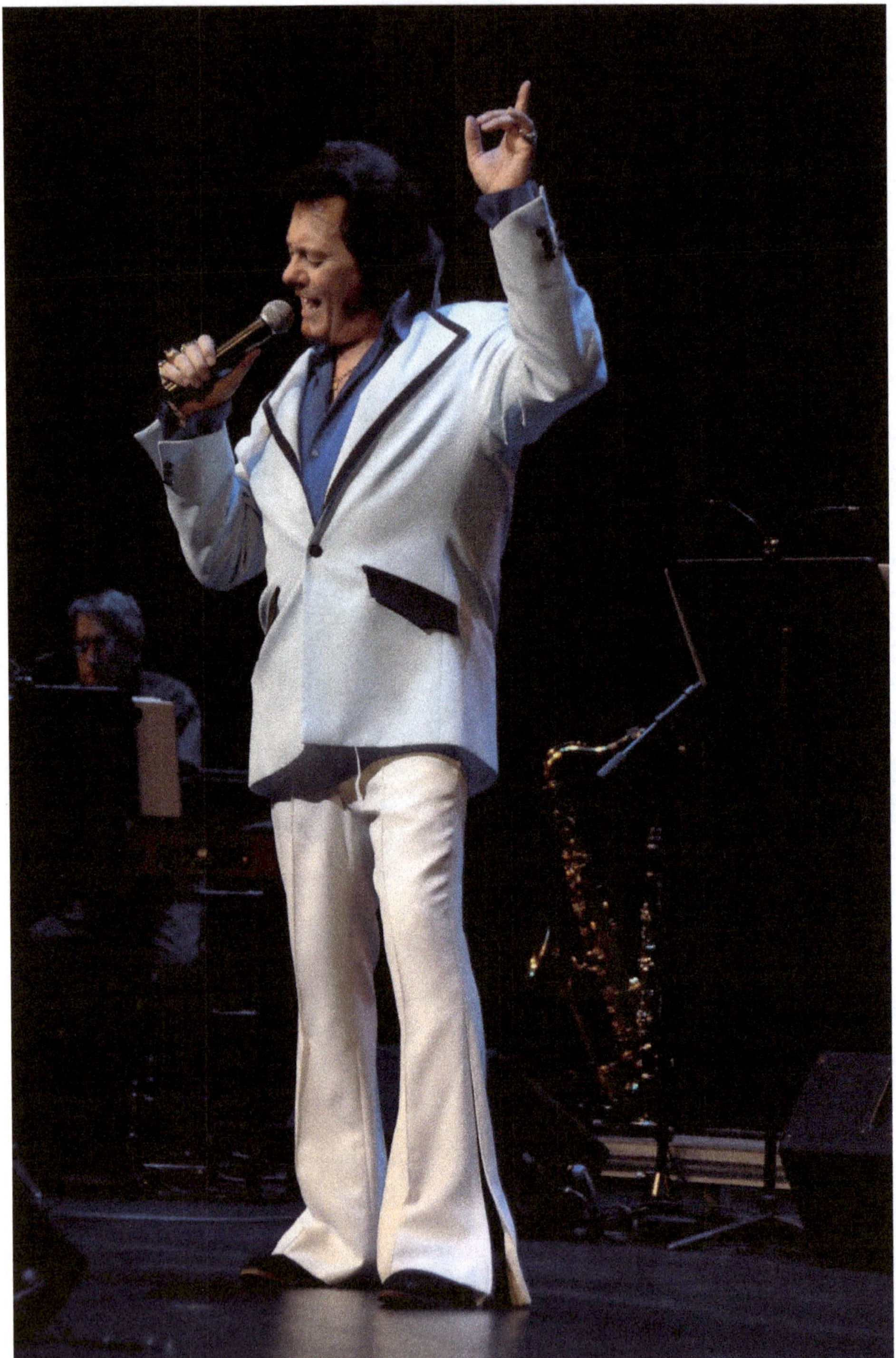

Costume Conversation # 18
George Gray a.k.a. Elvis Presley

Society for Creative Anachronism (SCA) investiture ceremony for the Barony of Unser Hafen in the Kingdom of the Outlands. Back row (l to r): Matthew Willis (Seamus MacRae), Meria Willis (Angel d'Auvergne), Mary Beth Ward (Ylva), Tristan Gilman (Syr Torstein), Susan Lin (Shostrangh), Binhan Lin (Hayashi Norikata), Jacob Waid (Vagn Egilsson) Front row (l to r): Stewart Fairburn (Freana), Ann Fairburn (Richenda de la Selva), Richard Brown (King Barekr), Mark Anderson (Baron Dubhghall), Elizabeth French (Countess Ansteys)

Realities for Children volunteer event. Back row (l to r): Brian Messick (Groot), Casey Barrett (Batman), Sarah Paul (Harley Quinn). Middle row (l to r): Matt Gnojek (Captain America), Heather Martin (Peggy Carter), Cara Logan (Rocket Racoon), Kayla Kelley (Elsa), Kathrynne Watson (Queen Anna), Mackenzie Johnson (Cinderella). Front row (l to r): Nathalie Costello (Spidergirl), Ashley Phillis (Ghost Spider)

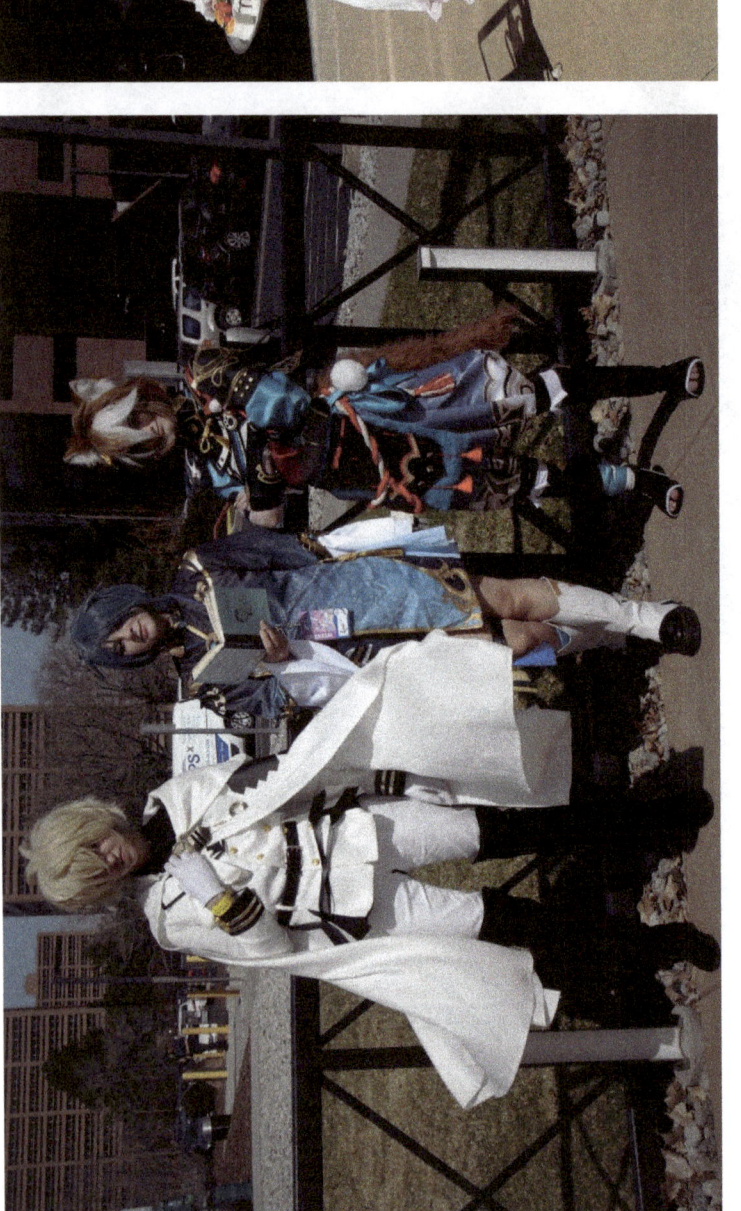

Colorado Anime Fest

Photo on left (l to r): Ella Swift Heminger (Mikaela Hyakuya, *Owari no Seraph*), Aysia Muller (Xingqui, *Genshin Impact*), Jessica Cooper (Gorou, *Genshin Impact*)

Photo on right: Diana Austin (Mitsuri, *Demon Slayer* [maid costume])

Deadwood Alive

Left to Right: Patrick Harpel (Potato Creek Johnny), Elizabeth Harpel (Dr. Flora Hayward Stanford), Ty Sanford (Daniel Boone May), Sean Baxter (Jack McCall), Andy Moser (Con Stapleton), Jake Fogle (Sherriff John Manning), Zachary Ziegenbein (technical assistant), Les Nuckles (Seth Bullock), Sean Henderson (Lame Johnny)

Greeley Monster Days

Top photo: George Gray (Zombie Elvis)

Bottom photo: Brittany McNellis (left) and Jesse Thomas promote "Terror in the Corn: Mile of Mayhem"

New Orleans, LA

Top Photo: Patrick Long (*The Mask*) promotes his "New and Used Vehicles" business by entertaining on world famous Bourbon Street
Bottom Photo: Tourist Anecia Woolcock tries on parade wear at Carl Mack's interactive "Mardi Gras Museum of Costumes and Culture"

Busking in California

Photo Above: Tim Barchard (right), as Zach Galifianakis's *Hangover* character Alan Garner, posing with *Minion* Johnny "One Song Johnny" Shakespeare, across from Grauman's Chinese Theater on Hollywood Blvd.

Opposite Page: Lenny "Lenny the Great" Hoops entertains crowds on the Santa Monica Pier

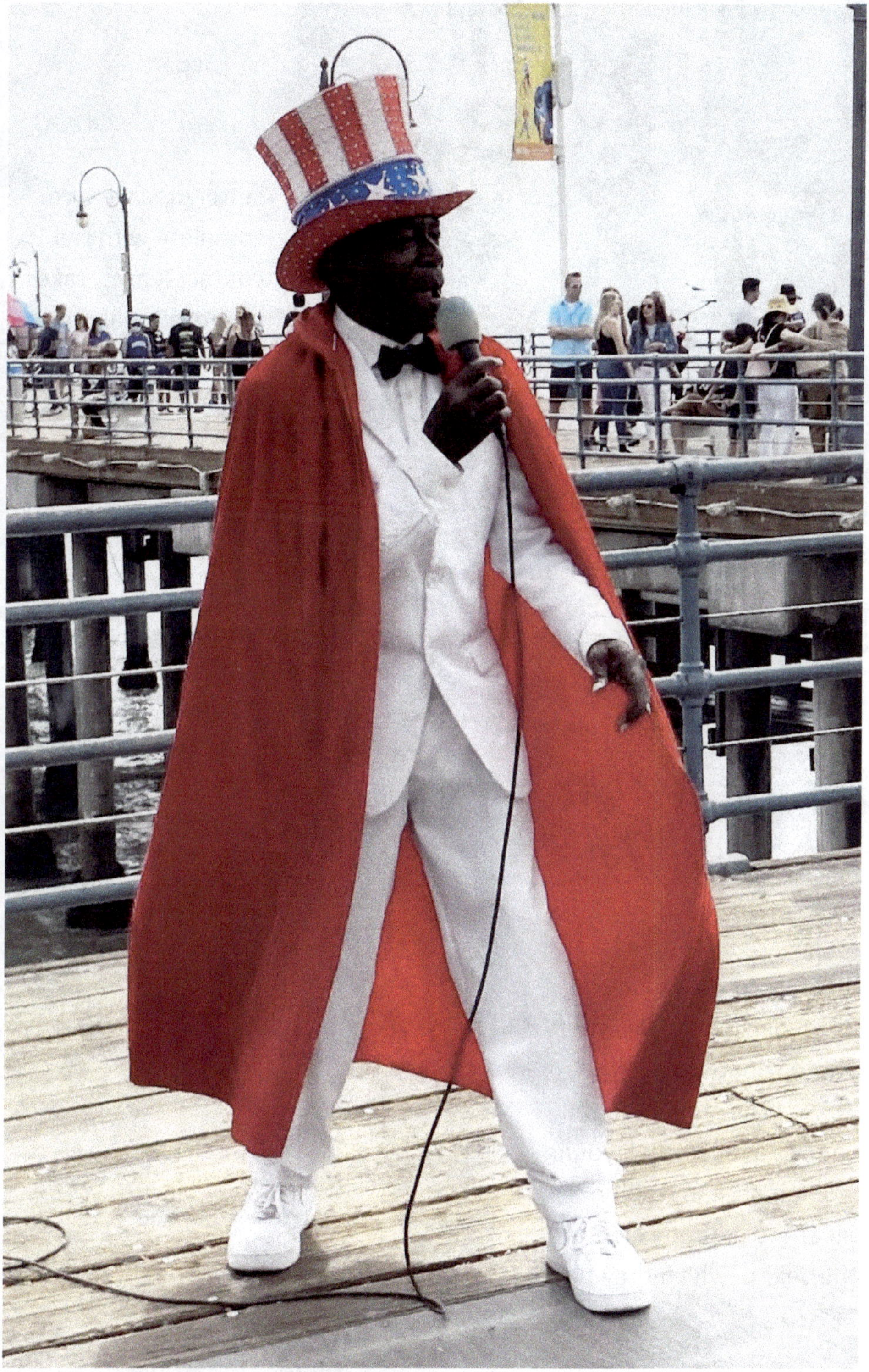

Japan

Left: Kurosaki Kuro, complete with red contact lenses, takes a smoke break from work in the Dotonbori shopping district in Osaka

Right: Mao Maeda allows us to join in her *seijin-no-hi* photo shoot outside the Tokyo train station. In this coming of age ritual, young women pose in traditional Japanese garb to celebrate the year in which they turn age 20

CPSIA information can be obtained
at www.ICGtesting.com
Printed in the USA
LVHW050737160523
747052LV00007B/112

9 781959 681090